LEGISLATIVE POLITICS
IN THE ARAB WORLD

LEGISLATIVE POLITICS in the ARAB WORLD

The Resurgence of Democratic Institutions

Abdo Baaklini, Guilain Denoeux, and Robert Springborg

LYNNE RIENNER PUBLISHERS

BOULDER
LONDON

Published in the United States of America in 1999 by
Lynne Rienner Publishers, Inc.
1800 30th Street, Boulder, Colorado 80301

and in the United Kingdom by
Lynne Rienner Publishers, Inc.
3 Henrietta Street, Covent Garden, London WC2E 8LU

Library of Congress Cataloging-in-Publication Data
Baaklini, Abdo I.
   Legislative politics in the Arab world : the resurgence of
democratic institutions / Abdo Baaklini, Guilain Denoeux, and Robert
Springborg.
        p.   cm.
   Includes bibliographical references and index.
   ISBN 1-55587-839-3 (hc. : alk. paper). — ISBN 1-55587-840-7 (pb.
: alk. paper)
     1. Legislative bodies—Arab countries.   2. Democracy—Arab
countries.   3. Democratization—Arab countries.   4. Arab countries—
Politics and government—1945–   I. Denoeux, Guilain.
II. Springborg, Robert.   III. Title.
JQ1850.A71B33   1999
328'.0917'4927—dc21

                                                                                        98-46654
                                                                                             CIP

British Cataloging in Publication Data
A Cataloguing in Publication record for this book
is available from the British Library.

Printed and bound in the United States of America

The paper used in this publication meets the requirements
of the American National Standard for Permanence of
Paper for Printed Library Materials Z39.48-1984.

5 4 3 2 1

To Soumaya, who has been a source of strength and inspiration.
—Abdo Baaklini

To Eliza, with gratitude for her love and encouragement.
—Guilain Denoeux

To Suzy and Greg, for their support.
—Robert Springborg

Contents

3
Conclusion

Acknowledgments

We are very indebted to the United States Agency for International Development (USAID) for making it possible for us to undertake much of the field research out of which this book developed. In addition, we would like to thank the members and staff of the parliaments we studied for taking the time to answer our questions, for sharing their knowledge of their legislatures' inner workings, for their willingness to engage in an intellectual debate over their respective parliaments' evolving political roles, and for putting at our disposal many of these institutions' internal documents.

The authors are also very grateful for the first-rate research assistance provided by Katherine Charbonnier, William Barndt, and Omar Sanchez at Colby College. The countless hours that Kate, Will, and Omar spent in Miller Library collecting data and tracking down sources contributed much to the completion of this project. Many thanks as well to the Center for Legislative Development, University at Albany, State University of New York, for providing us with all the working documents it had about the legislatures studied in the following chapters.

At Lynne Rienner Publishers, Jean Hay's perceptive feedback on the first draft of the manuscript was instrumental in enabling the authors to make judicious cuts and other improvements. Sally Glover and Shena Redmond expertly shepherded the manuscript through production. And careful, outstanding copyediting by Libby Barstow also significantly enhanced the quality of the final product.

Last, but not least, the task of writing this book was greatly facilitated by the advice and expertise generously provided for many years by W.M.G. on matters of style and composition.

—*The Authors*

Introduction

Human beings have invented only a few routines to govern themselves in peace, and representative government through assemblies is one of them; parliaments tend to persist, and to be reinvented if they disappear.
—Patterson and Copeland 1994: 7

Political scientists specializing in the Arab world have largely ignored legislatures. When discussed at all, Arab parliaments are usually derided as window dressing for authoritarian regimes or as artificial transplants that are meaningless in the political and socioeconomic context of Arab societies. Such perceptions help explain why Arab legislative institutions have not been studied.

The paucity of writings on Arab legislatures has left us poorly equipped to appreciate the significance of the increasingly visible role these institutions have come to play in the region's politics. Indeed, the efforts that several Arab regimes have made since the 1980s to open up their political systems have been accompanied by the emergence or reemergence of legislatures as important platforms in political life. In fact, the new prominence of Arab legislatures—whether measured by their number, influence, or the presence within them of active and vocal oppositions—has become one of the major trends in Arab politics in recent years. This phenomenon can be better understood by examining it in the context of the six Arab countries that constitute the focus of this study: Lebanon, Morocco, Jordan, Kuwait, Yemen, and Egypt.

Resurgent Parliaments in the Arab World: An Overview of Six Countries

In August and September 1992, for the first time in two decades, the Lebanese elected a new Chamber of Deputies. In the four years that followed, this legislature asserted its prerogatives, which had been enhanced as a result of constitutional amendments adopted in 1991. Led by its influential speaker, Shiite leader Nabih Berri, the legislature forced Prime Minister Rafiq Hariri into embarrassing retreats on several occasions. It also made significant headway toward developing its internal capacity. Although the elections that took place in August and September 1996 yielded a parliament more supportive of Hariri and his policies, it also included deputies who were quick to force the cabinet into significant compromises and retreats.

Although the Lebanese parliament has emerged as an important player in the process of political reconstruction following a fifteen-year civil war, in Jordan, Morocco, and Kuwait the legislature has become a major arena in which the double drama of democratization and "reinvention" of monarchical or family rule is played out. In all three countries, the 1990s saw two sets of legislative elections. That these elections took place as scheduled—even when regional tensions complicated the electoral process, as was the case in Jordan in 1993 and 1997 and in Kuwait in 1996—should be seen as an indication of the routinization and consolidation of democratic practices. Furthermore, each election produced an active legislature in which the opposition was well represented. In Morocco, in fact, the opposition's strong showing in the November 1997 elections to the lower house paved the way for the appointment of Socialist party leader Abderrahmane Youssoufi as prime minister on February 4, 1998. More important, in all three polities, parliament has been at the very center of a strategy intended by the ruler to ensure the survival of the monarchy (in Jordan and Morocco) or dynastic system (in Kuwait) into the twenty-first century. It is primarily by expanding the prerogatives and visibility of an elected legislature that the emir of Kuwait and the kings of Jordan and Morocco have sought to respond to popular pressures for increased political participation and governmental accountability. Evidence presented in Part Two will show that these rulers have enjoyed significant success in implementing this strategy.

Parliament has also played a central role in the Republic of Yemen, which was established in May 1990 when the Yemen Arab Republic (North Yemen) merged with the People's Democratic Republic of Yemen (South Yemen). The new country's constitution, ratified by a popular referendum held in 1991, gave significant prerogatives to a 301-member Chamber of Deputies. (Before the cabinet could be installed, for instance, it had to receive a vote of confidence from the Chamber.) In 1991 and 1992, the Chamber passed important laws on the press, political parties, and elections, thus setting the parameters within which political activity was to take place. Parliament's centrality was further demonstrated in April 1993, when Yemen organized the first multiparty elections ever on the Arabian Peninsula. Women were allowed to participate, both as voters and as candidates, and voting was deemed by foreign observers to have been free and fair. Even during the civil war that disrupted Yemen's democratization experiment between April and June 1994, parliament continued to function, providing one of the few arenas within which leaders of the contending forces could interact. And when new elections were held on April 27, 1997, eleven out of fourteen parties took place in them, despite earlier reports of a possible massive boycott. This circumstance suggests that most political actors understood the importance of being present in the legislature to further their respective agendas. Since the end of the civil war, in fact, the Chamber has been the only national institution in which all major political forces are represented, and it is with the Chamber that hopes are vested for the renewal of the country's democracy-building process.

In Egypt, by contrast, the legislature now plays a less significant role than in the other five countries. It is struggling to assert its influence against a powerful executive jealous of its prerogatives. The balance of power between executive and legislative branches, which has always favored the former, tilted yet further in that direction during the 1990s. Most opposition parties boycotted the 1990 parliamentary elections in protest against an electoral system that places the responsibility for organizing and administering elections in the hands of the Ministry of the Interior. The opposition's share of seats dropped from around 20 percent in the 1987–1990 parliament to less than 5 percent in the 1990–1995 parliament. That token representation was still further reduced in the 1995 elections, despite the fact that opposition political parties conducted vigorous election campaigns. Those elections were far from being free and fair, as is evidenced by the fact that not a single representative of political Islam was elected. Egypt is thus the only country under study here in which the legislature is playing a less important role than it did in the 1980s or even the 1970s.

The Renewal of Parliamentary Politics in the Arab World: Causes and Significance

The increased centrality of Arab legislatures results from two mutually reinforcing trends. The first is the desire of governing elites to enhance the role and visibility of their respective parliaments. The second is the attempt by these same parliaments to assert themselves by taking advantage of both their new constitutional prerogatives and the broadened political space afforded to them by incumbent regimes. In other words, legislatures have become more important because governments have made them a primary vehicle of their reform efforts and because opposition forces are struggling to enhance their influence within and through them.

For a variety of interrelated reasons, Arab regimes have tried to reinvigorate legislatures so as to:

- broaden their popular base and increase their domestic and international legitimacy;
- mobilize public support for specific policies, ranging from austerity measures to the repression of Islamic militants;

- respond to growing demands for political participation while making sure that these demands will be channeled through the official political system;
- lessen political tensions by integrating the moderate opposition into the system and providing safe outlets for the expression of grievances that might otherwise fuel sedition;
- project a more liberal image to the outside world, a strategy that has become critical to gaining access to new international loans or better refinancing terms for accumulated debts;
- create a national forum where policy agreements can be negotiated and bargains struck with opposition elites on the rules of the political game;
- improve overall linkages between state and society; and
- enhance governmental performance by strengthening the legislature's ability to scrutinize the bureaucracy.

To make legislatures more credible political arenas, however, regimes have had to make significant concessions to them. Accordingly, the regimes have increased the constitutional prerogatives of parliaments, allowed for more competitive elections, and displayed greater tolerance of parliamentary criticism. Legislatures, for their part, have been swift to capitalize on their new power and freedoms. They have become more active in initiating legislation and in seeking to influence public policy. Through parliamentary debates, question-and-answer sessions (during which ministers have to address the questions asked by parliamentarians), and the formation of investigative committees, legislatures have publicized instances of bureaucratic negligence, corruption, and abuses of authority by government officials. In short, they have begun to exercise their constitutional functions of oversight of the executive branch. They also are becoming more effective in assisting their constituents to obtain services from the executive branch. Furthermore, despite insufficient resources, space, qualified staff, and experience in legislative matters, members of parliament (MPs) and the political and administrative leaders of Arab legislatures typically take their roles very seriously. In working with Arab parliaments during the 1990s, the authors noted repeatedly that the cynicism and malaise that pervade the region's executive bureaucracies are much less evident in legislatures. MPs and their staffs are typically genuinely interested in building their institution into a major force for democracy.

Even in those Arab countries in which parliaments have only limited influence over decisionmaking and legislation, they can still play a critical role in the political process because they deal with important matters. The critical issues of the day—economic reform, associational and press freedoms, electoral codes and procedures, civil liberties, ownership of and control over the media, governmental accountability and political pluralism—are all hotly debated in parliaments. In fact, during the 1990s, Arab parliaments have dealt with topics that only a decade earlier were still considered taboo, outside the realm of legislative debates—for instance, human rights and political prisoners (in Morocco), the normalization of relations with Israel (in Jordan), or the role of the ruling family in managing the country's overseas investments (in Kuwait).

Underlying the new prominence of Arab legislatures has been a deeper political transformation affecting the region: the gradual but steady shift from ideological to procedural concerns, a shift that reflects the increasing preference for constitutional-representative forms of government over the former model of popular mobilization under state auspices. As a result, since the late 1980s, the key political debates in Arab countries have been less over irreconcilable ideological differences than over the rules that govern political competition. These rules center on five main areas:

1. constitutional arrangements and the relationships they specify between branches of government (especially the executive-legislative relationship);
2. electoral codes (which define how elections to representative institutions are to be organized and conducted);
3. party laws (the laws that affect the formation and operation of political parties);
4. the regulatory framework for nongovernmental organizations (NGOs);
5. laws and regulations that determine the prerogatives and degree of political autonomy of the media.

Most of the preceding points share three features: They regulate access to the legislature and influence within it, they determine whether parliament can function as an arena where substantive political issues are debated and whether these debates can be followed by a national audience, and, most important, they delimit the legislature's prerogatives relative to the executive branch. Therefore, the struggle for democracy in the Arab world revolves to a large extent around changes designed to make legislatures more representative, autonomous, and influential. Parliaments have consequently become the focal point of Arab efforts to expand and institutionalize political participation. They can no longer be dismissed as mere rubber stamps, designed to deceive domestic public opinion and foreign donors into believing that progress toward democratic governance is being made. Instead, they lie at the heart of tentative efforts by regimes and oppositions alike to negotiate and institutionalize transitions toward more open political systems. They have become arenas in which incumbents and opponents experiment with new sets of political rules and novel ways of relating to each other. Indeed, they may be in the process of becoming what legislatures are supposed to be in free and competitive societies: the highest forum in which key players fight their political battles.

Thus, after a long period of political decline, most Arab parliaments are making a comeback. To the extent that new competition has been introduced in Arab political systems, much of it has been aimed at increasing the diversity and prerogatives of existing legislatures. These institutions, as a result, have become central actors in the renewal of politics in the Arab world. It is vitally important, therefore, that their functions, procedures, strengths, and weaknesses be better understood. This book is a first step in that direction.

Content and Organization of the Book

This book has three primary objectives: (1) to demonstrate that a focus on parliamentary institutions provides a useful perspective from which one can better understand the dynamics of democratic transition and consolidation in the Arab world, (2) to highlight the many contributions that legislatures make to the halting and incremental process of democratization currently under way in the Arab world, and (3) to provide information about legislative development in six key Arab countries: two in North Africa (Morocco and Egypt), two in the Levant (Jordan and Lebanon), and two on the Arabian Peninsula (Kuwait and Yemen).

The material is organized to suit these different interests. Part One consists of four chapters that frame the historical, comparative, and theoretical perspectives for the six case studies presented in Part Two.

Chapter 1 attempts to explain why political scientists who focus on the Arab world have paid so little attention to legislatures and discusses the combination of developments that has led to a renewed interest in institutional analysis, such as that conducted in this book.

Chapter 2 highlights the distinctive features of democratization processes in the Arab world, identifies an Arab path to democracy consisting of three main stages, and discusses the role of the legislature in each stage.

Chapter 3 concentrates on the functions legislatures perform in the process of democratic transition, with particular attention to the ability of parliaments to provide linkages between government and citizens; to process political demands into public policy; to hold the executive branch accountable; to increase popular interest in, and understanding of, political life; and to regulate and decrease political conflict.

Chapter 4 presents a typology of Arab parliaments revolving around two variables: centrality and capacity. *Centrality* refers to the extent to which a country's constitutional framework and political dynamics allow the legislature to play a meaningful role in the political system. *Capacity* describes the resources and organizational factors that shape parliament's ability to play the role to which it can aspire as a result of constitutional and political conditions. By combining centrality and capacity, we then classify the parliaments analyzed in this book into three main types.

Part Two consists of case studies in legislative development in Lebanon, Morocco, Jordan, Kuwait, Yemen, and Egypt. These countries were chosen because they represent distinctive subregions of the Middle East and North Africa, because they reflect the range of parliamentary politics in that part of the world, and because the authors were able to gain access to their legislatures, whether as independent scholars or as consultants. Indeed, for each of the parliaments examined in Part Two, the authors reviewed all key relevant internal documents, attended numerous legislative sessions, and conducted hundreds of interviews with MPs and the political and administrative leaders of these institutions.

Each of these chapters is organized chronologically, in order to provide the reader with a sense of how legislatures have changed over time and have influenced their respective countries' political evolution. To emphasize the analytical underpinnings of the book, the case studies are structured so that they address critical questions that emerge from the study of Middle Eastern legislatures, including the following:

- What functions do parliaments perform in relatively closed political systems?
- What do legislatures contribute to the process of democratizing authoritarian regimes?
- What can be learned from Arab experiments about the requirements for successful parliamentary openings?
- How do parliaments (and, by implication, other political bodies), which first emerged in the West, coexist and interact with distinctly Middle Eastern institutions such as the Jordanian or the Moroccan monarchies? Does the expansion of parliamentary prerogatives necessarily compromise the survival of monarchical or dynastic regimes?
- What specific roles do parliaments play in a multisectarian society such as Lebanon or in a setting still heavily influenced by its tribal heritage, such as Yemen?

The Conclusion summarizes the book's main findings. It highlights lessons that will be of interest to Middle East specialists, students of democratic transitions, and policymakers intent on using legislatures to facilitate the democratization process.

PART ONE

Arab Legislatures: A Framework for Analysis

1

The Neglect and Rediscovery of Arab Parliaments

At a time when parliaments are playing an increasingly central role in Arab politics, the literature on Middle Eastern legislatures remains strikingly underdeveloped. Three main factors account for this phenomenon. The first is the demise, during the 1940s and 1950s, of the parliamentary systems that had existed in the Arab world since the 1920s. As will be shown below, this collapse of parliamentary politics was accompanied by the rise of ideologies that were explicitly hostile to legislatures and that led to (or were used to justify) their marginalization. A second factor relates to the assumptions and methodologies that shaped the research agendas of political scientists studying the Middle East during the 1960s and 1970s. These assumptions and methodologies, it will be argued, were not conducive to an emphasis on legislative institutions. Therefore, even though there was substantial interest in legislatures within the political science community in the United States as a whole during the late 1960s and early 1970s, that interest had little influence on Middle Eastern studies. Finally, political obstacles have also made it difficult for Western academics to study Arab parliaments.

The Historical Roots of Arab Legislatures

Arab legislatures are frequently described as imported pieces of governmental machinery artificially transplanted by Western colonial powers into the region. The historical record, however, contradicts this interpretation. We will show this by looking at the emergence of the concept of political representation, as well as the attempt to give institutional meaning to it, in the Ottoman Empire during the nineteenth century. The historical roots of legislatures in the region will then be further illustrated by examining the first wave of parliamentary experiments in the Arab world from the 1920s through the 1950s.

Concepts and Forms of Political Representation in the Late Ottoman Empire

As Ergun Özbudun observed, "the idea of representation is older in Ottoman history than is generally realized. It was an established custom for the Ottoman government to convene an assembly of leading civil, military, and religious officials to discuss important matters of policy, especially in times of stress" (Özbudun 1987: 329). Özbudun went on to note that, shortly after acceding the throne, Ottoman sultan Selim III (1789–1807) gathered such a body to discuss the modernizing reforms that he intended to introduce. To be sure, the assembly was not truly representative, for all its delegates were chosen by the sultan, and it operated at his discretion. Nevertheless, it is revealing that the Ottoman authorities felt it useful to call for an assembly that, as Özbudun points out, "gave support to the notion that important policy decisions should be based on deliberations and consultations in a broader council" (Özbudun 1987: 329). In the Middle East as elsewhere, therefore, rulers have long understood the necessity of securing a measure of public consent for key policies, and they have seen the convening of assemblies as the most effective way to do so.[1]

There is abundant evidence of repeated Ottoman efforts to institutionalize the practice of consultation during the nineteenth century (Davison 1963). For instance, in 1838 Sultan Mahmud II established an advisory body known as the Supreme Council of Judicial Ordinances, assigning it responsibility for preparing and discussing new regulations. The powers of the council were expanded by Mahmud's successor, Abdülmecid I, who entrusted it with drafting and debating new laws on matters of taxation and personal freedoms. Although this council only had advisory powers and its members were all appointed by the sultan, its internal rules and proceedings were similar to those of a legislature. Most important, its impact was real, since many of its recommendations for far-reaching reforms were acted upon by the sultan (Shaw 1970: 57–62).

Other attempts to introduce semirepresentative institutions into the Ottoman Empire soon followed. In 1848, provincial councils of local notables were established to provide a counterweight to the power of provincial governors. During the 1860s, the Armenian, Greek, and Jewish communities were allowed to elect assemblies endowed with the power to legislate in areas concerning their own communal affairs. Even more significant was the creation in 1868 of an empirewide Council of State, in charge of proposing legislation. This new body brought together local leaders chosen by provincial governors, city officials, and heads of religious communities and guilds. Although not elected, these individuals represented a cross section of the empire's population. As Özbudun noted, "the emergence of the notion that major social groups and classes of the empire should be represented in its central legislative council and become involved in the law-making process was an important beginning" (Özbudun 1987: 330).

By 1870, the establishment or empowerment of representative institutions had become a primary goal of most political reform movements in the Ottoman Empire. In December 1876, Sultan Abdülhamid tried to ride this wave—and hold Western powers at bay—when he promulgated a constitution that provided for an elected Chamber of Deputies (Heyet-i Mebusan) and an appointed Senate (Heyet-i Ayan). Although the Chamber of Deputies sat for only two sessions (in 1877–1878), it represented a landmark in the evolution of the late Ottoman Empire (Lewis 1994: 50). The Chamber elected in 1877 was fairly representative of the religious, ethnic, linguistic, and occupational makeup of the empire (Devereux 1963: 147–148; Özbudun 1987: 333; Turan 1994: 110). It was outspoken and often critical of the government. Shortly before the sultan prorogued parliament, some of its members had gone so far as to demand the indictment of the former prime minister and the generals who had lost the recent war against Russia. Most important, despite the limited franchise and flaws that marred the electoral process, the two elections of that period gave legitimacy to the notion that the political opinions of the population deserved to be taken into account. In this sense, they helped promote the concept of citizen, as opposed to subject.

It is also significant that the struggle to restore constitutional rule became one of the most important political forces in the empire after 1878. That struggle was ultimately successful when in 1908 the Young Turks reinstated both the 1876 Constitution and parliament.[2] This second constitutional experiment lasted until the empire's final disappearance in 1920 and included five elections (one in 1908, two in 1912, one in 1914, one in 1919). For all their flaws, these elections gave further legitimacy to the notion of constitutional, representative government. They also exercised an important mobilizing effect through the campaign rallies and press coverage they generated (Kayali 1995: 282).

The rise of constitutionalism was also reflected in Tunisia and Egypt— Arab lands nominally under Ottoman sovereignty but in reality under the control of semi-independent dynasties. In both cases, ideas of representative government were first introduced by westernized intellectuals, who saw in them a way of curbing arbitrary government. But the rulers of Tunisia and Egypt soon tried to appropriate these ideas for themselves, largely to enhance their domestic and international legitimacy at a time when they were confronted with the threat of Western interference (on Egypt, see Chapter 10). In 1861, for instance, the bey of Tunis (as Tunisia's rulers were known then) promulgated the first constitution ever issued in the Islamic world. The constitution provided for a hereditary monarchy, the prerogatives of which were partly tempered by a Grand Council of sixty members, most of whom were appointed by the bey. Legislative powers were divided between the bey and his ministers on the one hand and the Grand Council on the other. Both the bey and his ministers were responsible to the Council. Although this constitutionalist experiment did not last long (the bey put an end to it in 1864, following a popular uprising), it served as an inspiration to reformers not only in Tunisia but in other parts of the region as well.

As these examples demonstrate, the quest for representative government has deeper historical roots in the Middle East than is usually recognized. Although active support for constitutionalism during the nineteenth century remained limited to a handful of intellectuals, that period saw genuine attempts to give concrete meaning to the notions of governmental accountability and checks and balances. This was usually done by establishing councils or assemblies, which served as the precursors of twentieth-century Arab legislatures.

Arab Parliamentary Experiments Between the Two World Wars

The 1920s and 1930s witnessed more fully developed attempts at parliamentary politics in the Arab world. The three countries that historically have vied for regional leadership—Egypt, Syria, and Iraq—all had functioning and active parliaments in the interwar period, and so did Lebanon. The political roles and significance of these legislatures, however, have been downplayed in the literature. The principal arguments are familiar. One is that parliaments exercised only very limited influence over decisionmaking. Real power was vested in the executive branch and, even more decisively, in the colonial or mandatory authorities (the British in Egypt and Iraq, the French in Syria and Lebanon). Another argument is that parliaments were not representative of the population. Most of the electorate lived in rural areas dominated by landowning families (or, as in Iraq, tribal leaders) who could buy votes through influence, patronage, and the manipulation of the traditional bases of social solidarity. In the cities, elections were usually won by wealthy merchants and other notables. As a result, parliaments were dominated by a tiny elite with little or no popular base. Moreover, elections were marred by administrative interference and other irregularities. The same individuals—the scions of the most influential families in the region—were almost always reelected to their parliamentary seats.

A third argument is that political parties existed in name only. They usually came to life only at election times. They lacked internal structure, nationwide representation, and a clear ideology and program. More often than not, they consisted of the personal following of prominent individuals and families. Elections, therefore, did not present the population with a clear choice among policy alternatives and ideologies. Finally, it is said that the general population cared little about parliamentary activity, understanding neither how parliaments worked nor the functions they were supposed to serve.

A closer examination of the historical record, however, suggests that Arab legislatures already performed vital functions between the two world wars. Particularly important was their contribution to nation building and the fight for independence. In those countries where the sense of national identity was the least pronounced (Lebanon, Syria, and Iraq), the legislature was the only place where representatives of the various regions, sects, and ethnic groups could meet to discuss national issues, exchange views, and learn how to cooperate with each other. As will be shown in Chapter 5, Lebanon's Chamber of Deputies played that role. The integrative function of legislatures can also be observed during that period in Jordan (then known as Transjordan) and Iraq. It is ironic, therefore, that during the 1950s Arab parliaments would come to be denounced as divisive. In reality, they did as much to foster a sense of national identity as the authoritarian regimes that disbanded them.

Insufficient attention has also been paid to the critical role that legislatures played in mobilizing public opinion, both internally and externally, against colonial and mandatory rule. Here again, Lebanon provides only a more dramatic manifestation of a phenomenon observable elsewhere. It was the Lebanese Chamber of Deputies that, in 1926, won a written constitution for the country. Afterward, it constantly agitated for greater autonomy from France, forcing the mandatory authorities into numerous concessions that paved the way for independence. Throughout the 1930s and until independence was finally secured in 1943, the Chamber acted as a check on the arbitrary authority of the French high commissioner and the Lebanese president of the Republic (who was better disposed toward France than toward the legislature). The Chamber's assertiveness led to frequent dissolutions by the French authorities. But although they repeatedly suspended the legislature, the French always ultimately reinstated it. This action was, in part, in order to project an image of respect for legality and constitutional norms, but it was also because the legislature could not be ignored. Indeed, the more the Chamber of Deputies assumed a militant posture in opposing French influence, the more it became a symbol of national resistance, so the more difficult it became for the French high commissioner to subdue it.

The French encountered similar problems in their dealings with the Syrian parliament. In 1933, for instance, French high commissioner Comte De Martel proposed a Franco-Syrian draft treaty that would have terminated the mandate, but with the Druze and Alawite regions remaining separate from the Syrian republic. This provision, as well as several others in the draft treaty, was strongly opposed by the National Bloc, the political party formed in the late 1920s by Syrian nationalists. As a result, the draft treaty was defeated in the legislature after several weeks of tumultuous debates and a boycott of parliamentary sessions by the National Bloc. In response, the French suspended the Chamber for four months (Khoury 1987: 393–394). The following years witnessed similar confrontations between parliament and the French authorities. In 1934, after the legislature was once again dissolved, National Bloc leaders organized a Committee for the Defense of Parliamentary Institutions that denounced France's "illegal dictatorship" and "irregular methods of financial and political administration" (Khoury 1987: 443). Throughout this period, parliament remained one of the main engines of agitation for national independence, which was finally won in 1946.

The Marginalization of Arab Parliaments (1950s–1960s)

Arab legislatures continued to play an active role in the immediate postindependence era, shaping public debate over national issues and criticizing government policies that members felt were wrong. Parliaments were heavily involved in budget matters and the allocation of resources. Parliaments were instrumental in seating and unseating cabinets—sometimes by forcing the replacement of senior government officials by others more acceptable to the legislature. They deliberated over general policy directions and influenced the setting of policies. Legislators also provided an important bridge between state and society by serving as intermediaries between their constituencies and impersonal bureaucracies.

Had circumstances been different, these parliaments might have developed their institutional capacities and asserted their political influence, thus contributing to the emergence of democratic political systems in the region. Shortly after a number of Arab countries became independent, however, their parliamentary systems were replaced by authoritarian, one-party regimes. This was the case in Egypt, Syria, and Iraq, where the legislatures were tightly subordinated to the executive. Only in Lebanon and Kuwait did relatively strong legislatures survive through the 1970s.

The downgrading of Arab parliaments during the 1950s and 1960s was part of a broader "revolt against democracy" sweeping across the area (Badeau 1959). The very concept of democracy came under attack by nationalist politicians and intellectuals. Legislatures in particular were condemned on several grounds. One principal argument was that they assumed a degree of political sophistication that did not yet prevail in the region. It did not make much sense, in this view, to have elections and parliaments if people voted merely on the basis of traditional loyalties and showed no interest in parliamentary life and politics in general. Before true representative democracy could be adopted, a civic and participatory political culture had to take root. Modernizing leaders, it was claimed, should not be subjected to the whims of an ignorant electorate motivated by particularistic interests.

A related argument against legislatures held that the masses could not be trusted to use elections to express their "true" political preferences or act upon their long-term interests. Traditional elites, through their control over land and other resources, would always end up "hijacking" the electoral process and the parliaments based on it. Thus, Western-style liberal democracy would not become a viable political system until far-reaching social and economic reforms had been implemented to free the individual from domination and manipulation by "reactionary" landed and commercial elites. Egyptian leader Gamal Abdel Nasser articulated this reasoning during an interview he gave to an Indian journalist in 1957:

> We were supposed to have a democratic system during the period 1923 to 1953. But what good was this democracy to our people? I will tell you. Landowners and Pashas ruled our people. . . . You have seen the feudalists gathering the peasants together and driving them to the polling booths. There the peasants would cast their votes according to the instructions of their masters. . . . I want the peasants and the workers to be able to say "yes" and "no" without this in any way affecting their livelihood and their daily bread. This in my view is the basis for freedom and democracy. (Quoted in Owen 1993: 21)

Another criticism of legislatures was that they were inherently divisive and posed a threat to national unity. Many feared that parliamentary debates would highlight and accentuate the sharp sectarian, regional, ethnic, and ideological cleavages that already characterized several Arab countries. This criticism was a powerful one, considering that Arab leaders at the time perceived nation building as one of their top priorities.

Even more fashionable was the argument that parliaments were ill suited to the urgent task of promoting social and economic development. After all, Arab legislatures had historically been dominated by traditional elites that were bound to oppose the extensive reforms needed to overcome poverty and underdevelopment. During the interwar period, furthermore, these elites had been closely tied to the colonial Western powers and therefore could hardly be trusted to protect national independence.

Finally, across the Arab world, the postindependence period was characterized by tremendous optimism and confidence in the new "modernizing leaders" who controlled the executive branch. It was widely believed that these men, often drawn from the military, would be able to bring about rapid social progress and economic development while restoring the Arab world to a position of power on the international scene. By contrast, owing to their emphasis on debate, consensus building, and procedure, legislatures were generally seen as institutions that would slow down the process of modernization. What was now needed, in the view of many, was not lengthy and arcane parliamentary procedures and debates but solidarity behind a revolutionary elite dedicated to social transformation and improvement of the well-being of the population. Through centralized decisionmaking, this new elite would mobilize scarce resources and march the country down the road to development.[3]

In this atmosphere, it is not surprising that legislatures were marginalized. By the early 1960s, many Arab parliaments had been abolished; others had become pale copies of their former selves and were ignored by political scientists specializing in the region. As a result, when parliaments slowly reemerged as significant platforms in the political life of several Arab countries in the late 1980s and early 1990s, Middle East scholars were ill equipped to analyze this important phenomenon.

Research Agendas and Legislative Studies

The scholarly neglect of Arab legislatures also reflects certain assumptions and methodologies within political science. Two of these factors—the "decline of parliament" thesis and the behavioral revolution—deserve particular attention.

The "Decline of Parliament" Argument

The theme of "declining parliaments" can be traced back to the early 1920s, when Lord Bryce's influential *Modern Democracies* was published in Great Britain (Bryce 1921). Bryce expressed the disillusionment of many Western intellectuals with the evolution of legislatures. Earlier writers had assumed that legislatures would emerge as the dominant policymaking arenas of modern democracies and that their members would dedicate their time exclusively to resolving the problems facing their nations. They had also believed that parliaments would resemble an academy of science, in which individuals discuss issues primarily on their merits. By the early twentieth century, however, it had become clear that executives, not legislatures, played the dominant role in formulating public policy. Western parliaments had even been marginalized in the area of lawmaking. In addition, rather than being concerned exclusively with the "public good," the rowdy members of these legislatures had repeatedly shown themselves to be selfish, power oriented, tied to particular interests, and prone to bickering. Parliamentary proceedings had generated little public enthusiasm, thus failing in the "civic education function" they had been expected to play.

The "decline of parliaments" theme was resurrected during the 1960s, when several experts expressed doubts that parliaments could survive in a modern technological society (Wheare 1963; Butt 1967; Loewenberg 1971). These observers suggested that parliaments would never regain the power they had lost to the executive, political parties, and the bureaucracy; that parliaments no longer maintained the real power of the purse; and that they no longer initiated much legislation. The experts highlighted the growing partisanship and corruption that plagued many legislatures and noted that the public had lost faith in the ability of legislatures to deliver.

Yet, far from being condemned to irrelevance, legislatures experienced a resurgence from the 1970s onward, and by the 1990s they emerged stronger than ever before. In established democracies, legislatures have been reinvigorated and have assumed new roles. Meanwhile, among the emerging democracies of Latin America and Central and Eastern Europe, new legislatures have been established and old ones resurrected after a long period of authoritarian rule. These legislative revivals in the North, South, and East are examined separately below.

Although the most dramatic example of an old legislature reasserting its power is provided by the U.S. Congress following Watergate, similar changes have occurred in Western Europe. For instance, the world's oldest chamber, England's House of Commons, has become far more capable of challenging the cabinet than in the past. It also displays a greater ability to educate the public and to mobilize support for particular public policies. Even though the cabinet remains the key policymaking institution, the House has seen a sharp increase in its political influence and ability to meet popular expectations (Norton 1991, 1994).

Scandinavian parliaments, for their part, have become far more active, as shown by the intensity of floor debates and committee work, the nature of the questions asked of ministers, and the amount of time that members spend in the plenary (Damgaard 1992). These changes reflect the growing freedom of maneuver that parliaments in Denmark, Norway, and Sweden enjoy, at a time when executives in these countries have been weakened by diminishing party discipline and the practice of forming minority governments that can no longer rely on automatic legislative majorities. Indicative of their new influence, legislatures in Nordic countries have become the target of intense lobbying efforts by outside groups, firms, and organizations (Daamgard 1992).

More generally, parliaments once seen as ossified and static are now described as vibrant and dynamic bodies that have been able to adjust to changing environments, have reinvigorated themselves, and are initiating broad societal transformations. This new perspective is reflected in the titles of books and book chapters published on Western parliamentary institutions since the early 1990s, most of which include the words *reform* or *change:* "The Changing Face of Parliament" (Norton 1991), *The Postreform Congress* (Davidson 1992), *Parliamentary Change in the Nordic Countries* (Damgaard 1992), *The Atomistic Congress* (Hertzke and Peters 1992), *Reform in the House of Commons* (Jogerst 1993), and *Parliaments in the Modern World* (Copeland and Patterson 1994). The internal restructuring of the U.S. Congress in the wake of the political earthquake created by the Republican landslide in the November 1994 elections is already adding to this considerable literature on legislative transformations (Evans and Oleszek 1997).

The reassertion of legislatures has not been limited to old liberal democracies. Indeed, legislative development has been a priority in countries undergoing democratic transitions or trying to consolidate their new democratic system. Since the early 1990s, this phenomenon has received increased scholarly attention. For instance, an insightful volume explored the role that parliaments played as "central sites" for the transition to, and consolidation of, democracy in Italy, Portugal, Greece, Spain, and Turkey (Liebert and Cotta 1990). Several books have analyzed the contribution of postcommunist parliaments to the transition toward multiparty politics in Russia and in Eastern and Central Europe (Remington 1994; Ágh 1994; Hahn 1996). The new legislatures of Central and Eastern Europe were also the focus of a special issue of *The Journal of Legislative Studies* in 1996. Another recent collection has filled important gaps in our understanding of Latin American legislatures and their role in the democratization process (Close 1995). The present book is intended as a contribution to this growing literature.

The Impact of the Behavioral Revolution

The paucity of writings on Arab legislatures also reflects the "behavioral revolution" of the 1950s and 1960s, which had a lasting impact on political science research. The behavioral revolution was largely a reaction against the institution-centered approach that had dominated the study of politics. This narrow focus on institutions had caused scholars to overlook such critical forces as norms, values, and the social and economic determinants of politics. The challenge of building a genuine "science of politics," the behavioralists argued, called for developing hypotheses to account for political behavior as opposed to merely describing the institutional framework in which that behavior was taking place.

The behavioralists' arguments prompted a dramatic change of emphasis within the discipline. By the 1960s, constitutional analysis and public law studies had largely given way to a new preoccupation with political parties, political culture, political socialization, political economy, and public policy analysis. By contrast, institutional studies became rare and were thought of as outdated. Furthermore, those few institutions that were studied were not legislatures but bureaucracies, political parties, or military structures.

The behavioral revolution had a particular impact on those subfields concerned with the Third World, where formal political institutions were typically less developed than in the West. It is significant that, from the late 1950s through the 1970s, the most influential works on Middle Eastern politics concentrated on the political consequences of modernization (Lerner 1958; Halpern 1963), the role of the military (Be'eri 1969; Hurewitz 1969), political culture (Waterbury 1970; Zonis 1971), and elites (Waterbury 1970; Dekmejian 1971; Zonis 1971; Bill 1972; Hermassi 1972; Tachau 1975; Lenczowski 1975; Springborg 1982; Zartman 1982).

The rise of neo-Marxist and dependency approaches during the 1960s and 1970s reinforced scholarly disinterest in institutions. In Marxist and neo-Marxist analyses, political processes were depicted as manifestations of underlying class conflicts. Institutions were not believed to be autonomous of socioeconomic interests, and hence they were not seen as having an independent impact on political outcomes. Instead, they were described as instruments used by the dominant classes to perpetuate their power. Dependency approaches, for their part, suggested that the politics of developing countries was shaped primarily by the unequal distribution of global economic and political power. From this perspective, indigenous political institutions were seen as largely irrelevant. The literature on bureaucratic authoritarianism similarly approached politics within a framework of economic determinism (O'Donnell 1973).

Even political scientists who stressed institutions actually portrayed them more as abstractions than as living organisms. For instance, despite its nominal emphasis on institutionalization, Samuel Huntington's *Political Order in Changing Societies* (1968) contained no detailed analyses of specific political institutions. In Huntington's mind, furthermore, institutions meant strong executive branches, bureaucracies, and mobilizing parties—not legislatures, about which *Political Order in Changing Societies* had virtually nothing to say.

Similar myopia characterized the resurgence of interest in "the state" in the political science literature of the late 1970s and early 1980s (Stepan 1978; Trimberger 1978; Skocpol 1979, 1980; Evans, Rueschemeyer, and Skocpol 1985; Hall 1986). For all its emphasis on the autonomy of the state and the ability of ruling elites to shape society through their control of bureaucratic organizations, this literature rarely concentrated on the internal rules, organization, or behavior of specific institutions. Middle Eastern scholarship, for one, has largely failed to describe state institutions in any detail. The few exceptions deal with the bureaucracy and its impact on development.[4] As late as the 1990s, there were still only a handful of studies of Middle Eastern legislatures—many of them written in the 1970s (Abu Jaber 1972; Khatib 1975; Baaklini 1976; Khalaf 1984; Baktiari 1996).

Technical and Political Obstacles to the Study of Legislative Institutions in the Arab World

Four other factors have played a role in the scholarly neglect of Arab legislatures. First, Arab governments have been very reluctant to open up parliaments and other politically sensitive institutions to systematic analysis. The authors of this book were able to overcome this problem only because of their work as consultants to efforts financed by the U.S. Agency for International Development to help Arab parliaments develop their institutional capacity. Second, few political scientists are equipped to study Arab legislatures. In addition to knowledge of Arabic, such analysis calls for expertise in public administration, legislative studies, and Middle Eastern politics—a combination of skills that few individuals possess. Third, to analyze a legislature requires an understanding of both the internal workings of the institution and the political context in which it operates. Arab legislatures may not be as complex as the U.S. Congress, but they are far from being simple, undifferentiated institutions. Finally, because familiarizing oneself with the functioning of legislatures requires substantial time in the field, interested scholars need extensive financing, especially to conduct comparative studies. Such financing, however, is increasingly scarce. There was more support—from both public and private sources—for major social science projects twenty or thirty years ago than is the case today.

The Rediscovery of Institutions

Whether defined as rules or as organizations, institutions influence how actors determine their interests, preferences, and objectives; they shape what is feasible and not feasible in a given society; and they create incentives and disincentives for action. Yet, in part as a result of the behavioral revolution, political scientists long underestimated the impact of institutional arrangements on political outcomes.

Economic historians were first to "rediscover" the importance of institutions. As early as 1962, Alexander Gerschenkron had demonstrated that strong and effective state institutions had made a critical contribution to economic development among the "late industrializers" of the nineteenth century (Gerschenkron 1962). During the 1970s and 1980s, other economists emphasized the importance of legal and institutional frameworks in creating environments conducive to economic development (Adelman and Morris 1973; North 1981). They saw the performance of market-based economies as dependent on the existence of institutions and legal systems that protected property rights, helped enforce contracts, reduced uncertainties, and lowered transaction costs. Some went so far as to argue that innovations in the institutional rules governing property rights had been the primary determinant of economic growth in Western Europe between the tenth and the eighteenth centuries (North and Thomas 1973).

By the 1980s, the "new institutionalism" had spread to political science (see March and Olsen 1984, 1989). One widely read book, for instance, explored the ways in which institutions have affected governing capacity, policy outcomes, and regime stability and legitimacy in various types of polities

(Weaver and Rockman 1993). Symbolic of this new emphasis was the fact that in early 1995 both the *American Political Science Review* and *Comparative Politics* devoted review articles to recent works in institutional analysis (Koelble 1995; Ostrom 1995).

The new institutionalism sees institutions as variables in their own right, not merely as reflections of other social, economic, and political phenomena. For instance, a legislature is not merely an arena in which preexisting social and political forces compete with each other. The degree of autonomy and the relative influence of a parliament affect the distribution of political power in society. An active legislature can generate greater popular interest in, and understanding of, the political process and thus have a catalyzing effect on civil society. Parliamentary debates or the adoption of a new law can mobilize a formerly quiescent constituency or provide disparate social interests with an incentive to form a coalition. Conversely, rivalries between two or more political parties over access to legislative privileges can unravel a preexisting political alliance. Finally, even though it is well understood that a party's ability to gain representation in parliament is related to the level of popular support for it, it is sometimes forgotten that how well a party plays its cards once inside the legislature will affect its image in society, and, therefore, its political future.

The new institutionalism has had a major impact on recent research on democratic transition and consolidation. This literature revolves around two central questions: Under what conditions can societies move from authoritarian to democratic rule? How can nascent and fragile democracies be consolidated into stable ones? Since the late 1980s and early 1990s, the answers provided to these questions have increasingly stressed the importance of institutional arrangements. Political scientists had previously emphasized the cultural and socioeconomic prerequisites of democracy. Cultural prerequisites were said to include the existence of a consensus over the fundamental principles around which society and the political system ought to be organized. Also deemed essential was the presence of a "civic culture" characterized by tolerance, trust, a propensity to compromise, feelings of "efficacy" (the belief that one can influence the course of public affairs), and the "right mix" of participatory tendencies and respect for the authorities (Almond and Verba 1963). Those writers who stressed the "socioeconomic preconditions" of democratic development paid particular attention to levels of per capita income, literacy, urbanization, and social and national unity. Lipset, for instance, highlighted the correlation between economic development and democracy (1960). Implicit or explicit in such analyses was the notion that democracy was highly unlikely to survive in societies characterized by widespread poverty, high illiteracy, and religious and ethnic heterogeneity. The presence of an educated public, a large middle class, and a dynamic civil society was believed to be essential for democratic transitions to take place.

This literature on the cultural and socioeconomic preconditions of democracy was implicitly pessimistic. Before stable democracy could develop, a country had to be "ripe" for it. There was little or nothing elites could do to facilitate democratic transitions in countries that were culturally or socioeconomically "unfit" for democracy.

By the early 1990s, however, these approaches had been largely discredited. Most scholars now agree that political cultural approaches to democratic transitions suffer from both empirical and logical flaws. Empirically, the 1980s and 1990s have witnessed transitions to democracy in countries in which the political culture had long been described as inimical to democratic development. Logically, it is not clear whether a certain type of culture is required for democracy to develop, as political culture explanations claim, or whether it is instead the presence of a democratic political system that fosters the development of democratic norms, beliefs, and values. Civic culture, in other words, may be more the consequence of democracy than its cause. As for socioeconomic explanations, they too have been undermined by historical developments. For instance, democracy survived in a poor country such as India for more than four decades. Since the 1980s, furthermore, some of the least developed countries of the world have undergone partial democratizations. Yemen, which will be dealt with in this book, is a case in point. Finally, far from promoting democracy, economic development has sometimes caused democratic breakdowns—as in Latin America, where democratic regimes were replaced by authoritarian ones during the 1960s and 1970s (O'Donnell 1973).

As the weaknesses of previous approaches became apparent, a far more persuasive literature emerged. This new scholarship began with a devastating criticism of what various writers called the "futile search" for the cultural and socioeconomic "preconditions" of democracy and concluded that democracy could be "crafted" in societies that earlier writers would have considered unprepared, provided that political elites displayed the required will and skills (Karl 1990; Di Palma 1990a). This new literature on "democratic craftsmanship" highlights the crucial role that institutional arrangements play in the process of democratic transition and consolidation, noting that certain types of institutions are better suited than others to foster democratic governance (Di Palma 1990a, 1990b; Remmer 1991; Karl and Schmitter 1991). Jorge Dominguez, for example, attempted to explain why democracy has survived among so many Caribbean nations, despite major economic crises. As he noted, "no other region in what has been called the Third World has had, for so long, so many liberal democratic polities" (Dominguez 1993: 2). One of the variables he highlighted is the legacy of the political institutions that the British left behind. In his words, "the point is not that the Caribbean's political leaders were born democrats. . . . It is that [institutions] set constraints that made domestic authoritarian outcomes less likely, while inducing political leaders to learn about democratic politics" (1993: 17).

East Asian experiences, too, demonstrate that the very act of introducing democratic institutions can help create a democracy. One reason is that "once the institutions of democratic government are established, it does not take long for vested interests to emerge that are determined to perpetuate those institutions" (Curtis 1997: 141). In Japan, for instance, the introduction of a competitive party system and the creation of labor unions, business associations, and other groups during the period of U.S. occupation "helped to make dissent and overt opposition to government policies a normal and accepted part of Japanese political culture" (Curtis 1997: 141). In other words, institutional change shapes and reshapes political cultures, and the latter therefore do not create insurmountable obstacles to democratic development.

Among scholars concerned with the consolidation of new democracies, an important debate has been raging since the early 1990s about the respective merits of presidential and parliamentary forms of government. The central question around which this debate revolves is whether parliamentarism or presidentialism provides better prospects for the consolidation of emerging democracies. Juan Linz (1990) argued that presidential systems are far more vulnerable to the breakdown of democracy. He traced this flaw back to the winner-take-all logic of presidentialism and to the fact that the executive does not need the support of an elected parliament to stay in power. In Linz's view, the very presence of an elected legislature and the executive's accountability to it in parliamentary systems constitute a key factor in the ability of a recently democratized country to sustain democratic governance over time.

Some scholars have taken issue with Linz's view of the superiority of parliamentarism over presidentialism in countries undergoing democratic transition (Horowitz 1993). Many others, however, have built on Linz's original thesis, arguing that for the following reasons parliamentary systems are more conducive to democratic consolidation (Stepan and Skach 1993):

- They tend to minimize the risk of legislative impasses, whereas presidential systems maximize them.[5]
- They encourage the formation of broad coalition governments that represent all major political forces in the country.
- They are more responsive to society's demands, since in a parliamentary system changing political preferences in society are more likely to force the executive to alter its policies or to bring about its replacement.[6]
- They make it easier for the executive to implement its programs, because they provide parliamentary majorities on which the cabinet can draw for support. By contrast, presidential systems encourage minor-

ity governments that find it necessary to govern by decree-law to implement painful but needed austerity measures.

- They make it difficult for the executive to flaunt the constitution without incurring immediate retribution by the legislature. In presidential systems, by contrast, presidents often do not control a majority in the legislature. Frustrated by the absence of parliamentary support, they may be tempted to bypass the legislature and disregard its constitutional prerogatives. Presidential systems, furthermore, offer few if any constitutional devices that allow for the prompt removal of a president who has become discredited and who governs either unconstitutionally or at the margin of constitutionality. The impeachment process provided in presidential constitutions is typically a protracted and costly way of remedying presidential violations of the constitution.

Thus, scholars who study democratic transitions may disagree about which type of constitutional framework works best, but they share a concern with the political consequences of institutional design and a belief that the institutional arrangements adopted by democratizing states will determine their ability to develop into stable democracies. Furthermore, in light of this book's concern with legislative institutions, it is significant that much of the debate about the relationship between constitutional frameworks and democratic prospects revolves around the centrality of the legislature in the political system and its degree of autonomy from the executive.

Unfortunately, like writings on "the state" during the 1980s, the "new institutionalism" in political science has remained too general and abstract. Discussions about the institutional context of democratic transitions would be more persuasive if they were accompanied by empirically based connections between institutional design and political performance. For all the talk about "crafting democracies," there has been surprisingly little interest in exploring the specific institutions through which this crafting actually takes place. As subsequent chapters in this book will show, parliaments constitute arenas that are central to the process of democratic transition and consolidation. It is often in them that new political agreements are forged and that competing elites experiment with new, more democratic rules of the game. To become successful legislative leaders, politicians must learn the merits of compromise, restraint, and accommodation—which are also the skills that the political class as a whole must display if democracy is to emerge and survive. In this sense, an active and influential parliament can socialize its members into the values of democracy. It is surprising, therefore, that so few studies concentrate on the role that parliaments play in the process of democratization and that even fewer provide a detailed analysis of the internal organization, rules, procedures, and resources of legislatures in countries that are in the throes of democratic transitions. The authors hope that this book will contribute to filling these important gaps in the literature on democratization.

Notes

1. See Marongiu 1968 for medieval parallels.

2. The Young Turks came to power through a military coup d'état in 1908. In another coup d'état in 1909, they deposed the Sultan and sent him into exile.

3. Unity, Discipline, and Work—the slogan of the Liberation Rally, the first single party created by Nasser in the mid-1950s—was highly revealing of this worldview.

4. See, for example, Palmer, Ali, and Yassin (1988) or the special issue of *Journal of Asian and African Studies* entitled "Bureaucracy and Development in the Arab World" (volume 24, 1989).

5. This is because parliamentary systems offer deadlock-breaking devices: A government that cannot muster a legislative majority will either dissolve the assembly and call for new elections or be removed through a vote of no-confidence by the legislature. Presidential systems do not offer similar constitutional means of eliminating legislative impasses, since they provide for independently elected presidents and legislatures that have their own, fixed mandates.

6. In presidential systems, by contrast, heads of government are elected for fixed terms and are independent of the legislature. Therefore, unless they violate the constitution (in which case they may be impeached), they cannot be constitutionally removed from office, even though they may have lost the support of civil and political society.

2

Negotiated Transitions to Democracy in the Arab World

Arab Democratic Transitions in Comparative Perspective

A particularly useful typology of democratic transitions distinguishes among three main types: "transition through regime breakdown or collapse," "transition through extrication," and "transition through transaction" (Mainwaring and Share 1986). The first type, transition through regime breakdown, is the most common process through which authoritarian polities are turned into democratic systems. It takes place when an authoritarian regime has become so thoroughly discredited that its leaders have no choice but to leave office. The collapse of the authoritarian order is typically brought about by its inability to face up to a domestic or external challenge, such as an economic crisis (as in the case of the former Soviet Union) or a defeat in war (as in the cases of Germany and Japan in World War II or Argentina in 1982–1983). The sudden delegitimization of an authoritarian government does not always lead to a more democratic political order. It can result in civil war or the establishment of another authoritarian regime. In many instances, however, one of the ways in which the discredited elite tries to cope with a situation it no longer controls is by relinquishing power and holding elections, thus providing an opportunity for a sudden breakthrough to democracy.

A second mode of democratization, transition through extrication, occurs when an authoritarian government has been seriously weakened, albeit not as much as in a transition through regime breakdown. The authoritarian elite realizes that it will not be able to hold on to power for much longer, but it retains enough control over the political process to negotiate its exit, thereby extricating itself from the responsibilities of government, with as little pain as possible. It attempts to do so by using its remaining power to influence the timing, scope, and form of political change. And, initially, it is usually still strong enough to dictate important terms of the transition—for instance, when elections will take place, who will be allowed to participate in them, and what kind of electoral system will be used. What generally occurs, however, is that the authoritarian elite loses control over subsequent stages of the democratization process. Once national elections take place, that process acquires a life of its own. At that point, the former authoritarian elite's main preoccupation becomes surviving the transition and proving that it remains a political force that must be reckoned with. To meet that challenge, it is usually forced to "reinvent" itself—to regroup and reorganize, acquire a new name, redefine its ideology and program, and learn how to play by the new rules of democratic politics. That is by no means an impossible task, as was shown during the 1990s by the political comeback of former communist elites in Eastern and Central Europe.

The least common type of transition is through transaction. In this book, we also refer to it as "negotiated transition" or "transition from above." Since this mode of transition closely fits current efforts at political reform in the Arab world, its main characteristics should be identified. They are as follows:

1. The transition is initiated and led by the incumbent regime. Because the balance of power between state and society remains heavily skewed to the former's advantage, the regime can dictate the pace of democratic progress as well as the nature and scope of the concessions it makes. Even though its control over the political system declines somewhat over time, the ruling elite remains the dominant actor throughout the democratization process. There is a general agreement, or feeling of resignation, that those in power will stay there.

2. The transition is characterized by slow and gradual changes. It displays few sudden, major leaps forward and is marked by both advances and setbacks. The overall trend, however, is progress toward a more democratic polity.

3. Although the regime tries to maintain control over the speed and breadth of the reform process, it makes a genuine effort to allow the moderate opposition to play a greater role in the political system. It does so by broadening freedom of speech, of the press, and of association and, more generally, by relaxing political controls.

4. The regime usually calls for and tries to establish a dialogue with the opposition, although groups that the government considers unacceptable are excluded from this dialogue, as is the case regarding many Islamist organizations in the Arab world. One central objective of this dialogue is to reach an agreement on new rules to govern access to, and influence within, decision-making institutions.

5. The authoritarian elite initiates the process of political liberalization not to bring about democracy but to retain power. Democratization is intended as a survival strategy—ruling elites seek to maintain or reestablish control over a more pluralistic, diverse, and politicized society by making concessions to it. They understand the benefits to be derived from accommodating

the reformist demands of civil society. They hope that by permitting more political participation, and by integrating moderate elements into the ruling
coalition, they will enhance their legitimacy, marginalize radical forces, and
increase their long-term survival prospects.

6. Because the initiative for reforms comes from above and because the incumbent elite remains in control, liberalization measures are met with a high
degree of suspicion by the opposition, the general public, and outside observers.
Many among them believe that the piecemeal concessions made by the regime
do not amount to real democratization and do not change significantly the way
power and authority are exercised. All realize that reformist measures can easily
be taken away if those in power feel genuinely threatened.

In the Arab world, therefore, democratization is following a pattern that
is less rapid and spectacular than it was in Latin America and Eastern Europe.
Neither the supply of political reforms nor the demand for them has culminated in the replacement of incumbent elites by new ones. Instead, political
change in the region has been gradual and uneven. Instead of manifesting itself through the downfall of existing regimes, change has taken the form of attempts at relegitimizing the system through elections and the incorporation of
new groups into the institutions of the state.

The forces driving this process differ significantly from those at work in
other regions. Latin American transitions to democracy during the 1980s were
caused primarily by the poor economic performance of military-dominated
regimes and by the demands placed on the state by more vigorous and assertive populations. The restoration of civilian rule was forced upon the military by resurgent civil societies seeking to impose accountability upon governments that had failed to engender sufficiently rapid economic growth and,
in many cases, had wantonly violated human rights. In Eastern Europe—a
clear case of transition through regime breakdown—democratization was
made possible by the collapse of the Soviet Union and communism. In East
Asia, democratization occurred mainly as a result of the social and political
changes brought about by rapid economic growth. Socioeconomic differentia-
tion, higher literacy rates, the expansion of the middle class, and the emergence of more dynamic civil societies forced governments such as those in
Taiwan and South Korea to respond to rising demands for political participation and governmental accountability.

In the Arab world, negotiated transitions are being impelled by several
forces. One is the enhanced political awareness caused by the social mobilization that has transformed the region over the past few decades. Increases in
literacy, urbanization, and exposure to the mass media and the outside world
have created a public that is more politically aware and better equipped to engage in the political process. Democratization, in this context, provides a way
to accommodate growing demands for political inclusion.

Democratization in the Arab world has also been caused by the economic failures of single-party systems, their successive military defeats at the hand of Israel, and, more generally, their inability to resolve the conflict with the Jewish state in a way deemed acceptable by much of their populations. The impression of government incompetence and powerlessness on the regional and international scene has spurred a radical opposition to Arab regimes, usually one that has taken the form of militant Islam. The resulting unrest and violence have forced regimes to seek to build new, broader coalitions against radical challengers. One of the ways they have attempted to do so and to relegitimize themselves has been by opening up the political arena and permitting greater political participation and contestation.

In the end, however, perhaps the most important force driving negotiated transitions in the region has been the shift of material resources from states to civil societies. From decolonization until the mid-1980s, most Arab states enjoyed a huge preponderance of resources relative to the societies they governed. That preponderance was due initially to the nationalization of resources that had been generated under colonial or quasi-colonial rule. Because the economy was brought under government control, societies lacked the wherewithal to build autonomous political organizations capable of constraining the arbitrary exercise of state power. The overwhelming extent of the state's control over existing resources tied the economic interests of virtually all social groups to those of the political leadership and denied a potential opposition the assets it needed for independent political action. As elsewhere, however, the Arab world's state-dominated economies performed poorly; consequently, the regimes that presided over them were ultimately faced with economic crises. At about that time—the early 1970s—a sudden infusion of new revenues was provided thanks to the oil boom. This boom bought a new lease of life for authoritarian regimes in the region, including those that exported little or no oil but benefited considerably, through workers' remittances and government-to-government aid, from the two consecutive oil price increases of 1973–1974 and 1979.

From the mid-1980s on, however, state revenues such as oil earnings and foreign assistance experienced a sudden and sharp decline relative to resources accruing to private individuals. Most Arab states, therefore, were caught in a financial and political crunch. They had overextended in the previous period—socializing their economies and offering their populations implicit "social contracts" that involved state-provided economic benefits in exchange for political quiescence. Populations had tacitly agreed to surrender the right to participate in the political process in return for the state's guaranteeing them satisfactory material rewards. The shift of economic resources from state to society undermined these social contracts and forced a redistribution of political power in the same direction.

Economic liberalization policies and the accumulation of wealth in private hands are beginning to have serious political consequences. As one analyst has observed, "there are now too many people, and wealth is dispersed in too many different directions, for the state to exert the same degree of systematic control" (Harrold 1995: 18). State-based elites have been deprived of the patronage resources required to maintain the personalistic networks through which they ruled. As a result, they have had little choice but to renegotiate economic and political relationships with their citizens. The thrust of these negotiations is a trade of increased taxation for greater representation. To gain acceptance for higher levels of taxation (understanding that a cut in subsidies and social benefits is the equivalent of a tax increase), governments have conceded more representation. Citizens have been asked to give up jobs in state-owned enterprises, pay higher prices for basic commodities, and submit to higher levels of direct and indirect taxation. In return, they have been given more rights to voice their political opinions (through democratization) and to pursue private economic interests (through economic liberalization). Bargaining over the terms of the trade of taxation for representation is driving the transition to democracy.

The renegotiation of state–civil society relations is a protracted, lengthy process. State-based elites use the process to enhance or reestablish their legitimacy, muster support for structural adjustment programs, and isolate radical challengers (most of whom are Islamists). Citizens, for their part, are attempting to take advantage of democratic reforms launched by the state to gain greater access to decisionmaking bodies and exert more influence on public policy. In sum, democratization in the Arab world is being driven primarily by the changing distribution of resources between state and society. Considering that this redistribution is a gradual process, it is perhaps only natural that the accompanying shift of political power also usually occurs slowly. Because of their incremental nature and because they pale in comparison with the rapid transitions that took place in Eastern Europe and Latin America, negotiated transitions to democracy in the Arab world are being overlooked. But when viewed in their own light—rather than being compared to the unique condition of a collapsing empire in Eastern Europe or the historic alternations between civilian and military rule in Latin America—Arab negotiated transitions have been making real, if limited, progress.

The Three Stages of Arab Democratic Transitions

Arab transitions to democracy share features that distinguish them from democratization experiments in other parts of the globe. For analytical purposes, they can be said to pass through three stages: *al-mithaq* (the pact), *al-hiwar al-qawmi* (national dialogue), and the phase at which the legislature asserts its authority. These stages are not mere academic constructs. An Arabic political lexicon has grown up around them. Arab political actors themselves use the words *pact (al-mithaq)* and *national dialogue (al-hiwar al-qawmi)* to characterize stages in their countries' democratization process. They refer to pacting between rulers and ruled and to the conduct of national dialogues between incumbent and opposition elites. Headlines in Arabic newspapers frequently contain the terms *al-mithaq* and *al-hiwar*. As for the assertion of legislatures, it is reflected in elections that are becoming more open and contested and in increased media coverage of parliaments and the debates within them.

Stage One: Al-Mithaq

Pacting begins when the incumbent elite declares new, more open rules of the political game. Typically, the elite is moved to do so by growing manifestations of civil dissatisfaction with the regime's performance, its lack of accountability, and the restrictions it places on political participation. In response to mounting opposition, which may include demonstrations and other violent forms of political protest, the regime unilaterally announces its decision to liberalize the political order.

Pacts involve an implicit or explicit trade-off, or "new deal," between the regime and the population. The regime accepts the principle that different political interests and views exist and need to be reconciled. This is a step forward, since formerly the myth of national political unity prevailed, reinforced by a ban on political parties or by a one-party system. When the regime declares a pact, it also usually relaxes controls over the press and allows greater freedom of expression and participation in professional organizations, student associations, chambers of commerce, think tanks, and other such forums that have no authority over policymaking but that in the preceding authoritarian era were under strict governmental control. The regime may go so far as to legalize a few opposition parties, as long as these do not appear to threaten its control over the political process. Society is expected to show its appreciation for this modest political opening by conceding to the incumbent elite the right to rule and by agreeing to operate within the confines set by the pact.

In the pact stage, governments may permit relatively free activities within service-oriented and single-issue organizations that appeal to narrow constituencies, but they discourage the formation of political parties that might aggregate the interests of broad segments of civil society. Although it is a far cry from real democracy, this arrangement may be satisfactory to both the regime and the opposition in the early stages of transition. The government benefits because the opposition blows off steam in relatively harmless arenas.

The opposition, for its part, may initially be content with the new opportunities that it is offered to propound its views and attract new followers.

When pacts are issued, incumbent elites are still comparatively strong. They believe that by *declaring* rather than *negotiating* new political rules, they will forestall further demands. In exchange for political quiescence, they are offering *consultation*, not *representation*. In the pact stage, therefore, access to the legislature is strictly limited and so is the autonomy and power of that institution. As a result, ruling elites remain unconstrained by institutionalized restraints on their exercise of power.

The pact stage may go through several iterations and be prolonged, or it may be declared once and for all, and then quickly give way to a more advanced stage. The examples of Tunisia, Egypt, and Jordan provide us with three different scenarios. Each of these examples deserves some elaboration, in order to illustrate the points discussed above.

On November 7, 1987, Zine el-Abidine Ben Ali, then Tunisia's prime minister, removed aging President Habib Bourguiba from power. Shortly thereafter, the new president did away with some of the more repressive aspects of his predecessor's regime. He oversaw the adoption of legal measures to improve civil liberties, limit police powers, and prevent extrajudicial practices. He ordered the release of thousands of political prisoners. During the spring of 1988, his government passed new, more liberal party laws and legalized several opposition parties. Ben Ali also opened a dialogue with the opposition, including Islamists. In September 1988, he met with representatives of business, labor, and political parties and with an unofficial representative of al-Nahda, the main Islamic group in the country, to discuss the content of a new political charter for the country. And on November 7, 1988—exactly a year after his ascent to power—Ben Ali signed the National Pact. This historic agreement was intended to symbolize the consensus of all the main political forces in the country on the rules of the political game, the institutional framework, and the general orientations of the country on foreign and economic policy matters. In exchange for recognizing the legitimacy of the new president, Tunisians were being offered a limited measure of pluralism and the promise of further progress toward democracy.

This political opening ultimately took the form of multiparty parliamentary elections in April 1989. Soon afterward, however, the government backtracked, largely out of fear that the process of liberalization would result in the acquisition of significant political power by the opposition, especially Islamist activists. The credible performance of Islamist candidates (who had run as independents) in the legislative elections, the ascendancy of the Islamic Salvation Front (FIS) in Algeria, and evidence pointing to a radicalization of al-Nahda all contributed to a violent confrontation between the state and the Islamist opposition in 1991–1992. By mid-1992, the Islamist movement had been repressed. Its leadership was either in jail or in exile. Its rank and file had been intimidated into silence.

The regime's determination to eradicate the Islamist movement also put an abrupt end to Tunisia's brief political opening. The search for a new political consensus, embodied in the National Pact of November 1988, had lasted approximately one year. From 1989 onward, the government became increasingly heavy-handed in its handling of the local media and foreign journalists. Opponents were denounced as "objective allies of the Islamists." The freedom to express criticism of government policies was sharply curtailed. Arbitrary arrests, human rights violations, censorship, and extrajudicial practices became more frequent. For all intents and purposes, therefore, Ben Ali's pact was stillborn.

Pacting in Egypt began much earlier than in Tunisia. Following his catastrophic defeat in the June 1967 war, Egyptian president Gamal Abdel Nasser was faced for the first time with popular demonstrations against his regime. He responded by convening a gathering of representatives of diverse political views, which in 1968 in turn ratified the so-called March 30 Program, also known as the National Pact of Working Forces. This pact provided official recognition of the existence of different political opinions within the regime's ruling coalition. It also enhanced freedom of speech and participation in relatively powerless forums such as professional syndicates.

Nasser's liberalization never moved beyond this initial stage. Nor, ultimately, did that of his successor, Anwar al-Sadat. Sadat's October Working Paper, drafted in the wake of the October 1973 war, was a somewhat more liberal version of Nasser's pact. It led to relatively free elections in 1976 and to the legalization of political parties the following year. But from 1978 until his assassination on October 6, 1981, Sadat backtracked from his commitment to democratize in the face of mounting opposition to his pursuit of peace with Israel.

At the outset of his presidency, Husni Mubarak renewed the spirit and much of the substance of Sadat's earlier pact. He retreated from the confrontational policies adopted by his predecessor between 1979 and 1981 and instead emphasized consultation and dialogue. This change in tone and style brought political quietude for most of the 1980s and appeared to presage a more thorough liberalization. As it turned out, however, Mubarak reimposed a more authoritarian order at about the time of the 1990 Gulf crisis. In the early to mid-1990s, this order became more repressive. Stepped-up activities by radical Islamist groups became as much a justification as a cause of this repression.

Egypt's political dilemma in the late 1990s is that although increased political demands and the widespread perception that democratization has stalled have rendered earlier pacts obsolete, the population is much less willing to be mollified by the declaration of a new one. The regime's call for a national dialogue in 1993 at first appeared genuine and designed to pave the way to significant reforms. But the dialogue that was finally held in July 1994 was stillborn, for the government stacked the dialogue conference with its own supporters and refused to allow significant political forces, especially the Muslim Brotherhood, to participate. Parliamentary elections held in late 1995 were the least free and fair of the Mubarak era, thereby confirming that the government was intent on subduing the opposition, rather than negotiating with it. Egypt, in short, has been more or less stalled in the pact stage since its first attempt at pacting in the wake of the 1967 war.

Jordan's experience with the pact stage of transition was much briefer and far more successful than either Egypt's or Tunisia's. Indeed, of the three countries, Jordan is the only one to have negotiated the transition to a more advanced stage.

A few months after serious rioting in the south of the country in April 1989, King Hussein appointed a sixty-member Royal Commission to draft a document that came to be known as al-mithaq al-watani, the National Charter. The commission included representatives from all major political forces in the country, from the Muslim Brotherhood to the Communist Party. Its main responsibility was to develop guidelines to regulate the legalization of political parties—it being understood that, as the king had instructed the commission, only parties that recognized Jordan as a constitutional monarchy could be tolerated. By appointing this commission, the king was trying to ensure that the process of political liberalization he was initiating would not spin out of control, because it would be guided by principles on which all the major political forces had agreed. The failure of Jordan's earlier experiment with multiparty politics in the mid-1950s probably inspired Hussein's desire to proceed carefully and cautiously in developing the institutional framework that would make possible the emergence of a viable multiparty system in the country. The charter, in short, was expected to embody broad national consensus on the process through which Jordan might ultimately be transformed into a genuine constitutional monarchy.

In June 1991, the king finally promulgated the National Charter, which he described as a contract between the monarchy and the Jordanian people and one that had been agreed upon by all the major political forces in the country. That the Muslim Brotherhood accepted the principles stated in the charter was considered a particular achievement. The charter clearly spelled out the rules that were now expected to govern Jordanian politics. Although it provided for a dominant role for the monarchy, it also offered guarantees for personal liberties and paved the way for the legalization of political parties.

Operating according to the rules stated in the pact, the Jordanian political system quickly demonstrated that increased access for the opposition was not incompatible with a ruling monarchy. Organized political Islam, in the form of the Muslim Brotherhood, shied away from testing the king's right to rule and chose instead to contest specific policies. As a consequence, the regime gained confidence and entered into negotiations with the opposition over further liberalization measures, thereby taking Jordan into the second stage of negotiated transition, that of national dialogue.

Stage Two: Al-Hiwar

Al-hiwar (the dialogue) or *al-hiwar al-qawmi* (the national dialogue) is initiated by incumbent elites for one or more of the following reasons:

1. Entering into the dialogue may be the means by which the regime attempts to enhance its legitimacy and broaden its base of popular support.

2. The dialogue can be a response to the "exhaustion" of the pact stage of democratic transition. That stage, as was shown, permits elections and freedom of speech in professional associations and other nongovernmental organizations (NGOs), but these organizations do not have the power to affect public policy. Ultimately, oppositions tire of having only such limited outlets for political participation. They covet access to representative institutions that have constitutional and legal powers to make policy and constrain the executive branch. They thus urge the government to open negotiations over new political rules that will provide them opportunities to be represented in such institutions. If and when the government agrees to discuss access to representative institutions, the process of national dialogue begins.

The transition from pact to national dialogue is greatly facilitated by the frequency and intensity of interactions between elites and counterelites. Small-scale, traditional societies typically provide more venues for such interactions and hence greater possibilities for members of the government and the opposition to come to know one another, exchange views, and bargain over politics. The political culture of Jordan, for example, is highly interactive, therefore more conducive to democratization than Egypt's, which is more impersonal, hierarchical, and structured and thus provides comparatively fewer venues for elite/counterelite interactions.

3. National dialogues may be launched by governments in order to gain endorsement for unpopular policies. In this case, the critical factor is the need to broaden public support for painful austerity programs (as was the case in Jordan in 1989–1990) or for emergency security measures that the leadership feels are required to contain extremist movements (as in Egypt since the early 1990s). The moderate opposition, for its part, seeks to trade support for these policies in exchange for political concessions by the regime.

4. Finally, dialogues also can commence as a result of a widely perceived possibility that political order may break down completely unless fundamental changes are made. Yemeni elites, for example, initiated a dialogue in a vain

effort to avert the 1994 civil war. Alternatively, dialogues may begin because political order already has broken down, and competing elites agree on the need to negotiate its restoration. That was the case in 1989 when Lebanese parliamentarians met in Ta'if, Saudi Arabia, to participate in a conference that produced the accord by which the country is now governed (though neither the essence nor the content of that agreement has been fully respected).

Repeated but unsuccessful attempts at national dialogue have also taken place in Algeria since the coup that canceled the second round of legislative elections scheduled for January 1992. That military intervention triggered a civil war that has been raging ever since. In an effort to avert total political collapse, attempts have been made on several occasions to bring the main political forces in the country to the negotiation table. In January 1994, for instance, the regime convened a Conference on National Consensus, which failed to bring about reconciliation. The violence continued owing to the refusal of most political parties (including the FIS and the National Liberation Front [FLN]) to participate in the conference. In January 1995, a meeting in Rome of eight opposition parties brought together secular and Islamist forces, including the FIS. The participants agreed on a fourteen-point document, known as the Sant Egidio platform, which called for the legalization of the FIS in exchange for a commitment by that party to respect democratic practices. Although the Algerian government had been invited to participate in the conference, it declined to do so and rejected the platform. Since then, hardliners in the military-dominated regime have thwarted efforts to agree on a compromise that would involve genuine power sharing.

In September 1996, a Conference of National Understanding took place at the initiative of President Liamine Zeroual. That conference brought together some one thousand delegates, many of whom belonged to the opposition. However, it was marred by the absence of the FIS (which remained outlawed and was not invited) and of two important, Berber-dominated parties—the Socialist Forces Front (FFS) and the Rally for Culture and Democracy (RCD), both of which refused to participate. Since then, little progress has taken place by way of forging a national consensus behind the principles that should guide the process of political reconstruction. A dialogue between the government and a broad spectrum of the opposition, including nonviolent Islamists, remains the only way out of the current impasse in the country. A step in the right direction took place with the parliamentary elections held in June 1997. The result of these elections was that most of the country's main political forces are represented in the lower house and the opposition as a whole controls approximately 40 percent of the seats.

As Chapters 6 and 7 will show, the experiences of Morocco and Jordan suggest that dialogues are facilitated when incumbent elites feel confident that they can make concessions and still retain power. In both countries, the proper role of the monarchy in the political system is no longer a major divisive issue, as it was in Jordan in the 1950s or in Morocco during the 1960s and early 1970s. Opposition leaders now accept the centrality of the monarchical institution and its claim to have the right to set the basic domestic and foreign policy orientations of the country. Because of this, both King Hassan II and King Hussein have been willing to concede greater freedom of maneuver to their prime ministers and cabinets in managing the day-to-day affairs of their respective countries. In Morocco, these changes even paved the way for the monarch's February 1998 decision to appoint Socialist Party leader Abderrahmane Youssoufi as the head of a coalition government.

The recent histories of Lebanon, Yemen, Algeria, and Egypt demonstrate that dialogues are also on the agenda when the situation is so catastrophic, or threatens to become such, that key actors decide it is better to compromise than to continue to pursue their interests in single-minded fashion. The case of Lebanon is of course somewhat different from the others, in that the dialogue in Ta'if was not between an incumbent regime and an opposition but between the political leaders of the country's various sects. Moreover, the object of that dialogue was not how to bring about greater democracy but how to end the civil war by redistributing power among religious groups.

In its first phase, a national dialogue typically brings together representatives of the government and the moderate opposition. Initially, the negotiations are likely to progress only slowly. The political distance between the regime and the opposition is too great to be bridged suddenly and without extensive confidence-building measures. Yet, the very act of dialogue helps build trust and mutual understanding. It also threatens to isolate radical forces and thus provides an incentive for them to join in the process.

As dialogue takes place and as incumbent and opposition elites probe and test one another, new political rules slowly emerge. The regime's main preoccupation at this point is to limit the elasticity of the new rules. By contrast, the opposition constantly tries to see how far these rules can be stretched. Even then, however, the opposition will most likely refrain from crossing certain "red lines," knowing that to do so would prompt the regime to respond in ways that would endanger the gains that the opposition already has made. Eventually, the confidence required for major compromises may be reached.

The slow pace of negotiations may actually be more of an asset than a liability. Long, painstaking negotiations may undergird the development of a greater commitment to the rules of the democratic game than might be the case if dramatic political reforms were suddenly agreed upon. Furthermore, unlike pacts, which are general in content and phrased in lofty, idealized terms, dialogues usually result in formal, legal political documents that specify in precise language mutual commitments and new rules of the game, identifying the exact powers and roles of key institutions and participants. Clear ground rules, in turn, make it easier for the process of transition to be sustained, consolidated, and expanded.

When incumbent elites initiate dialogues, the deal they propose to the opposition consists essentially of greater opportunities to participate and influence public policy, in exchange for recognizing the legitimacy of the regime and for providing support for specific policies. If the opposition accepts, the dialogue that ensues determines the terms under which political access and participation will be exchanged for acceptance of the current elite's incumbency and its key policy preferences.

Opposition leaders who engage in dialogues with incumbent elites are less concerned with influencing specific policies than with rewriting the rules that determine access to formal institutions and to the power that those institutions should wield. Although the opposition is usually heterogeneous (with the policy preferences of some of its members being closer to those of government than to those of other opposition forces), what unites its members is the desire to obtain guarantees for more effective political participation. As discussed in the Introduction, these guarantees are reflected in the following five areas: (1) constitutions and what they specify both about relationships among branches of government and about the means by which executive power can be limited, (2) laws governing the formation and operation of political parties, (3) rules and regulations defining how elections to participatory bodies are to be conducted, (4) rules and regulations defining the role and prerogatives of the media, and (5) codes and institutions meant to protect personal political freedoms and basic human rights.

Close examination of these topics for negotiation between incumbent and opposition elites suggests that access to parliament and this body's overall political influence are central objectives of national dialogues. Debates over electoral and party laws are important mostly because they determine who will gain access to the legislature and other decisionmaking bodies, such as local government institutions. Similarly, the call for constitutional revisions is usually largely driven by the desire to increase the legislature's influence and autonomy. Finally, a stronger parliament is better placed to protect and expand political freedoms, and an independent press can be more effective and objective in its coverage of parliamentary debates.

In short, the most hotly disputed political issues in the national dialogue stage—constitutional reform and changes in the rules governing political parties, elections, the media, and personal freedoms—regulate both access to the legislature and the visibility and power of that institution. It is also significant that new rules on elections, the media, and political parties are usually submitted to parliament, which is where they are further negotiated, modified, and then ratified (or not). When the legislature is not permitted to debate these new rules (as in the case of Jordan's new electoral law in 1993), participants protest what they see as a deviation from the democratic process.

Stage Three: Assertion of the Legislature's Authority

A central objective of a national dialogue is to broaden access to representative institutions and expand those institutions' prerogatives. Once this is done, the conditions must be created that will allow elected bodies to assert themselves and perform their functions more effectively. When this process takes place, the third phase of negotiated transition has been reached. Having succeeded in establishing accepted rules for access to decisionmaking arenas—of which the national legislature is far and away the most important—the national dialogue is superseded by a more advanced phase of democratization.

During that stage, elected and other democratic institutions such as the media endeavor to render the executive branch more accountable by subjecting it to oversight. Parliament typically supplants informal or extralegislative venues that were created to host the national dialogue in the absence of a representative legislature. Access to parliament having been opened up, it becomes the principal arena for further modification of the rules of the political game. As the legislature progressively asserts its power relative to the executive, it is faced with the critical task of modernizing its procedures and developing its capacity to make public policy and oversee policy implementation.

In sum, Stage Three is characterized by a gradual redistribution of power away from the executive—a process that may require amendments to the constitution. It is in this third stage of transition that institutions vital to democratic government are converted from largely symbolic and powerless bodies into organizations that aim to circumscribe executive power—a task that they can perform satisfactorily only if their capacities are developed. Once that occurs, the transition to democracy has been completed.

Of all the countries studied in this book, Lebanon is the only one to have reached an early phase of the third stage of negotiated transitions—and even there, Syria's overwhelming influence constrains very significantly what parliament can and cannot do. Morocco, Jordan, and Kuwait are not far behind. Since 1991–1992, these three countries have made very significant progress in developing a national consensus about new, more democratic rules of the game and in broadening both access to representative institutions and the prerogatives of these institutions. Yemen has not been as fortunate, since its advance toward the third stage was derailed by the April–June 1994 civil war. That country is now struggling to revive its earlier democratization experiment. As of 1998, it seemed back to the pact stage, with President Ali Abdullah Salih declaring—as opposed to negotiating—the rules of the game and with an opposition far more constrained than it was in 1992 or 1993. In Egypt, finally, the 1995 parliamentary elections produced a parliament in which over 95 percent of the seats are held by members of the ruling party or independents associated with it. During the campaign, several Muslim Brotherhood leaders were arrested by the police, then tried before military courts that sent them to prison for periods of up to five years. The vote itself was marred by administrative interference and fraud. These events confirmed that serious dialogue with the opposition was no longer on the government's agenda.

Toward Sustainable Democracy

Attempts to negotiate transitions from authoritarianism are taking place throughout the Arab world. Driven by the need to broaden support, several Arab regimes appear to be following a path of democratization that can be conceptualized as passing through three stages. In the first one, the pact phase, incumbent elites unilaterally declare new, more liberal political rules. The legislature, however, remains closed to the opposition. Stage Two, the national dialogue, sees the opposition and the regime renegotiate the rules that govern the political game and, in particular, those that determine access to the legislature and that institution's role in the political system. Stage Three is characterized by the assertion of parliament's authority. When that phase is completed, the transition to yet another stage—sustainable democracy— might conceivably occur. Only the general outlines of this final stage can be sketched, since no Arab country has reached it thus far and since the prospect of one's doing so anytime soon appears remote. If it ever develops in the Arab world, sustainable democracy is likely to present unique features. It is highly improbable that Arab democratic institutions and processes will be mere copies of those existing in the West. Still, it is possible to highlight the four basic characteristics that a political system needs to display to be described as having reached the stage of a sustainable democracy: (1) widespread agreement among all key participants on the rules governing access to state institutions and on the respective prerogatives of these institutions, (2) national consensus on proper procedures for the peaceful resolution of disputes, (3) guarantees of broad and fair access to the legislature and other representative bodies (such as local government assemblies), and (4) mechanisms designed to protect the autonomy of legislative, judicial, and other democratic institutions against infringements by executive elites.

Juan Linz and Alfred Stepan offered another useful perspective on what is required for a country to have reached the stage of sustainable (or "consolidated") democracy. They argued that the transition to democracy can be considered completed when democracy has become "the only game in town" (Linz and Stepan 1996: 5). Concretely, this means that three conditions must be met. First, none of the key political players, groups, and institutions must seek to achieve its objectives in ways that involve attempting to overthrow the democratic order or using violence. Second, even when the political system is confronted with a severe political and/or economic crisis, the overwhelming majority of the population must believe that decisions to address these problems must be reached through democratic procedures and institutions. Third, it must be taken for granted throughout the polity that political conflicts will be resolved through the laws, institutions, and procedures embodied in the democratic order (Linz and Stepan 1996: 5–6). Despite the significant political reforms implemented by several Arab regimes since the 1990s, no country in the region appears capable of meeting these conditions in the near future.

Conclusion: The Neglected Merits of Democratization Experiments in the Arab World

Although they are frequently derided as face-lifts for authoritarian regimes, the negotiated transitions currently under way in much of the Arab world have the potential to eventuate in genuine democracies. There is a constituency to support them among incumbent and opposition elites. They offer a relatively low-risk path that does not require a sudden and dramatic change in political personnel and institutions. Their incremental nature militates against the political breakdowns that frequently take place when transitions are accompanied by a sudden shift of power that threatens entrenched interests and thus invites violent confrontation. Transitions from above rest on the logic that recalcitrant elites are likely to be prodded into compromise by increasingly restive oppositions and that concessions made by those elites will be piecemeal rather than wholesale. Thus far, only the Algerian elite has sought to circumvent a negotiated transition and democratize rapidly through a high-stakes election. The resultant catastrophe has reinforced the appeal to Arab elites—including those in Algeria—of more cautious approaches.

Negotiated transitions are unlikely to proceed in unidirectional fashion. Two steps forward (toward greater political freedoms) may be followed by one step backward (toward a more limited tolerance of opposition and dissent). Gradual improvements, with periodic setbacks, are to be expected in transitions that result from lengthy bargaining between elites and oppositions. At first glance, such slow and limited change appears to be a liability, especially when compared to the rapid and dramatic democratic breakthroughs that reshaped the political map in Eastern Europe. But sudden breakthroughs are usually made possible by the collapse of state authority, which in turn is typically caused or accompanied by economic chaos and social dislocations. Breakthroughs that are the product not of negotiations, but of sudden, dramatic alterations in the political balance of power, thus leave unresolved a host of questions about political and economic relationships. They may signal the beginning of the process of democratization and economic reform, but they can also lead to instability or the emergence of new forms of authoritarian rule. Recent history suggests that transitions that take place in the wake of abrupt political changes tend to be very fragile. There is much to be said in favor of a process that advances in a more measured, controlled fashion.

In the Arab world, a sudden lifting of political controls would probably transfer power to radical, anti-Western forces—not to committed democrats. Polarization between entrenched governments and Islamist oppositions virtually guarantees that a dramatic opening would result not in stable democracy but in instability and violence. Significantly, in the two Arab countries that experimented with rapid democratization—Algeria and Yemen—the results proved unsustainable. Most Arab governments and oppositions are in the early stages of building the trust and devising the procedures and institutions required for democracy to work. Such negotiations are themselves central to the democratization process, because they are essential to accomplishing the required redistribution of political power and because they foster the skills and attitudes essential to democracy.

Arab negotiated transitions, including expanded roles for parliaments, are still precarious and incomplete. They are precarious because they have been orchestrated from the top. They can still be suspended if the interests of those who initiated them are seriously challenged. They are incomplete because even though they have broadened recruitment into and participation within the political elite, the original incumbents retain disproportionate shares of power and resources.

It is worth remembering, however, that over two centuries ago French indictments of incremental reforms in Britain—which included a gradual transfer of power from monarch to parliament—were based precisely on the grounds that these reforms were precarious and incomplete. The position of French revolutionaries was that change had to be sudden and thorough to be meaningful. History has shown, however, that evolutionary change has just as great a potential as a revolution to lead to a fundamental and lasting transformation and that it is less likely to produce a backlash.

Arab legislatures are beginning to take on characteristics reminiscent of the parliaments of Britain and other European countries in the early stages of those countries' democratization process. It may well be that these historical precedents, which were gradualist and incremental, are more appropriate than the examples of contemporary Eastern Europe, where change was spawned by the collapse of an empire—a historical occurrence that cannot now be duplicated in the Middle East–North Africa region. Latin American models, too, may be inappropriate because civil societies there tend to be more developed and economies less state controlled. Moreover, Latin American experiments with democracy, and the role of the legislature in them, have reflected what has been, until the 1990s at least, the primary struggle for power in that region, that is, the competition between civilians and military officers for control of government. Accordingly, in Latin America dramatic oscillations in the authority of legislatures have been primarily a function of whether the military is seizing or being ejected from power. That pattern does not apply to the Arab world, where military rule has been either absent, as in Jordan and Morocco, or more diluted and counterbalanced by other forces—as in Yemen. There tribal influence and, in the south, the power of the single party, have been significant forces affecting the pace and direction of democratization. Arab militaries have not been exclusive wielders of power—even though they play a major role in Algeria, Libya, Egypt, and Syria. Even in Arab countries where the military appears to be in control, the army usually does not rule as a corporate institution (Algeria being an exception) but serves instead as the instrument through which the rule of an individual or a minority group exercises itself. In this context, negotiation, gradual incorporation of social and political forces, and progressive enhancement of the prerogatives of the legislature provide a viable path of democratization.

3

The Functions of Arab Parliaments and Their Role in Democratic Transitions

Because parliaments have been analyzed mostly within the framework of established democratic polities, their role in regime transition remains a neglected area of study. This is unfortunate, for not only does the importance of legislatures increase in countries that undergo democratization, but also legislatures contribute to that process in significant ways: (1) They improve society's ability to express political demands and to follow and influence debates on public policy issues, (2) they enhance the political system's capacity to process and satisfy societal demands, (3) they help legitimate government decisions, (4) they provide channels through which the actions of the executive branch can be subjected to oversight, and (5) they contribute to the regulation and management of political conflict.

Legislatures and the Expression of Political Demands

Legislatures facilitate the articulation and aggregation of political preferences in civil society both by strengthening the institutional capacity of political parties and by generating greater public interest in, and understanding of, the political process.

Legislatures and Party Strengthening

A democratic political system must offer channels through which individual citizens can express their political preferences. In liberal democracies, such channels typically consist of political parties and interest groups. In the West, these organizations often control sufficient resources—financial assets, trained personnel, and access to information—to allow them to formulate programs, evaluate government policies, propose policy alternatives, publicize their views, and attract a clientele. Some of this institutional capacity is autonomous, possessed independently by those organizations. But another portion typically comes through access to legislative bodies that themselves enjoy informational and analytical capacities for public policymaking and policy analysis. In parliamentary systems, and to a lesser extent in presidential ones, governing parties can also draw on the resources of the executive administration.

In the Arab world, however, the political infrastructure of interest groups and political parties is less well developed. These organizations typically have only rudimentary capacities for policy analysis. Such weaknesses contribute to their inability to articulate coherent, detailed political programs. The problem is particularly acute for opposition parties. In their competition with progovernment parties, opposition groups suffer from the disadvantage of not having access to patronage. As a result, their potential appeal to the electorate rests almost exclusively on their ability to propose convincing alternatives to the policies carried out by the incumbent elite. Unfortunately, most political parties in the Arab world still lack the resources to do so.

In this context, Arab parliaments can make a critical contribution to the strengthening of the institutional capacity of political parties and therefore to society's ability to articulate and aggregate political demands. Once political parties gain representation in the legislature, they can draw on the resources controlled by that institution, including trained staff, access to specialized data, and connections to individuals in the bureaucracy, the government, academia, think tanks, and the press. Individual members of parliament, as well as the political parties with which they are affiliated, benefit greatly from gaining access to such resources. Consequently, through participation in a legislature, parties can develop their capabilities. They can mobilize the expertise and information that will enable them to put forward the detailed programs and concrete policy proposals that will enhance their credibility and ability to affect public policy debates.

The institutional strengthening of political parties—especially moderate opposition parties—is all the more important considering that democratization is unlikely to proceed without it. As William Zartman noted, the weak structure, organization, and capacity of mainstream opposition parties constitute a major obstacle to Arab democratic transitions (Zartman 1994). As long as these parties fail to produce credible alternative programs capable of attracting broad segments of the population, the main source of opposition to discredited ruling elites will come from radical movements, religious or secular, that are ill prepared to assume the responsibilities of government and are not necessarily well disposed toward democracy. In such situations, fear that democratization will benefit radical forces will remain a powerful disincentive for regimes to liberalize their political systems. The same concern will cause segments of the population to support quasi-secular authoritarianism as the lesser of two evils and to lapse into the cynicism, apathy, and indifference that so strongly militate against democratic transitions.

The relationship between party building and legislative development is of course a two-way street. Although parliaments that develop their institutional capacity can by the same token strengthen political parties, stronger party organizations also make for more capable and better-institutionalized parliaments. One reason for this phenomenon is that strong political parties can help legislatures mobilize the popular support that they need to defeat attempts by executive elites to limit or encroach on their prerogatives.

The Educational Function of Legislatures

The enhanced visibility and centrality of legislatures also improve prospects for democracy by generating greater public interest in politics. In many of the countries that will be discussed in Part Two, legislative debates are televised (sometimes live, as in Morocco, but more typically on a delayed and abridged basis). These debates sensitize the public to emerging issues. In addition, the radio and the print media provide regular coverage of parliamentary proceedings. Where it is active, the opposition press relays the questions raised and the complaints made by opposition deputies and does not hesitate to denounce what it sees as the government's "unconvincing" responses to the charges leveled against it by parliamentarians. During legislative debates, important and sensitive issues are discussed that otherwise might not become part of the public agenda. And as people's interest in parliamentary proceedings grows, populations become more knowledgeable about public policy. Politicized and educated strata can even draw on the studies produced by parliamentary committees, where and when these are made public.

As legislatures become more active and influential, they facilitate the expression of political demands in other ways. For example, parliamentary elections provide opportunities for mobilization of civil society through campaigns. Significantly, public interest and participation in electoral campaigns appear to be a function of (among other variables) the extent of a parliament's centrality. With the exception of Tunisia, voter turnout for parliamentary elections in Arab countries seems to be roughly correlated with the representativeness, autonomy, and influence of the legislature. Turnout in Jordan, Kuwait, and Morocco, for example, is consistently higher than in Egypt, where parliament has failed to become as central to the country's political system. Therefore, as legislatures become more visible institutions, the importance of elections is heightened, which in turn forces political elites to develop campaign skills. Such changes tend to make for a political system in which both participation and contestation increase and in which competing elites are compelled to fight their political battles in the open, thus creating the basis for a better-informed and more active citizenry.

A more influential legislature also contributes to the development of civil society by providing a power center to which interest groups will be attracted. As individuals become aware that the legislature can affect policymaking, those who share common interests will organize themselves, or activate pre-existing solidarity networks, to lobby parliament. In this fashion, a stronger legislature can both energize civil society and create greater linkages between the people and their government.

As parliament becomes a more respected and dynamic institution, public interest in, and understanding of, the political process increase. A more active and capable legislature helps individuals feel that their needs and aspirations are addressed by the system. It fosters a better understanding by the population of what democracy involves, including accountability in government, give-and-take, alliance building, and, ultimately, compromise. Such a legislature can also be effective in reducing political apathy, increasing confidence in the country's political institutions, and generating feelings of identification between rulers and ruled. These contributions are critical, particularly in the early stages of democratic transitions.

Arab legislatures do not yet perform their educational function as effectively as they should or might, although notable progress has been made in this area during the 1990s. Linkages to the press, research organizations, think tanks, advocacy groups, and academic institutions are still insufficiently developed. Broadcasting of debates remains intermittent and subject to varying degrees of censorship. Reports issued by parliamentary committees and records of these committees' proceedings are rarely made available to the public. (This is in part because channels through which dissemination would occur are weak and because governments tend to discourage such dissemination by classifying reports or by simply not producing them in adequate numbers.) In short, Arab legislatures have much greater potential than is currently being realized to contribute to a better-informed and less politically alienated citizenry.

Legislatures and the Processing and Satisfaction of Political Demands

Three critically important ways in which Arab legislatures help process and satisfy political demands is by passing legislation; by drafting, analyzing, and approving the budget; and by providing constituency services.

The Legislative Function

Constitutions in Arab countries typically empower legislators to propose bills in all areas of public policy. The practice, however, has been for legislation to originate in the executive branch and be transmitted to parliament for approval. Legislation proposed by the executive is typically vague, providing only general policy guidelines. Ministers and other executive branch officials are thus given leeway to specify both details and implementation procedures. This is usually done through executive decrees that are not subject to legislative approval. As a result, in a country such as Egypt, even though a typical annual session of parliament produces several hundred pieces of legislation, ministerial decrees, which have the force of law, number in the thousands over that same period.

The concentration of bill-drafting capabilities in the executive branch is a crippling disadvantage for Arab legislatures. It sharply restricts their ability to convert societal demands into public policy. To improve their contribution to democratic transitions, Arab legislatures must begin to initiate more legislation, directly or in consultation with the executive branch. To do so in turn requires that they be politically—and not merely constitutionally—permitted to do so. They must also acquire the expertise and resources needed to assist legislators draft bills. Such capacities are currently in short supply in most Arab legislatures.

Even though Arab legislatures lack the political and technical capacities to introduce much legislation, they nevertheless make significant contributions to lawmaking. The nature and scope of these contributions can be assessed by looking at the legislative process, which typically consists of three stages.

1. Once a bill is received by the legislature, it is considered pro forma by the whole body and immediately referred to one of the subject matter committees for consideration.
2. The committee reviews and debates the bill. Experts, as well as ministers or their representatives, may testify before the committee and respond to the questions of its members.
3. The committee's report on the bill is submitted to the whole assembly for approval. The bill can be debated again during the plenary session, and the sponsoring minister may again be called to justify or explain the proposed legislation.

This process provides the legislature with opportunities to influence legislation in several ways. First, because the executive sometimes uses plenary debates and committee proceedings to air a policy initiative and gauge the public's reaction to it, the legislature can affect the policymaking agenda. Second, whenever there is substantial disagreement within the executive bureaucracy over a particular issue, the role of the legislature is typically enhanced. A lack of consensus within the bureaucracy can cause executive agencies to seek external support, sometimes among legislators, for their respective policy preferences. This gives the legislature leverage over both the executive and policymaking. Third, committee proceedings and plenary debates provide the executive or members of parliament with ideas for new bills. Merely by listening to parliamentary debates, the executive can also make its future programs or legislation more effective and in tune with popular desires. The legislature thus enables the executive to become better informed about the effects of its actions and about people's reaction to them. Furthermore, whether or not they are incorporated into legislation, some of the points raised during legislative debates are often taken into consideration when the executive branch embarks upon the complex process of translating into concrete measures the general policy guidelines embodied in a law. Finally, both in committees and during plenary sessions, members of parliament can call upon the executive to defend the legislation it introduced. They can make suggestions and offer amendments to the bill that is being considered. Although it is up to the cabinet to accept these amendments, the executive often finds it easier to seek an accommodation with the legislature than to fight changes proposed therein.

The ability of Arab legislatures to contribute to policy formation varies greatly not only from one country to another but also from one area to the next. On foreign policy, military, and security issues, Arab legislatures almost invariably defer to the executive. In less sensitive areas, such as taxation, spending on education and health care, agricultural policymaking, or public works, the executive frequently allows parliament to debate and even genuinely amend its proposed bills. These general rules, however, do not always apply. Legislators may insist on their right to debate highly sensitive foreign policy issues, before or after the fact. In Jordan, for example, a large minority of the eighty-member lower house was able in early 1995 to force a debate on the 1994 peace treaty with Israel—a development that embarrassed the government and placed considerable political pressure on it. Conversely, in countries where the executive is bent on marginalizing and bypassing the legislature, the latter may not even be able to seriously discuss and alter domestic policy initiatives by the executive. That repeatedly has been the case in Egypt since the ruling National Democratic Party captured more than 90 percent of the vote in the December 1995 parliamentary elections. In early 1997, Mubarak did not even bother to consult with parliament on his decision to launch one of the most significant infrastructural projects ever in the country's history: the multi-billion-dollar Tushka irrigation program in Upper Egypt.

Budget Formation and Analysis

Another function usually performed by legislatures—one that allows societal demands to be translated into public policy—is the compilation, review, and approval of the budget. The U.S. Congress, recognizing the vital nature of this function and the disadvantage of executive control over it, created the Congressional Budget Office to augment its already substantial constitutional and institutional capacities to formulate and analyze budgets. Control of the purse strings is indeed one of the most important functions that a legislature can perform, since budgets can be thought of as political balance sheets. If politics is about who gets what, when, and how, then budgets lie at the heart of the political process. They determine how bureaucracies use the financial resources that accrue to them. They reveal which social groups are called upon to make sacrifices and which ones are the beneficiaries of state largesse. It is through the budget that national priorities are set and resources allocated among competing programs. The more civil society can influence budget formation, the greater its ability to shape its future.

All the parliaments that will be studied in Part Two are constitutionally authorized to study and approve the budget. In practice, however, their contribution to this aspect of public policy is minimal. One reason is that the budget, as it is transmitted by the executive to the legislature, usually provides general principles rather than specific appropriations. The executive is thus left with a wide margin of discretion to determine actual allocations in the implementation stage. In addition, although in theory the legislature can reject the budget, only rarely does it exercise that power and directly challenge the executive, for doing so could lead to parliament's dissolution. Most important, Arab legislatures lack the institutional capacity to contribute to budget formation and analysis. In order to play a significant role in the budgetary process, legislatures must have professional staffs with capacities to provide fiscal analyses and to develop budgetary information systems that can be utilized effectively by legislators. That is not yet the case in the Arab world.

Political and technical constraints thus seriously limit the contribution that Arab legislatures can make to the elaboration and review of the budget. Nevertheless, the parliaments that will be examined in Part Two take their role in the budgetary process very seriously. The budget committee is usually one of the busiest and most prestigious committees. Its members typically study the budget carefully, comment on many of its components, and make recommendations to the cabinet. Although the latter is free to reject these suggestions, it frequently accepts some of them and takes them into account when implementing the broad guidelines specified in the budget. Finally, individual legislators, especially those in leadership positions, act as lobbyists for programs and services to their districts and constituencies. Even in legislatures dominated by one party, legislators often form regional blocs to press for programs of importance to their regions. The executive is usually attentive and receptive to such legislative requests, especially when they originate among the regime's supporters in the legislature. As mentioned earlier, distributive policies (state spending on education, health, social policy, public works, and so on) are considered a legitimate domain for legislative influence.

Enhancing the capacity of Arab legislatures to contribute to the budgetary process would increase their ability to promote democratic transitions in the region. For example, the development of Arab civil society is constrained by current patterns of revenue extraction and allocation, which still favor civilian and military bureaucracies. Legislatures have the nominal power to tax and spend and therefore to address this constraint. Yet they need to translate this constitutional prerogative into reality. The acquisition of the relevant budgetary capacities can help legislatures push for more equitable public policies that correct the imbalance in material resources (and therefore political power) between executive authority and civil societies.

Provision of Constituency Services

The most significant way in which legislatures contribute to the satisfaction of political demands, at least in the early stages of democratization, is by providing constituency services. This vital function, which helps tie citizens to government, typically accounts for the bulk of a legislator's activity. It is performed comparatively well by the parliaments that will be studied in Part Two, largely because this function is in line with prevailing political and social norms. Arab populations expect their members of parliament (MPs) to provide constituency services, and parliamentarians see this function as one of their primary responsibilities. For its part, the executive branch typically does not prevent MPs from playing that role, as long as legislators do not encroach on executive prerogatives.

In several Arab countries, the legislature has been able to move into the political vacuum created by the inability of parties and interest groups to articulate and aggregate demands adequately. Legislators typically have better access to government than do activists in political parties and interest groups, and they can use that access to assist their constituents. Working as middlemen between the public and government enhances the personal political power of legislators and provides them with the experience necessary to craft policies that address recurrent problems.

Although the performance of constituency services is widely accepted as a legitimate activity of Arab legislatures, those legislatures provide few resources to help parliamentarians respond to the personal demands of their constituents. Instead, MPs must draw upon their own resources and personal networks to serve their constituents who request assistance. Enhancing the ability of Arab legislatures to provide constituency services would therefore build more bridges and stimulate information flows between state and civil society.

Legislatures and the Legitimation of Government Decisions

The emphasis in the previous section was on the ability of legislatures to make governments more aware of, and receptive to, the political preferences of their citizens. As was shown, parliaments do so by facilitating the expression and aggregation of political preferences and by transforming these preferences into authoritative policies. Effective legislatures, however, also make the population more likely to abide by governmental decisions. That, after all, was their original purpose in medieval Europe, where kings convened consultative assemblies of influential individuals in order to ensure those individuals' willingness to comply with royal policies—particularly policies likely to create resistance, such as requests for additional taxation. The historical contribution of legislatures to restricting the arbitrary use of royal authority is usually well understood, but the same is not true of their role in allowing royal authority to be exercised in the first place. Yet Britain's kings could never have developed the vast scope and depth of power that they did had it not been for the support of Parliament. In Bertrand De Jouvenel's words, "a parliament is needed to take any decision of importance. The reason is not that the king is 'not entitled' to take decisions without parliament . . . but that he is under the practical necessity of convoking this assembly, because it consists of the men whose goodwill and entire support are necessary to the success of any plan whatever" (De Jouvenel 1957: 176). The English historian A. F. Pollard made a similar point when he observed that during the Middle Ages the kings' attempts to concentrate authority in their hands ironically compelled them to consult regularly with their most powerful vassals on matters of public interest. These gatherings, he notes, made a critical contribution to the growth of sovereignty. "Before the days of parliament," Pollard observed, "there was no real sovereignty at all: sovereignty was only achieved by the energy of the crown in parliament, and the fruits of conquest were enjoyed in common" (Pollard 1964: 230).

Building the political support that will facilitate the effective implementation of policies, especially unpopular ones, remains a critically important function of legislatures. This is especially true in democratizing countries, where the authority and legitimacy of governments are often not well established. When these governments must carry out belt-tightening measures, they seek means through which they can demonstrate a degree of public consent for these policies. A legislature, in this context, can prove a very valuable political tool. A parliament can also provide for broad representation of a democratizing polity's varied interests and viewpoints, which in turn can help create the consensus that is required for the new political institutions to survive. It is not surprising, therefore, that in all the countries studied in Part Two, governments have gone out of their way to have parliaments ratify important and often sensitive policy changes—even when doing so has forced them to compromise on aspects of their policies. Democratizing regimes usually have seen such compromises as well worth the benefit of securing parliament's seal of approval on the measures that they have put forward. A legislature's capacity to generate popular consent explains why governments are often willing to engage in extensive bargaining and give-and-take with it.

Legislatures and Executive Accountability

Overseeing the executive branch is one of the most important contributions that parliaments can make to democracy building. When asked how they think their institution contributes to democratization, Arab legislators invariably respond by stressing scrutiny of the executive. This is hardly surprising considering that constraining the arbitrary exercise of executive power constitutes perhaps the most universal and widely accepted function of a legislature. Parliaments should ensure that administrative bureaucracies implement policies in ways that are lawful. Democratic political systems also rely on legislatures to operate as counterweights to the executive branch and to prevent the latter from concealing its actions or usurping the powers of other institutions. Analysts often describe elections as the single most important way in which governments can be made to answer to citizens. Between elections, however, it is legislatures that must perform the greater part of that role. (To the extent that they are independent from government control, the media, the judiciary, and civil society also contribute to watching and controlling the government.)

One of the most significant ways in which parliaments are usually authorized to perform this oversight function is through their power to inspect both the allocation of resources by the executive and the latter's management practices. In well-established democracies, legislatures have armed themselves with a number of capabilities to carry out these prerogatives. Some of these capabilities are used routinely (as is the case for the Congressional Budget Office in the United States); others, such as parliamentary investigation committees, are employed in unusual circumstances, such as looking into potential violations of the law by leaders of the executive branch.

In the Arab world, the oversight function is not performed systematically. Even in Arab countries in which democratic transitions are under way, parliaments possess neither the political leverage nor the institutional resources to ensure that the executive branch is genuinely accountable. For instance, the capacity to audit executive agencies is usually located in the executive branch, not in the legislature. When the legislature has such power, as it does in Egypt, reports prepared by the auditing agency responsible to parliament are distributed only to the legislature's leadership (which in Egypt's case is largely subservient to the executive). Across the region, auditing and program evaluation tend to be dominated by the executive, even when they are nominal prerogatives of parliament.

These limits notwithstanding, Arab legislatures do perform oversight functions, albeit to varying extents and with uneven results. One way in which they exercise some control over the actions of the executive is through their involvement in the budgetary process. This role allows them to affect the amount of financial resources available to executive agencies. Even limited influence over the purse strings permits the legislature to reward effective per-

formance and penalize mismanagement within the executive branch. Legislatures also promote governmental accountability by drawing attention to government wrongdoings, inefficiencies, and corruption. Some of the techniques
that parliamentarians can use to do so include the following:

1. *The request for information.* In all the countries studied in Part Two,
the constitution allows individual members of parliament to ask ministers to
provide written answers to specific questions. This information may subsequently be used by parliamentarians to compel the cabinet to account for its
policies or to alter them.

2. *The oral question-and-answer period.* Constitutions typically provide
for one parliamentary session in the week to be reserved for oral questions
asked by deputies. During that session, the minister directly responsible for the
area covered by the question must answer that question in person and in front
of the entire parliament. Question-and-answer periods can lead to harsh questioning and acrimonious exchanges. Ministers are frequently taken to task and
forced to justify their policies or account for the actions of the agencies or personnel under their jurisdiction. This is the case even in countries such as
Kuwait, where the minister in question may belong to the ruling family.

3. *The deliberation of parliamentary committees.* In all of the countries
under discussion, ministers attend and participate in the deliberation of parliamentary committees. On such occasions, they must answer the questions of
the committee's members. This often forces them to justify their actions, defend their records, or divulge information that the executive branch would
rather keep to itself.

4. *General parliamentary debates.* During these debates, the government's overall performance is reviewed and evaluated, and a vote of no confidence is at least a constitutional possibility. Even in legislatures dominated by
a single party, parliamentary debates force the executive to act in public,
thereby providing the population with an opportunity to judge the government's effectiveness and commitment to its promises. In contrast to policies
secretly adopted by bureaucratic agencies, discussion of public policies in the
legislature provides the media and the public with a standard against which
they can measure the actions and achievements of the regime.

5. *Special investigation committees.* In most of the countries under review,
the constitution allows the legislature to establish committees to investigate allegations of mismanagement, corruption, and abuses of power. To conduct such
investigations, these committees rely on information reported in the press, on
the input provided by citizens negatively affected by government actions, and
on the questioning of individuals who might have benefited from violations of
the law by government personnel. Conflicts pitting bureaucrats or administrative agencies against each other occasionally lead to the leaking of information
to legislators (as a way of embarrassing or compromising competitors). In some

cases, the chief executive may even encourage parliament to undertake an investigation, so as to achieve one or several of the following objectives:

1. demonstrate responsiveness to popular concern with governmental corruption;
2. shore up the legitimacy of the political system by proving that wrongdoings by senior officials do not always go unpunished;
3. project the image of a chief executive that is above the fray of bureaucratic politics and is not implicated in administrative intrigues and corruption;
4. send a signal throughout the bureaucracy that abuses of power will be curbed;
5. discredit or scapegoat opponents and make possible the adoption of policies that they have opposed;
6. reshuffle the political elite, possibly bringing into it reform-minded individuals.

Across the region, the 1990s witnessed several cases of high-profile and widely publicized investigations by legislatures. In all instances, the focus was on incompetence, mismanagement, or financial misconduct by senior government officials. In Jordan, for example, the investigation of former ministers and even one prime minister (Zaid al-Rifa'i) revolved around illegal benefits from government contracts. The conduct and results of the investigation, which commenced in 1990, were reported prominently in the press. In Lebanon, an investigation into charges of illegal commissions paid on purchases of Puma military helicopters from France occupied a large part of the work of parliament in 1992 and 1993. One of the former officials accused of financial wrongdoings was no less than former president Amin Gemayel, who by then was living in Paris. The results of parliamentary investigations generated much public interest and were widely reported in the press and the audiovisual media. In Egypt, following the earthquake that hit Cairo in 1992, parliament looked into allegations of collusion between senior government officials and contractors. Press reports had charged that such collusion had resulted in the substandard, unsafe housing that had been a primary reason for the high number of casualties caused by the earthquake. The distribution of public housing units and violations of civil liberties caused by the government's counterterrorism policies were also investigated by parliament, and the findings of the investigation were widely reported in the press. In Kuwait, finally, the reconvening of the legislature in October 1992 was followed by a parliamentary investigation into the ruling family's conduct when Iraq invaded Kuwait on August 2, 1990. The report eventually issued by parliament documented the al-Sabah family's inability or unwillingness to organize resistance against the invasion and their hasty flight from the country. That document proved a real public embarrassment to the ruling family.

Other parliamentary investigations followed that exposed widespread corruption and kickbacks in weapons procurements by the Defense Ministry. These reports had significant political and policy consequences. Not only did they bring pressure to bear on many individuals in high places, but they also forced certain changes in military purchases.

Legislatures and Conflict Regulation

A legislature's greatest contribution to the success of a democratic transition may lie in the area of conflict resolution. In fact, in the early stages of democracy building, a parliament's conflict regulation function is likely to be far more decisive than its decisionmaking responsibilities.

More than any other governmental institution, a legislature reflects in a very public way the political disagreements that exist in a polity. This attribute may actually constitute a parliament's most defining characteristic. As Olson observed:

> Because they express conflict . . . legislatures appear messy, contentious, and argumentative to the public. . . . The other entities of government, instead, hide their internal disagreements. They, too, can be full of conflict. The heated and important battles within the executive branch—for example, over the annual budget—may be the subject of innumerable leaks to the press, but the public never sees the officials engage in actual conflict. Furthermore, there is no public record of who said what to whom, and with what result. There is, likewise, no public record of the conferences, much less private discussions, through which judges arrive at their decisions. By contrast, the legislature is open to public view. Its floor meetings and perhaps committee hearings are televised. All may be publicly available in printed text. (Olson 1994: 8–9)

Parliaments, however, should not merely reflect societal conflicts. They are also expected to offer avenues and mechanisms through which these conflicts can be resolved peacefully. When they do, they can serve as an example to the wider society, demonstrating that it is acceptable and even healthy to disagree and that there are better ways of resolving disputes than through violence. This demonstration effect is particularly important in societies that are just exiting authoritarian rule or civil wars. Needless to say, legislatures may not always perform this function satisfactorily. For example, during the first half of the 1990s, politics in Eastern and Central Europe was frequently dominated by parliaments that seemed to exemplify and exacerbate the flaws of the new democratic politics: excessive posturing and positioning by politicians, inability or unwillingness of leaders to strike the necessary bargains, arrogant behavior by the new elites, and, most important, a lack of well-established internal rules and procedures to overcome these problems (Ágh 1995).

Legislatures may also reduce societal conflicts by helping incorporate into the political system forces that, were they to remain outside it, might undermine the political order. Arab legislatures are certainly not unique in this regard. A thorough analysis of parliaments in southern Europe during the 1970s and 1980s concluded that one of their primary functions was to have facilitated the integration of major political and economic forces and to have contributed to the peaceful resolution of political conflict among them (Liebert 1990a: 18–22). The crucial role of legislatures in this area is neither well understood nor sufficiently appreciated by either scholars or policymakers and thus deserves a closer examination.

Governments can reduce political tensions by utilizing legislatures to socialize former antagonists. Regimes undergoing transition to democracy frequently have to integrate parties that until recently were illegal and operating underground. They must also convince the leaders of these parties to join in the game of democratic politics—even though these leaders' commitment to democracy is often tenuous at best. Active and influential legislatures can help a regime achieve these goals, for they offer significant incentives for leaders and organizations to operate within the system. Membership in a legislature can provide a political party with prestige, visibility, financial resources, staff, sources of information, and the opportunity to publicize its views. To join the legislature, however, a party that had expressed radical positions must typically moderate its claims. Once in parliament, furthermore, its leaders must usually eschew their former hard-line rhetoric and learn to bargain in pursuit of limited objectives—for if flamboyant, radical rhetoric is the tool of extrasystem opposition politics, the art of forging compromises is the key to success in legislative bodies. In these and other respects, a reinvigorated legislature can promote more responsible and pragmatic party leaderships that adopt a problem-solving approach to politics and are capable of working with individuals who do not necessarily share their views. If properly structured, committee work and debates in the plenary will foster such an outlook and progressively marginalize hard-liners and ideologues. This is particularly true of committee proceedings. As Olson noted,

> partisanship can be relaxed in committees more than is possible on the floor. The small size permits personal friendships to form across party lines, and the lack of publicity encourages personal candor. Furthermore, the experience of working together over time encourages a common view against outsiders such as administrative agencies, government ministers, or even the leaders of their own legislative parties. (Olson 1994: 140)

This is why legislatures can prove ideal channels for hammering out agreements among elites and for testing new political rules and conflict resolution devices.

In short, a more influential and visible legislature can help rival politicians realize that politics is not necessarily a zero-sum game and that accommodation and compromise can be mutually beneficial. By providing an arena for the peaceful resolution of political differences, parliament contributes to the crystallization of a democratic ethos within the elite. A legislature offers "a forum which brings various segments of the country's power elite together under one roof to communicate and exchange views. Often a sense of camaraderie develops between members of different ideological persuasions. In times of conflict this cushions the animosities that can develop among the elite and makes conflict resolution more feasible" (Khoury 1981: 436).

The Lebanese and Yemeni civil wars provide dramatic illustrations of the costs associated with not taking advantage of parliamentary venues for conflict resolution. In both cases, an active legislature existed that might have provided a forum through which rival political elites could have resolved peacefully some of their differences. Instead, in both instances, key political actors chose not to explore this venue to find a way out of a major political crisis (the Palestinian presence in Lebanon and the division of power between north and south in Yemen, respectively). The result was two devastating civil conflicts. In Yemen, the north prevailed after only seventy days, whereas in Lebanon a fifteen-year war led to mutual exhaustion and no clear winner. Despite these differences, both wars ended with parliament being the primary symbol of national unity and, at least in Lebanon, a principal venue for hammering out institutional compromises and the foundations for a new political order.

4

Arab Legislatures:
A Typology

A legislature's ability to serve as a "central site" for democratic transition depends largely on its political strength. The stronger it is, the more likely that it can play an active role in the democratization process. It is important, therefore, that one be able to assess the political strength of a given parliament. That strength is primarily a function of two variables: institutional centrality and internal capacity.

Defining Centrality and Capacity

Institutional centrality measures the extent to which a country's legal-constitutional framework and overall political context provide parliament with the potential to play a meaningful political role. Centrality is high when the legislature meets the following conditions: (1) It is constitutionally and politically permitted to operate as an autonomous and influential institution, (2) it is capable of resisting actions emanating from the executive, and (3) it is able to formulate its own policy proposals and can affect the decisionmaking process in significant ways.

Internal capacity, by contrast, refers to a parliament's possession of the resources and expertise that will allow it to perform the functions to which it theoretically is entitled. For instance, a parliament's ability to contribute to legislation depends in part on the legislative skills of its members, on their experience, and on their access to bill-drafting capabilities. It is also influenced by the nature and quality of the institution's political and administrative leadership. Similarly, effective oversight of the executive branch and active involvement in the budgetary process require professional staff capable of performing fiscal analyses and audits. More generally, parliaments must provide their members with substantial technical and human resources if they are to discharge their responsibilities. The internal organization of the legislature and its access to informational and personnel resources have a critical bearing on the institution's ability to perform its constitutionally and politically mandated functions. This is particularly true of parliaments in countries undergoing transitions to democracy, because they are usually given a host of new responsibilities but very few resources with which to carry out their duties.

By defining a legislature's political strength as a function of centrality and capacity, we seek to account for the external and internal constraints that shape its behavior and influence. External constraints arise from the political context within which the legislature operates. Important variables affecting centrality include (see Olson and Norton 1996: 7–9):

- *The type of political system provided by the constitution.* As a rule, the autonomy and influence of the legislature tend to be greater in presidential systems than in parliamentary ones.
- *The number of political parties represented in parliament, the distribution of seats among them, and the extent to which party discipline prevails.* For example, legislatures dominated by one party that can enforce discipline among its members will have less room for autonomous action, especially if that party also controls the executive branch.
- *The number and strength of interest groups.* A political system that features numerous and well-organized interest groups will tend to provide the legislature with opportunities for independent action. This is particularly true if these interest groups are not able to affect policy-making through access to executive agencies. In that case, they will often seek to harness the legislature to promote their interests, thus enhancing the influence of that legislature.
- *The extent to which the executive branch and the administrative bureaucracy are united or divided.* The greater the divisions among senior political figures in the executive branch and among administrative agencies, the more likely these leaders and agencies are to try to mobilize legislators as foils in the battles among themselves and therefore the greater the bargaining power of the legislature.

External constraints thus determine what a legislature is empowered to do by the constitution and the political context. Internal constraints, in contrast, affect the legislature's functions. Internal constraints typically consist of resource deficiencies and/or inadequate utilization of existing resources. (The main types of internal constraints are described under "Assessing Internal Capacity.")

The relationship between external and internal constraints is complex. It is tempting to assume that fewer external constraints also means fewer internal ones, that is, that legislatures constitutionally and politically permitted to play a central role in the political system will necessarily have access to the resources they need. Empirically, however, that is not the case. For instance, the Lebanese parliament elected in 1992 proved quite assertive. Constitutionally and politically, it was one of the most influential Arab legislatures during the first half of the 1990s. Yet, its ability to perform its functions effectively was significantly limited by insufficient resources and internal organization problems. Conversely, during that same period, Egypt's lower house had the most abundant and sophisticated internal resources of all parliaments in the Arab world. But despite these resources, the Egyptian parliament had a very limited and circumscribed political role (that is, it operated under powerful external constraints). Thus, although Egypt's case suggests that access to resources does not enable a legislature to overcome external constraints under which it operates, Lebanon's experience demonstrates that centrality does not immediately generate capacity. This lack of correlation between internal and external constraints is certainly not unique to the region. For instance, under the authoritarian regime that ruled Brazil from 1964 until the early 1980s, the legislature had internal resources second only to those of the U.S. Congress. Yet during that period its role was minimal. The Costa Rican legislature, on the other hand, had few internal resources, but it performed critically important functions in the political system.

In fact, centrality and capacity are often inversely related to each other. It is not hard to understand why. When the legislature is subordinate to the executive, the latter is likely to be less apprehensive about giving resources to the legislature. Therefore, although weak legislatures often are given resources because they constitute no threat, strong ones typically must contest with the executive to obtain these resources. In other words, if a parliament is largely dependent on the executive branch, the latter may help it become better organized and better equipped. By contrast, if parliament possesses some constitutional and political autonomy, its ability to take advantage of this opportunity to maximize its room for independent action will increase with the resources that it can secure; that, however, is precisely why the executive branch is likely to be ill disposed toward allowing it to gain access to these resources.

Assessing Institutional Centrality

As noted in Chapter 2, in countries undergoing negotiated transitions, the single most important variable that shapes the influence of the legislature is how far political elites have moved toward reaching agreements on constitutional arrangements and on laws governing elections, parties, associations, and the media. Parliaments cannot emerge as meaningful arenas of political competition until some consensus on these matters has been reached. Societies in which the regime and the opposition have hammered out the needed compromises are more likely to have assertive legislatures. By contrast, in polities that still display substantial disagreements on how the political game ought to be played, parliaments will usually be quiescent and subordinate to the executive.

Several reasons explain why the influence of the legislature depends on the process of negotiating agreements on institutional and legal frameworks. First, as noted earlier, access to parliament and the power of that institution are largely determined by the constitution and the laws governing the formation and operation of political parties, the conduct of elections, and freedom of the press. Second, unless the ruling elite feels confident that the opposition sees the political system as legitimate and agrees to work within its confines, the elite will want to control parliament for fear that its opponents might use it as a power base to challenge the regime. By the same token, the opposition is unlikely to put much trust in, and emphasis on, parliamentary work if it does not believe that the existing rules of the political game provide the legislature with real influence. In fact, such a situation will encourage the opposition to resort to extraparliamentary means to press its demands. We thus may classify Arab countries according to how successful they have been in reaching a compromise on new political rules, hence in transferring political dialogue to the legislature. This approach yields a typology made up of three main categories.

Category One

The first category consists of countries that have succeeded in negotiating and establishing most of the institutional arrangements required for enshrining the legislature as the principal arena of political competition. According to the framework developed in Chapter 2, this category includes polities that have reached the third stage of democratic transition (assertion of the legislature's authority). Countries that belong to this category are characterized first and foremost by the fact that political incumbents and the main opposition forces agree on the basic rules of the political game, including the constitutional framework, the electoral law, and the laws regulating the formation and operation of political parties and voluntary associations.

As of mid-1998, Lebanon and Morocco broadly fit this description. In Lebanon, the October 1989 Ta'if Accord, which less than a year later was embodied in constitutional amendments, established a Second Republic built on widely accepted new rules of the political game. These rules provided a central role for the Chamber of Deputies, and their modification, when and if it occurs, will likely be discussed and approved by the Chamber. Since the rules were adopted, Lebanon has held two legislative elections (in 1992 and 1996). Both elections took place on schedule, and the second saw a significant rise in voter turnout, demonstrating that a much larger percentage of the population, including those in predominantly Christian areas, was now willing to play within the parameters of the Ta'if Accord and the Syrian-dominated political order.

Morocco, too, meets the requirements for inclusion in Category One, since it has been able to develop the degree of political consensus needed to make parliament a central institution. The key political actors—from the monarchy to the main parties on the left—no longer disagree over the basic rules of the game. Indeed, in the 1990s a general consensus has crystallized over both the nature of the institutions appropriate to the country and the mechanisms according to which political disagreements ought to be resolved. This consensus is apparent in the sharp contrast between the 1992 referendum on the new constitution and the 1996 referendum on the constitutional amendment creating an upper house. In 1992, the two largest opposition parties, the Socialist Union of Popular Forces (USFP) and the Istiqlal, called upon their followers to boycott the referendum. In 1996, by contrast, they supported the constitutional amendment. More generally, they no longer objected to the political framework provided for in the constitution, including the central political role of the monarchy. The overwhelming approval of the 1996 constitutional reform (99.6 percent of those who voted endorsed the amendment) highlighted the unprecedented national consensus on the country's institutions.

In February 1997, moreover, representatives of the government and of all the political parties were able to agree on the modalities for the organization of the forthcoming elections. A special, ad hoc commission (Commission de Suivi des Elections) was even established to ensure that these modalities would be implemented in a way satisfying to all the parties involved. For the first time in Moroccan history, therefore, a consensus emerged not only over the rules of the game but also over the ways in which it could be ensured that these rules would be applied fairly and systematically. The transcending of the old rivalry between "the Palace" and "the opposition" was made even clearer by the king's February 1998 appointment of socialist leader Abderrahmane Youssoufi as prime minister. For the first time in forty years, a leader of what had been "the opposition" was allowed to form the government and was given a strong and publicly expressed mandate by the king. The subsequent constitution of a cabinet representing a broad alliance of left-oriented and centrist parties, the traditionalist-nationalist current represented by the Istiqlal party, independent personalities, and individuals closely associated with the Palace (Driss Basri, Abdellatif Filali) underscored Morocco's new "sacred union." Such developments portend well for the future of parliament's role in the political system.

Category Two

A second category includes countries that have demonstrated substantial success in negotiating new political rules and that have begun to revitalize the legislature on that basis. These countries, however, still fall short of a clear national consensus on the rules of the game. In our democratic transition model discussed in Chapter 2, these are polities that have reached Stage Two (national dialogue) and begun to move into Stage Three. Their legislatures have become more representative, dynamic, and autonomous, although they still occupy a subordinate place in political systems that remain dominated by the executive branch. As of mid-1998, Jordan, Kuwait, and Yemen all belonged to Category Two. (Among the countries not included in the Part Two case studies, Algeria since the June 1997 legislative elections might be progressing into Category Two as well.)

Until Yemen's democratic experiment was disrupted by the civil war that broke out in May 1994, it even had prospects of moving from Category Two to Category One. The Yemeni legislature elected in April 1993 displayed its increasing centrality at the end of that year, when it assumed a leading role in the attempt to effect a reconciliation between President Ali Abdullah Salih (a northerner) and Vice President Ali Salim al-Bidh (a southerner). In fact, the Committee for National Reconciliation, which issued its recommendations for a compromise solution in January 1994, was originally composed of members of the parliamentary groups of the General People's Congress (GPC), controlled by President Salih, and the Yemeni Socialist Party, under Vice President al-Bidh's command. The civil war, however, had the effect of reducing the centrality of the legislature. Nevertheless, since new elections were held in April 1996, the Yemeni parliament has shown that it remains a force with which President Salih must contend. This is particularly true in light of two factors: (1) the power wielded by the speaker of Parliament, Shaikh Abdullah al-Ahmar, who is also the leader of the influential Islamic Islah party; and (2) the fragmented nature of the ruling party, which, as a coalition of diverse and frequently antagonistic forces, provides individual members of parliament (MPs) with much room for maneuver.

Jordan and Kuwait also belong in Category Two. In both cases, opposition forces are well represented in the legislature, and the latter's influence has increased markedly during the 1990s. Still, there remain significant unresolved issues that prevent the emergence of a clear consensus on the rules of the game. In Kuwait, for instance, women are not yet allowed to vote. In Jordan, the electoral law is widely contested. The Islamic Action Front—the political arm of the Muslim Brotherhood and the largest party in the Jordanian lower house until 1997—boycotted the November 1997 elections, as did eight smaller, mainly leftist or pan-Arab parties. All of them complained that the electoral law favors conservative, tribal candidates and that the government had failed to provide guarantees that the poll would be fair. Government critics had also accused the regime of seeking to marginalize the legislature and of imposing excessive restrictions on reporting (especially regarding the peace process). As of mid-1998, these and other issues continued to thwart Jordan's ability to "graduate" into Category One.

Category Three

Countries in this category have the following features: They have yet to begin, or remain in the very early stages of, broad-based negotiations over institutional arrangements; the constitution offers parliament only a limited role; party and electoral laws make it difficult for political forces not associated with the regime to gain seats in the legislature; and parliament has not been significantly involved in the design of constitutional amendments and in the writing of laws regulating elections, the media, and parties. Because of these characteristics, Category Three legislatures cannot serve as venues for meaningful national dialogues.

Egypt belongs to this category. Its parliament has been struggling to defend even the limited political space in which it has been operating for the past decade. Significantly, when in 1994 the Egyptian government convened a national dialogue, it had to do so outside of the parliamentary arena—in part because the legislature lacked credibility and in part because it did not include representatives of the most important opposition parties.

Assessing Internal Capacity

A parliament's political strength is not determined by external constraints alone. Factors internal to the legislature create other potential obstacles to its ability to play an influential role in the political process. Internal constraints are particularly relevant if the institutional framework provides the legislature with considerable prerogatives. As Olson noted,

> If a parliament is closely controlled externally, it makes little difference how it is organized internally. But if it has some latitude for independent thought and action, its ability to take advantage of those opportunities depends upon the extent to which it is internally organized. Its organization and resources define its internal capability for external action. (Olson 1994: 137)

Such observations are particularly relevant to countries engaged in a process of transition to democracy. As these countries experience sharp increases in political competition and participation, it becomes essential that parliaments be capable of adjusting to the new demands placed on them. This challenge can be met only by reducing the internal constraints—human, organizational, and informational—under which such parliaments operate.

Human Constraints

Human constraints arise from deficiencies of either the parliamentary staff or elected members. In most Arab countries, for example, the support personnel of legislatures remain limited and poorly trained. Assistance provided to Arab parliaments in this area has often been restricted to housekeeping and elementary management. Typically, little if any staff support is given to legislative committees or to individual legislators, which is where it is most needed if a parliament is to assert its constitutional and political prerogatives.

The limited legislative expertise of MPs may also constitute an important internal constraint. In countries with minimal or brief previous parliamentary experiences, MPs may lack both the skills and the common frame of reference needed to hammer out agreements through argumentation, negotiation, and compromise. Members from parties that were long outlawed and driven underground are likely to be ideologues skilled in the art of deceit and conspiracy. It may take time for them to learn how to operate in a system based on negotiated compromise.

The absence within the legislative institution of broadly accepted procedures and shared norms to handle disputes and interpersonal relations is often a particularly important internal constraint, although it is also one that is difficult to measure. In general, parliaments can operate smoothly and effectively only if members understand their obligations to each other and to the institution and if they share a similar understanding of the proper way of conducting parliamentary activities.

Another potential human constraint originates in the political leadership of parliament. Until recently, the leaders of almost all Arab legislatures were handpicked by the executive branch. Today, all the legislatures that will be studied in Part Two choose their own leaders. To perform their role effectively, however, these parliamentary elites need specialized skills. Whether they possess such skills or whether, if they do not, the system makes it possible for them to acquire the needed expertise has a critical bearing on how well the institution operates. The leadership issue is rendered all the more critical by virtue of another fundamental change now confronting several Arab legislatures. These legislatures are frequently moving from being dominated by a ruling party or a coalition of progovernment parties to becoming parliaments in which several opposition parties are well represented and active. As this shift takes place, new tensions appear within parliament between progovernment and opposition forces. It is incumbent upon the parliamentary institution as a whole to find ways of accommodating these internal strains. The main responsibility for doing so usually falls with the political leadership of the legislature, which thereby becomes far more critical to the future of the institution than when it was a mere transmission belt of the executive branch.

Organizational Constraints

The manner in which a legislature is organized, both politically and administratively, can be either a liability or a source of strength. Of particular importance are the following variables:

- Are parliamentary resources distributed among political parties in a fashion that these parties broadly see as fair?
- Are decisionmaking routines, procedures, and rules well developed and codified?
- How effective is the division of labor within the legislature? Are the various functions of the legislature performed by different, identifiable agencies within it? Is the scope of work for each agency appropriate? And do these subunits interact with each other in a logical and productive way?
- Do the leaders of parliamentary blocs and the chairs of committees have prerogatives and responsibilities of their own? Do they have the resources with which to discharge their functions? And do they relate to other sources of authority in the legislature (e.g., the speaker) in a manner that is conducive to the effectiveness of the institution?
- Are the number of committees and the nature of their staff consistent with the political challenges facing the legislative institution and the complexity of the issues with which it must deal?
- Is the relationship between the political and the administrative sides of the institution well defined? Do the two sides of the institution interact in fruitful and productive ways?
- Is the process through which a bill becomes law adequate?

These and other factors are critical determinants of a legislature's ability to carve out a meaningful place for itself in the political system. They also often are among those that prevent a legislature from assuming the role that it is constitutionally and politically permitted to play.

Informational Constraints

More than most other political institutions, legislatures require a very broad array of information to be able to discharge their functions. Unfortunately, Arab parliaments have largely been bypassed by the information revolution. Only since the early 1990s have some of them demonstrated an awareness of the importance of new information technologies and a desire to become better equipped in this area. Despite recent progress, however, most Arab parliaments still suffer from insufficient access to data and research facilities. They lack adequate information storage and management systems and do not have the ability to deliver information to their internal and external consumers in a timely and effective manner.

To suggest that a legislature lacks formal capacity does not necessarily mean that all of its members lack access to information, staff, or other critical resources. Members of parliaments can draw on their personal networks and assets to compensate for the weaknesses of the legislature. For instance, those among them who are lawyers, engineers, or businesspeople frequently have enormous resources at their disposal in their offices or companies, and they utilize these resources to facilitate their legislative work—for instance, to secure information or provide constituency services. Others use their contacts in the bureaucracy to obtain needed information. These contacts may have been developed by serving as a cabinet minister or through relatives and constituents employed by the bureaucracy. Still other members of parliament use acquaintances in the media or academia. However, although this type of information is extremely important for legislatures with limited formal institutional capability, it is unevenly distributed among members. It is available primarily to legislators who have previous national political experience, are independently wealthy, or belong to well-established families. Other members are denied these advantages and therefore are hindered in the performance of their legislative functions.

A Typology of Arab Legislatures

One can classify legislatures by combining the two variables of institutional centrality and internal capacity. For each variable, legislatures can be located on a continuum going from high (level of centrality or capacity) to low. When applied to the six Arab legislatures that will be studied in Part Two, this approach yields three main types of parliament.

Type One Legislatures

Type One legislatures are parliaments that rank high on institutional centrality but continue to display internal capacity deficiencies. By definition, such legislatures operate in political systems in which elites have been able to hammer out a compromise over the proper institutional frameworks. Because the obstacles that prevent these parliaments from becoming more powerful are primarily (although not exclusively) internal constraints and because internal constraints can more easily be overcome than disagreements over the rules of the political game, Type One legislatures display the greatest potential for further development.

The Lebanese Chamber of Deputies is the only Arab parliament that approximates a Type One legislature. The constitution assigns to it a broad range of powers, including electing the president of the Republic and approving the cabinet. The Chamber provides a power base for its speaker, who is one of the country's three key leaders (together with the president and the prime minister). Through question periods, general debates, motions of confidence, and a whole range of special investigatory powers, the Chamber creates a measure of governmental accountability. It contributes to all aspects of public policy, and it debates, amends, and approves the budget. One critical constraint on its centrality, however, is Syria's veto power on all key governmental decisions. Parliament, like all Lebanese political actors and institutions, must work within the parameters set by Damascus. Its speaker, like the president and the prime minister, makes regular trips to the Syrian capital, where he is informed of Syria's positions on the key issues of the moment. The Chamber also continues to display internal capacity weaknesses—though since 1993 it has been engaged in a major and sustained effort to overcome these constraints and has made significant headway in that direction.

Type Two Legislatures

Type Two legislatures consist of parliaments that have experienced a very significant increase in their institutional centrality since the early 1990s but that still operate under serious constraints, both external and internal. The legislatures of Morocco, Jordan, Kuwait, and Yemen can all be included in this category—Morocco having made the most progress, by far, and Yemen still having the most obstacles to overcome.

These parliaments have been among the main beneficiaries of the political openings that have taken place in their respective countries. Their centrality has been enhanced by constitutional reforms or amendments, the relaxation of political controls, a relatively successful dialogue between regime and opposition elites, and freer elections that have resulted in significant parliamentary representation for opposition forces. However, despite these advances, the political power of Type Two legislatures remains circumscribed by limitations arising from the institutional framework and/or a lack of internal resources. As far as institutional framework is concerned, the constitution and/or the political practice of three of these four countries subordinates the legislature to a monarchy (in Jordan and Morocco) or a ruling family (in Kuwait) that is placed above the political system. Parliament's autonomy and prerogatives are also limited by a distribution of power that favors the executive over the legislature. During the 1990s, the legislature has asserted its authority in Morocco and Jordan; in Kuwait it has reasserted itself after being reconstituted in the wake of the 1991 Gulf War. This process of political assertion or reassertion can be reversed, as the case of Yemen demonstrates. The Yemeni parliament had indeed become a "high centrality" legislature before the 1994 civil war, only to see its centrality sharply curtailed as a result of the conflict and the consolidation of power by President Ali Salih.

More generally, Type Two legislatures remain vulnerable to the changing political tactics of powerful presidents, kings, or emirs. As long as the individual who controls the executive branch—whether directly (as in the case of Ali Salih) or indirectly (as in the cases of Kings Hussein and Hassan II)—remains committed to using the legislature as a vehicle for democratic transformation, parliament can be expected to perform significant and expanding roles. But if these political leaders decide otherwise, legislative authority will be undermined, as was the case in Jordan in 1993, when King Hussein suspended parliament to prevent it from debating the new electoral law. Yet, kings, emirs, and presidents always pay a political price for curtailing or taking away the privileges that they recently have bestowed on legislatures. In the Arab world's increasingly complex and politicized environment, decisions seen as arbitrary or capricious can easily backfire, no matter how powerful those who make them. Thus, heavy-handed attempts to bypass, ignore, or repress the legislature are risky and cause major expenditures of political capital. This political calculus implies that parliaments have room to maneuver, as indeed the Moroccan, Jordanian, Kuwaiti, and Yemeni examples indicate.

The internal constraints that impede the performance of Type Two legislatures are also significant. They are greatest in Yemen, where skilled parliamentary staff is in very short supply, MPs often lack legislative skills, and parliament's access to information and ability to store and process it for legislative purposes remain very limited. By contrast, internal contraints are less pronounced in both Morocco (which is the only Arab legislature thus far to provide parliamentary groups with specialized staff) and Kuwait (which benefits from sumptuous facilities and is currently engaged in a major effort to increase its informational resources). The Jordanian parliament's internal capacity is greater than that of the Yemeni legislature but less developed than the internal capacity of the Kuwaiti or Moroccan parliaments. For instance, staff support for Jordanian MPs remains underdeveloped. Still, both Jordanian MPs and the administrative personnel who assist them have begun to grasp the art of serious legislative work. In general, since the early 1990s Jordan's legislature has made significant progress toward overcoming the considerable internal constraints that impeded its work when it was reconvened by King Hussein in November 1989.

Type Three Legislatures

Type Three legislatures consist of parliaments that rank very low on institutional centrality and suffer from far greater domination by the executive branch than Type Two legislatures. Such parliaments, however, are sometimes better endowed in internal resources than Type Two legislatures. That is the case of Egypt. As of mid-1998, the Egyptian legislature still had the largest and most qualified staff support of all Arab parliaments. This suggests that, should the regime in countries that have Type Three legislatures succeed in their attempts at national dialogue with opposition forces, their legislatures would be well equipped to discharge effectively their new political preroga-tives. Unfortunately, as of this writing, such a scenario seems very unlikely to eventuate in Egypt in the foreseeable future.

PART TWO

Case Studies

5

Lebanon

One of the features that sets Lebanon apart in the Arab world is the influential role that the legislature has played in that country's political system ever since the 1920s. During the French mandate (1920–1943), the Chamber of Deputies made important contributions to the emergence of a sense of Lebanese nationalism and to the struggle for independence. After 1943, the Chamber found itself at the center of a political system designed to accommodate the country's deep political and religious divisions by relying on two principles: (1) the distribution of political offices among the various sects in proportion to their share of the total population and (2) a process of intersectarian accommodation through bargaining among the leaders of these sects. The Chamber of Deputies thus became the cornerstone of a distinctive type of democratic system designed to allow various communities to live together while preserving their unique identities and traditions.

During the 1950s and 1960s, the Lebanese took great pride in their legislature, which contributed to the atmosphere of freedom that so sharply distinguished Lebanon from its neighbors. Even after civil war broke out in 1975, parliament continued to meet periodically. Unlike the army or the council of ministers, it never split into two or more contending factions. When in 1976 the spread of hostilities made the election of a new Chamber of Deputies impossible, the term of the legislature that had been elected in 1972 was extended. It continued to be extended (by the Chamber amending the electoral law—amendments signed into law by the president and prime minister) until August 1992, less than two years after the end of the civil war. Throughout, the Chamber continued to perform many of its constitutionally mandated functions, including the election of the president of the Republic (in 1976, 1982, and 1988).

It is interesting to note that none of the main actors in the civil war ever suggested that the Chamber of Deputies ought to be abolished. What came to be known as the Muslim-leftist alliance merely claimed that it wanted to make the Chamber more representative, better capable of assimilating new political forces, and more in tune with the country's changing demographic realities. As Iliya Harik noted in a perceptive article published as the hostilities were raging,

> the fact that warring factions in the recent civil war have not sought to over-throw the system is perhaps because they have invested fifty years of experience in their representative institutions and have to a considerable extent adjusted them to their changing needs. . . . Most groups and individuals have come to appreciate the advantages and virtues of a free representative system. (Harik 1980: 28)

More generally, at no point in the civil war were the foundations of the country's constitutional order a major issue to the key actors involved. Throughout the sixteen years of hostilities, not a single major warring group denied the legitimacy of the political institutions, including parliament. Legally, the country continued to be ruled by the president, the prime minister, the cabinet, and parliament—even after they became incapable of implementing their decisions uniformly throughout the country. In fact, each of the main factions in the civil war strove to associate itself with the symbols of legitimacy represented by state institutions. The leaders of these groups continued to serve in the cabinet and parliament, working side by side, each claiming to be the legitimate holder of constitutional authority. None of them ever chose to participate in a parallel government or parliament.

In light of this history, Lebanon—unlike the other countries examined in this book—cannot be described as going through a "parliamentary resurgence" or, more generally, a transition from authoritarianism to democracy. Instead, what Lebanon has experienced since 1990 is an attempt at political reconciliation and reconstruction under Syrian control. This process has had profound implications for parliament and its role in the political system, as will be discussed later in this chapter.

Legislative Institutions Under the French Mandate (1920–1943)

In 1922, two years after the League of Nations had given the French a mandate over the newly created state of Lebanon, they allowed the election of a Representative Council (RC). This RC did not turn out to be the compliant body that the French had anticipated. In 1925, it moved to exercise its constitutional right to choose the chief executive. Despite French objections, the RC was determined to elect Bishara al-Khuri, a Maronite who enjoyed the support of many Muslim leaders opposed to the French presence. The French high commissioner, Gen. Maurice Sarrail, repeatedly applied pressure on the RC to change its mind and choose France's preferred candidate, Emile Eddé. But the RC could not be swayed. In desperation, Sarrail dissolved the assembly, and elections for a second RC were held.

The Representative Council and the Making of the 1926 Constitution

From the moment it convened, the second RC worked assiduously to muster opposition to France's decision to proceed unilaterally in drafting a constitution for Lebanon. When a committee in the French Ministry of Foreign Affairs was set up to draft the document, the RC reacted quickly. Pointing to the articles of the mandate that called for the participation of the people of mandated territories to draft their own laws, albeit under the guidance and advice of the mandatory power, the RC unanimously passed the following resolution: "Since the RC represents the national authority in the country, we request that the mandatory authority presents the Constitution to us so that we may jointly work on it, in accordance with Article One of the Act of Mandate."

Fearing unfavorable reactions from members of the International Committee of the League of Nations (which was supposed to supervise the way in which the mandatory powers were fulfilling the provisions of their mandate), France requested that a French parliamentary commission rule on the question of whether the RC was entitled to draft the constitution. The ruling of the commission was favorable to the RC. Accordingly, the RC acted as a constituent assembly, and in 1926 it wrote and promulgated the constitution that remains in place today, although with several amendments (the most important of which were in 1927, 1929, 1943, and 1990). A body that many observers had initially dismissed as a "rubber-stamp assembly" had forced the mandatory power to back down and had made a lasting contribution to Lebanese political life. By insisting that it should draw and ratify the constitution, the RC had bestowed on that document an element of legitimacy that would help it survive the tribulations of the mandatory period.

Parliament in the 1926 Constitution

In its original version, the 1926 constitution had made parliament the cornerstone of the political system. This was hardly surprising, considering that it had been drawn by legislators who were hostile to the notion of a strong executive—particularly one subservient to the mandatory power. The legislature was initially divided into two houses, a Senate and a Chamber of Deputies. However, a constitutional amendment adopted in 1927 abolished the Senate. The constitution was amended again in 1929 at the initiative of the French, who wanted to strengthen the presidency at the expense of the legislature. Facing the threat of disbandment, the legislature had no choice but to approve these changes. As a result, the final document provided for a stronger presidency and a weaker parliament than had been originally envisioned. Yet, the legislature remained a powerful institution. For one, it still elected the president and was unlikely to select someone hostile to its interests. Furthermore, the principle of cabinet accountability to the legislature, which was enshrined in the constitution, made it inevitable that successive cabinets would be coalition governments representing the various forces present in the legislature.

The 1926 constitution, as amended in 1927 and 1929, provided the foundation for much of Lebanese politics until the late 1980s, although with some important changes along the way. Its main features were as follows:

1. The term of the Chamber of Deputies was four years. Two-thirds of its members were to be elected, the remaining third being appointed by the president of the Republic (this was changed in 1943, when it was decided that the Chamber of Deputies would henceforth be fully elected).

2. The president was elected by the Chamber for six years (by a two-thirds majority in the first round and by a simple majority in the second round). His term was nonrenewable. He was to be assisted by a council of ministers, led by a prime minister. One of his main prerogatives was to negotiate and sign treaties with foreign countries.

3. Each member of the Chamber had the right to ask the cabinet to submit to a vote of confidence any time during one of its regular or extraordinary sessions.[1]

4. Any project bill (a proposal of law drawn by the government) that had been rejected by the Chamber could not be resubmitted during the same session.

5. Members of the Chamber were given immunity against arrest or prosecution while performing their duties, unless they were caught in a flagrant violation. They could not be prosecuted for opinions they had expressed during a parliamentary session.

6. The president was constitutionally bound to promulgate the laws as passed by the legislature. He could not change these laws or make special exemptions. Laws passed by the legislature had to be promulgated within one month after they had been referred to the cabinet. If the legislature decided that a law was urgent, the president had to promulgate it within five days. He had no veto power over legislation passed. All that he could do was to refer the passed law back to the Chamber for reconsideration. Even then, he could do so only one time during the regular session, and the Chamber could overrule him by a simple majority. The president's main influence over legislation lay in what was termed the urgent method: With the approval of the council of ministers, he was entitled to promulgate by executive decree any bill that the

council had submitted to the legislature as urgent if the Chamber failed to act upon that bill within forty days.

7. The president was bound to carry out the budget, as passed by the legislature. He could promulgate the budget by decree only if the Chamber had failed to act, within the constitutionally allotted time, on the budget sent to it by the executive. The constitution gave the Chamber three months to pass a budget. If no consensus could be reached, the previous budget was enforced until the Chamber could agree on a new budget.

The Legislature as a Focus of National Resistance

As soon as the constitution was implemented, the French discovered that the Chamber could often prevent them from carrying out their policies, which were opposed by a majority of the deputies. Between 1926 and 1943, a constant tug-of-war pitted the high commissioner against the Chamber. In 1926, for instance, competition between the French-supported candidate for president and the candidate backed by the anti-French forces in the Chamber resulted in the selection of a compromise candidate, Charles Debbas, a Greek Orthodox. Compromise, however, was not always possible. When in 1932 the legislature threatened to elect a Sunni Muslim (Shaikh Muhammad al-Jisr), the high commissioner dissolved the assembly and appointed Debbas for another two years. Debbas was reappointed by the French in 1934. By 1936, when the Chamber was finally reconvened, the French were confident that their candidate, Emile Eddé, would easily receive the support of half the members of the legislature (one-third of which the French had appointed). Instead, Eddé won by only one vote. And in 1939, faced with the exigencies of the war, the French did not even trust the legislature to elect a president. Instead, they suspended the constitution, dissolved the Chamber, and appointed Eddé for another three-year term as president.

These examples suggest that a parliament that initially had been dismissed as no match for French power in Lebanon was actually able to stand up to the high commissioner and force France to come to terms with it. It is frequently claimed that the Chamber during that period was nothing but a "rubber-stamp" legislature. If that were the case, the French would not have bothered to disband it. France's repeated attempts to strengthen the president in relation to the Chamber demonstrate instead that the mandatory power knew very well that its interests were better served by a compliant executive than by a legislature that kept struggling for full independence.

One of the factors that allowed the Chamber to act as a catalyst for independence was its ability to integrate into a coherent whole the many regions and sects that made up the country. When the French had created Greater Lebanon in 1920, they had stitched together vastly different populations. The core of the new country was Mount Lebanon, which in late Ottoman times had enjoyed a semiautonomous status. To Mount Lebanon, however, the French had added substantial territories to the north, east, and south. Unlike Mount Lebanon, these territories were politically, ideologically, and economically oriented toward Syria. They differed greatly from Mount Lebanon and from each other in their outlook, traditions, temperament, and aspirations (Hourani 1976). If Lebanon were to survive, it was necessary that these people be tied to the central government in Beirut and that they develop a stake in the country's political system. No institution contributed toward this goal more than the Chamber, which brought together representatives of the various regions and sects and allowed them to cooperate in charting the future path of their country.

The Chamber's emergence as a focus for national resistance led the French to suspend or disband it on several occasions. Yet, every time France resorted to such measures, it found itself facing an increasingly hostile public. Eventually France had to agree to new elections, which usually yielded an even more defiant legislature. Finally, in 1943, candidates opposed to French control won a majority. The new Chamber immediately elected Bishara al-Khuri to the presidency and then endorsed al-Khuri's choice of Riadh al-Solh (a Sunni who also called for the end of the mandate) as prime minister.

Shortly afterward, the Chamber eliminated from the constitution all references to the mandate and the League of Nations. The powers of the president were extended to cover all aspects of foreign relations, including negotiations and the signing of treaties, without reference to the rights of mandatory power. This defiant act by the Chamber triggered an immediate response from the French, who declared the constitutional changes null and void and arrested the president of the Republic, the prime minister, and the entire cabinet as well as the president of the Chamber. Faced, however, with a popular outbreak that brought the country to a standstill and with pressure from other Arab countries, Great Britain, and the United States, France released the imprisoned political leaders. The latter immediately reassumed their constitutional powers and resumed the work they had begun toward extracting Lebanon's complete independence.

The Foundations of Parliamentary Politics in Postindependence Lebanon

Across the Arab world, the period that followed independence in general saw the decline of legislative institutions. Lebanon's experience, however, differs very significantly from this regional trend. From 1943 until the civil war—and indeed even after the outbreak of hostilities—the Chamber of Deputies played a pivotal role in the process of sectarian representation and intersectarian bargaining that sustained Lebanon's distinct form of liberal democracy. To understand this role, one must first analyze the context in which it was performed: the National Pact of 1943, the electoral system, and the contribution of parties to political life.

The 1943 National Pact

Shortly before independence, Lebanon's Maronite president Bishara al-Khuri and his Sunni prime minister Riadh al-Solh reached an oral agreement that came to be known as the National Pact. Although this compact was never written down, it became the bedrock of Lebanese political life and has survived, in modified form, until today.

According to the National Pact, political offices were to be divided among the various religious sects that made up the country. This arrangement, known as "confessionalism" or "consociational democracy," was seen as the fairest and most effective way of ensuring that the political and sectarian diversity of Lebanese society would be reflected in its political system. The distribution of power was to reflect the relative size of each sect, based on a census carried out in 1932. Since that census had shown that Christians outnumbered Muslims in a proportion of six to five, all positions in the bureaucracy, parliament, the cabinet, and even the higher ranks of the military were to be apportioned accordingly. Similarly, because the 1932 census had revealed that the Maronites were the largest sect (with 29 percent of the total population), they were given the most powerful office in the land, the presidency. The premiership was to be held by a member of the second largest sect, the Sunnis, who represented 22 percent of the population in 1932. Finally, the third largest sect, the Shiites, was given the relatively powerless position of speaker of Parliament.

Although in theory the distribution of political offices was meant to strictly reflect the size of each sect, in practice it was also driven by these sects' relative bargaining power at independence. This is shown by the Maronites' being given a clearly dominant position, even though by 1943 their actual share of the population was probably not above 27 percent. Similarly, among Muslims, Sunnis benefited disproportionately at the expense of Shiites, even though only three percentage points had separated the two sects in 1932 (22 percent as against 19 percent), and even though that difference had presumably narrowed by 1943, given the birthrate among Shiites was always much higher than among Sunnis. The 1943 National Pact thus embodied a few basic unwritten rules that were expected to define the parameters of Lebanese political life:

- Christians would have more power than Muslims.
- Maronites would prevail over all other sects. This was shown not only in the attribution of the presidency to a Maronite but also in the subse-

quent practice of putting Maronites in charge of key ministries (such as foreign affairs) and institutions (including the army and the Central Bank).

- Among Muslims, Sunnis would play a far more influential role than Shiites. Thus, the country would essentially be run by a tacit Maronite-Sunni alliance.
- A more general rule was that the political order would be maintained through a complex bargaining process among the leaders of the country's four main sects: Maronites, Sunnis, Shiites, and Druze. These leaders were expected to maintain control over their respective followings while reaching agreements with each other over the basic issues facing the country. The system was therefore a very elitist form of democracy—in which a handful of powerful individuals determined public policy through a process of intra-elite bargaining.[2] The stability of the system rested largely on the ability of the sectarian elites to understand and trust each other. Otherwise, the system might succumb to elite miscalculations and/or adventurism, possibly leading to violence. That, in fact, is precisely what ultimately happened in the 1970s.

Electoral Laws, Districting System, and Role of Political Parties

Between 1947 (when the first election after independence was held) and 1972 (when the last election took place before the civil war broke out), Lebanon had nine parliamentary elections. Although the number of deputies changed significantly over the years, it was always a multiple of eleven, in order to preserve the fixed ratio of six Christian members of parliament (MPs) for every five Muslim ones. (See Table 5.1.)

The number and size of constituencies also changed significantly during the 1947–1972 period. Originally, the basis was the *muhafaza* (plural *muhafazat*) or governorate, which is Lebanon's largest administrative division. In 1950, however, the *muhafazat* of North Lebanon and Mount Lebanon were subdivided into smaller units, in order to facilitate the reelection of powerful Maronite and Druze political figures. Two years later, smaller electoral units were adopted for the country as a whole, and Lebanon was divided into thirty-three wards. Finally, the electoral law adopted in 1960 redivided the country into twenty-six constituencies (for further details, see Ziadeh 1960: 367–368).

Each district was usually given several parliamentary seats. Between 1960 and 1972, for instance, only the city of Sidon in the south was a single-member district. The remaining twenty-five constituencies were multiple-member districts ranging from two to eight seats. These seats were divided among the different sects according to their share of the district's population.

Table 5.1   Distribution of Parliamentary Seats by Sects

	1947	1951	1953	1957	1960–1972
Christians					
Maronites	18	23	13	20	30
Greek Orthodox	6	8	5	7	11
Greek Catholic	3	5	3	4	6
Armenian Orthodox	2	3	2	3	4
Minorities	1	3	1	2	3
Muslims					
Sunni	11	16	9	14	20
Shiite	10	14	8	12	19
Druze	4	5	3	4	6
Total	**55**	**77**	**44**	**66**	**99**

In overwhelmingly Maronite districts such as Kisrawan, in Mount Lebanon, all the seats (four in that instance) were assigned to go to Maronite candidates. Similarly, the two seats assigned to the predominantly Shiite Bint Jbeil district in south Lebanon were to be filled by Shiite candidates (despite the presence of a Christian minority in that district). Most districts, however, had mixed populations. In those cases, seats were divided among the various sects represented in the district. For instance, of the eight seats of the Shuf district, in Mount Lebanon, three went to Maronite candidates, two to Sunnis, two to Druze, and one to a Greek Catholic.

This system, which remains in place today, ensured that each of the competing lists included politicians from different sects. It also compelled voters to select candidates according to the sectarian breakdown of their district. A Druze voter in the Shuf, for instance, was allowed to pick 8 candidates (the number assigned to his district), but only 2 of them could be Druze; the others had to be Maronites (3), Sunnis (2), and Greek Catholic (1). That voter could choose one of the existing lists (all of which were composed of 3 Maronites, 2 Sunnis, 2 Druze, and 1 Greek Catholic), or he or she could form his or her own list, by picking candidates from among the various lists and/or by selecting independents.[3] Therefore, although the electoral law always specified the number of seats allotted to each district, the voter was free to build his or her list in accordance with his or her own preferences, with no restriction stemming from formal alliances among candidates or political parties.

The main strength of this mixed-list system was that it reduced intersectarian rivalries and promoted communal integration. It did so in four ways. First, in each district, competition for a given seat was always among members of the same sect. Second, because candidates usually faced the voters as part of a multisectarian list, intersectarian accommodation among politicians was encouraged. Third, candidates knew that they could win only by appealing to

Table 5.2   MPs Affiliated with a Political Party, 1960–1972

	1960	1964	1968	1972
Phalange (Kata'ib)	6	4	9	7
National Liberal Party	5	6	8	7
National Bloc Party	6	2	5	3
Progressive Socialist Party	6	6	5	4
Tashnak	4	4	3	2
Other political parties	1	0	1	5
Total affiliated with political parties	28	22	31	28
Without party affiliations	71	77	68	71

members of sects different from their own. Therefore, extremists campaigning on narrow, sectarian platforms were unlikely to prevail. Fourth, the candidates elected on a given list would often continue to cooperate in the Chamber, thus creating crosscutting linkages among deputies from different sects.

A related advantage of the system was to make it very difficult for doctrinaire parties to gain representation in parliament, because electoral success was usually dependent upon a candidate's ability to join a list. Since these lists were usually headed by local leaders whom ideologically oriented parties considered "feudal" or "reactionary," joining the lists might lead party regulars to leave the organization in protest against what they might see as their candidate's "compromising" with "traditional forces." But candidates who did not cooperate with locally or regionally powerful politicians were almost certain to lose the election. This explains why the only political parties that managed to send representatives to the Chamber were, on the whole, nondoctrinaire, compromising parties that accepted political divisions in society as natural and healthy.[4]

Most of the candidates to the Chamber were not party members but were locally prominent individuals who understood their primary role to be servicing their constituents. Accordingly, elections were fought over local issues, not national ones, and the small size of electoral districts accentuated this phenomenon. As a result, political parties did not play a major role in electoral campaigns or, subsequently, in the Chamber. As shown in Table 5.2, all parties combined never commanded more than 30 percent of the loyalty of all MPs.

The five most significant political parties to operate within the Chamber were the Kata'ib, led by Maronite leader Pierre Gemayel; the Progressive Socialist Party (PSP), headed by Druze chieftain Kamal Jumblatt; the National Liberal Party (NLP) of Camille Chamoun (a Maronite); the National Bloc Party of Raymond Eddé (a Maronite); and the Armenian nationalist party (Tashnaq). The Kata'ib, which had the largest membership, was also the only party to have a nationwide organization. Even then, its appeal never extended much beyond the Maronite community.

Political parties were mostly vehicles to promote the personal interests and agendas of their leaders. They were defined less by adherence to a common program and ideology than by loyalty to the dominant personality around which they were built. The NLP, for instance, was "Chamoun's party," whereas the PSP was closely identified with Kamal Jumblatt. Accordingly, politicians affiliated with the PSP or the NLP were usually locally prominent individuals who, on national issues, tended to support the views of, respectively, Jumblatt and Chamoun.

Followers of a given party also tended to belong to the same sect, which has led some observers to argue that parties reflected and reinforced the "primordial" divisions within Lebanese society. Only the Lebanese Communist Party (LCP) and the Syrian Social Nationalist Party (SSNP; better known by PPS, the acronym of its French name [Parti Populaire Syrien]) ever managed to attract significant numbers of supporters from different sects. These parties, however, had little electoral success. Moreover, Deputies affiliated with them had usually won their seats in the Chamber less because of their party affiliation than because they belonged to locally influential families.

Electoral lists were almost always headed by a figure tied to one of the region's dominant families. Less influential candidates would attach themselves to that person and try to run on his list (or one of the lists led by his competitors). For instance, a Christian candidate in the district of Aley would typically seek to join the list headed by Druze leader Emir Majid Arslan, the dominant leader in that constituency. Only candidates connected to one of the country's preeminent families had a real chance; on their own, those who did not enjoy the backing of a prominent family lacked the social influence and economic resources required to win a seat. For that reason, truly independent candidates were a rare species; only in the 1972 elections were a handful of individuals with no ties to Lebanon's political establishment able to win seats in both Tripoli and Beirut. Still, even where political leadership was dominated by certain families, political competition within these families was often intense, and it was not uncommon to see brothers running against brothers or nephews against uncles.

Weaknesses of Pre–Civil War Parliaments

Lebanon's pre–civil war chambers were not fully representative of the electorate (the same could be said of most legislatures in the world). For instance, the division of the country into many electoral districts was in a way unfair to parties such as the PPS, the LCP, or the Baath party. At the national level, these parties together might have controlled perhaps as much as 10 percent of the electorate. However, because of the district-based electoral system, very few of their candidates ever made it into the Chamber. Understandably, these parties felt that the electoral system did not do justice to their real political weight. They advocated treating Lebanon as one single electoral district, and adopting a system of proportional representation.

Electoral districts also had been drawn in a way that overrepresented rural areas at the expense of urban ones. In the early 1970s, for example, although perhaps as much as 30 percent of Lebanon's population lived in the Greater Beirut area, it held only 16 percent of the seats in the Chamber. By contrast, even though Mount Lebanon contained no more than 20 percent of the country's population, it still held 30 percent of parliamentary seats (Kliot 1987: 63). Although such discrepancies were hardly unique to Lebanon (indeed, similar ones can be found in many "advanced liberal democracies"), they were detrimental to the Chamber's representative character. The same can be said of the growing gap between the fixed numbers of parliamentary seats assigned to each sect and these sects' actual proportion of the population. N. Kliot has aptly summarized the distorting impact of this phenomenon:

> In the mid-1940s, parliamentary seats were distributed among the various religious communities more or less in proportion to their respective populations. There was a slight over-representation of the Maronites and Druze, and a slight under-representation of the Armenians. But in 1982, the distortion in the representation of the various communities was conspicuous. The Maronites, who then constituted only 22 percent of the population, received 30.5 percent of the parliamentary seats, and there was over-representation for all other Christian communities. The Muslims were under-represented: the Sunnis, who comprised 26 percent of the population, received only 20 percent of the parliamentary seats, and the Shiites, who constituted 27.5 percent, received only 19.3 percent of the seats. According to the real size of their population, the Christians should have received only 38 seats, but they received 53. The Muslims should have received 61 seats, but they only got 45 seats. (Kliot 1987: 61)

Strengths of Pre–Civil War Parliaments

Despite the limitations identified in the preceding section, the Lebanese Chamber became more representative over time. Significantly, voter turnout increased regularly from 1943 to 1972 (Hudson 1968: 219–225). During the same period, elections became more competitive, as shown by the growing number of individuals running for parliamentary seats, the smaller margins by which successful candidates typically won, and the more frequent tendency for incumbents to be challenged and defeated (Hudson 1966: 174).

Elections held during the 1960s and in 1972 also led to a significant broadening of the social base of the parliamentarian elite. For instance, the number of deputies whose first occupation was "landlord" decreased from 46.5 percent in the Chamber elected in 1943 to 10 percent in that elected in 1968. During the same period, the percentage of professionals increased from 10.2 percent to 28 percent and that of businessmen from 10.2 to 17 percent (Harik 1975: 203). In the 1968 parliament, deputies whose primary or secondary occupation was in the professions or in business represented 83 percent of all deputies (Harik 1975: 205). These figures suggest that the socioeconomic transformations affecting Lebanon's population—in particular the growth of the "new middle class"—were being reflected in the Chamber's composition.

Finally, there was also a clear trend toward fewer incidents of electoral fraud and governmental interference in the electoral process. As Farid El-Khazen noted:

> While observers disagree over the extent and nature of irregularities in the 1950s and 1960s, they agree that the peak in fraudulent electoral practices was in 1947 and the peak of orderly and government free intervention was in 1972. . . . Elections in the 1950s were, by and large, less corrupt, freer and more representative than elections in the 1940s. In turn, elections in the 1960s were better handled than elections in the 1950s, while elections in 1972 scored better on all counts both in relative and absolute terms than previous elections. (El Khazen 1994: 129–133)

It seems appropriate at this point to dismiss the myth that Lebanese elections were never much more than a formality, since the same "neofeudal," aristocratic elite would always prevail, capitalizing on its economic power and social influence. In reality, elections were always hotly contested. Incumbents were constantly threatened and regularly unseated by challengers. Between 1943 and 1972, the average turnover of Lebanese deputies was a relatively high 40 percent (Khalaf 1987: 122). As Iliya Harik noted in the mid-1970s:

> The rate of change in the Lebanese parliament is higher than is often thought to be. The erroneous impression may be created by the fact that those few members of parliament who are often reelected are prominent and well known by the public. This gives the impression of a stable oligarchy entrenched in the Chamber. In fact, a career in the Lebanese parliament is quite insecure, and even among the dozen prominent members all but two have lost their seats at least once. (Harik 1975: 210)

The competitive nature of elections, and the relatively high turnover in the Chamber, point to a legislature that was actually more representative than is usually believed.

That legislature, furthermore, made important contributions to Lebanon's political development in four key areas: (1) overseeing the executive branch and regulating political succession, (2) acting as a training ground and pool of recruitment for positions in the executive branch, (3) providing constituency services, and (4) legislation.

Executive Oversight and Succession Regulation

Through floor debates, question-and-answer sessions, votes of confidence, and requests by parliamentary committees for information and documents from the government, the Chamber exercised significant oversight of the executive branch. Even the powerful office of the presidency could not ignore the legislature. In 1952, for instance, four of the Chamber's most prominent leaders—Camille Chamoun, Kamal Jumblatt, Ghassan Tweini, and Raymond Eddé—joined in a front with the avowed intention of unseating President al-Khuri. They accused him, among others, of having amended the constitution illegally after manipulating a general election. Through the parliamentary pressure they generated, as much as through the popular support they mobilized, they brought about the resignation of Prime Minister Sami al-Solh and then succeeded in forcing al-Khuri to step down in the summer of 1952, three years before the expiration of his second term. Six years later, after they were defeated at the polls during an election marred by governmental interference and fraud, key parliamentary figures organized the uprising that foiled President Chamoun's attempt to have his mandate renewed for another term.

Subsequently, under the presidencies of Fuad Shihab (1958–1964) and Charles Helou (1964–1970), parliamentary leaders such as Raymond Eddé and Albert Mokheiber played an instrumental role in organizing the resistance to the army's growing involvement in policymaking. Ultimately, with the election of Suleiman Franjiyeh as president in 1970, these leaders were able to curb the army's interference in the political process and succeeded in reasserting the influence of elected representatives over a military institution that was progressively attempting to usurp power. This was no small achievement in a region where during that period the army was often able to hijack power.

By selecting successive presidents, the Chamber also facilitated smooth transitions from one administration to the next. This contribution can be fully appreciated only when examined in the context of the Arab world's and Lebanon's turbulent history during the 1950s and 1960s. Even though one can only speculate about what might have happened if the election of the president had been done by direct popular voting, it is possible that the upheavals and uncertainties associated with such a process would simply have overwhelmed the political system and reduced its chances of survival. Thus, the selection of the president by the Chamber may have worked as a cushion against the disruptions often inherent in transfers of power.

Parliament as Training Ground

From 1943 through the civil war, the legislature was the main pool of recruitment to key offices in the executive branch. Presidents, prime ministers, and ministers invariably came from the Chamber (Harik 1975: 211). It was there that they acquired their political skills and experience and accumulated years of exposure to the stresses and strains of public life before assuming positions in the executive branch. Neither the army, nor the bureaucracy, nor political parties ever developed as alternative recruiting grounds for the highest executive positions.

One reason why the road to government responsibilities almost always passed through the Chamber was that in order to maintain parliamentary support for the executive branch, the president and his prime minister frequently reshuffled the cabinet so as to placate deputies by integrating them into the government. Through the rotation of ministerial positions among deputies, the Chamber developed a political leadership with extensive executive branch experience; that, in turn, enhanced the legislature's power, influence, and centrality in the political system.

Constituency Services

Lebanon's MPs were known to maintain particularly close relations with their districts. One of their main roles was to intercede with the bureaucracy on behalf of their constituents and to obtain jobs and favors for them. In fact, electoral lists always included one member, called *na'ib al-khadamat* (which loosely translates as "the deputy in charge of services"), who was mostly responsible for ensuring constituency services. Contributing to the strong ties that bound Lebanon's MPs to their home base was the fact that an overwhelming majority among them (90 percent in the Chamber elected in 1968) were born in the district they represented (Harik 1975: 215). Critical as well were the small size of the country and the ease of communications within it. These features kept parliamentarians in close contact with their constituencies, partially compensated for the lack of professional legislative staff, and prevented Lebanon from falling victim to the "absentee representative syndrome" in which deputies reside in the capital and rarely return to their constituencies.

Through the success they displayed in bargaining with the executive branch for services to their constituents, Lebanese deputies operated as key intermediaries between individuals and the broader political system. In so doing, they performed one of the most important functions that a legislature can discharge. In view of the competitive nature of elections, they had to remain extremely sensitive to their local bases in order to keep their jobs. As a result, they would devote much of their time and attention not only to mediating between their constituents and the bureaucracy but also to attending social, cultural, and religious events in their respective districts (Harik 1975: 215).

Legislative Function

Few commonly accepted ideas about Lebanese politics are more inaccurate than the proposition that the Chamber played little part in lawmaking. In fact, a close examination of legislative activity between 1953 and 1972 reveals the Chamber's active role in that area.[5] During that period, a total of 4,157 bills was introduced. Of these, the Chamber approved only 52.9 percent of the regular bills and 38.1 percent of the urgent bills.[6] The rest were rejected, remained in committees, were referred back to committees, were withdrawn by those who had introduced them, or were amended and then passed. The regular growth in the number and percentage of bills introduced by deputies also suggests that the Chamber was taking an increasingly active part in initiating legislation.

Through its strong legislative role, the Chamber made important contributions to the country's socioeconomic and political development. It passed legislation that allowed the government to carry out major socioeconomic projects in the areas of transportation, communication, education, health, agriculture, and energy. It also adopted legislation that protected or strengthened freedom of speech and political action as well as the rule of law. In so doing, it contributed to the climate of openness and pluralism that characterized Lebanon and enabled the country to realize its potential as a commercial and financial bridge between the West and the Arab world.

The Ta'if Accord

From September 30 to October 22, 1989, sixty-two members of the Lebanese parliament elected in 1972 met in Ta'if, Saudi Arabia. The gathering, sponsored by the Arab League, was the last in a series of efforts to agree on a formula to rebuild a political system shattered by years of harrowing civil war. It is significant that those chosen to conduct the negotiations were parliamentarians. Their presence in Ta'if suggests that the Chamber was widely seen as the one institution that, because it had been legally elected by the Lebanese people, was entitled to work out the details of a new political system for the country. Certainly, one could question the extent to which deputies elected seventeen years earlier were representative of Lebanese public opinion in 1989. However, the legitimacy of these individuals was not in doubt; it was based on their having been chosen according to due process and their belonging to a state institution recognized by the world community (Collings and Tansley 1992: 26).

Out of the Ta'if meeting came a Document of National Understanding, better known as the Ta'if Accord. Although calling for the abolition of confessionalism in the long run (a promise that was not to be taken too seriously[7]), this path-breaking agreement preserved, for the immediate future, the principle of dividing political offices among the country's various sects. However, it redistributed power among them in a way that reflected more accurately the country's new demographic and political realities. Its main provisions were as follows:

1. Parliamentary seats would now be divided equally between Christians and Muslims (instead of according to a 6:5 ratio to the Christians' advantage).
2. Within the executive branch, the balance of power among the president, the prime minister, and the council of ministers would be altered. The president would remain a Maronite, but his powers would be very significantly reduced, to the benefit of the cabinet and the prime minister (who, as in the past, would be a Sunni).
3. Parliament and its speaker (who would remain a Shiite) would be given expanded powers.

As this summary suggests, the Maronites lost much influence in Ta'if. The Sunnis, by contrast, emerged as clear winners; the Shiites gained some power but not as much as the size of their sect might have warranted.

Parliament in the Revised Constitution

On August 21, 1990, Lebanon's parliament approved sweeping constitutional amendments based on the Ta'if Accord. Signed in September 1990 by President Elias Hrawi, these amendments provided for a new political order, sometimes called Lebanon's Second Republic. The main features of the political system within which parliament has been operating since then can be summarized as follows: (1) a weaker presidency (most executive powers have been shifted from the president to the cabinet); (2) a powerful council of ministers, which now has authority for ensuring the execution of laws, proposing legislation, deploying and administering the army, and ratifying international treaties;[8] (3) a prime minister who is the dominant figure in the day-to-day running of the affairs of the country, acts as the cabinet's leader and spokesperson, sets its agenda, and oversees the operation of its various ministries;[9] and (4) a more influential parliament and speaker.

The constitutional changes of 1990 thus emphasized the parliamentary characteristics of the system and de-emphasized its presidential character—although in this respect they mostly codified informal understandings that had developed over the years.[10] Most important, the changes rectified the gap that had developed between the sectarian distribution of political power and the country's demographic realities. However, the logic of the confessional system was left untouched.

The new constitution strengthens parliament in four important ways. First, it mandates that the Chamber be closely involved in the process through which the prime minister is selected. Although the president still formally appoints the prime minister, he or she no longer chooses the premier. Instead, the premier is now chosen through binding consultations between the president and the parliamentary groups, in the presence of the speaker of parliament. Second, only parliament now has the authority to remove the prime minister (whereas before 1990 the premier could be dismissed by the president). Third, the method under which the executive can present urgent legislation has been amended. The constitution still enables the executive to declare a particular bill as urgent, but the Chamber now has forty days from the time it takes up the bill, rather than forty days from when the executive submits it, to act on the bill. (If the legislature fails to act within that period, the executive can promulgate the legislation as presented.) In effect, the Chamber has been empowered to determine whether to give a bill the character of urgency. Fourth, the speaker's role, too, has been enhanced. His or her term has been increased from one to four years, which gives him or her time to develop a power base within parliament and therefore increases his or her standing and bargaining power when negotiating with the prime minister or the president. In addition, the speaker benefits from the previously discussed constitutional clause that stipulates that prior to appointing the prime minister, the president must engage in "binding consultations" with parliament—consultations to which the speaker is privy. In effect, the speaker has been given the power to veto any of the president's choices for premier and can force the president to accept a compromise candidate. More generally, whenever the speaker feels that his or her views are not taken seriously by the president or the prime minister, he or she can derail key legislation and appointments.

One should also remember that, for all its power, the council of ministers is by no means independent of parliament. It will survive only as long as it retains the legislature's support, and its composition must consequently reflect the balance of power in the Chamber. For the same reasons, the prime minister's room for maneuver is constrained by parliament. The influence that the premier can wield depends largely on the skills that he or she demonstrates at building alliances and coalitions—within the cabinet as much as within the legislature—to support the policies that he or she advocates.

Overall, the 1990 constitution provides for a political system in which power is far more widely distributed than under the old one. Significantly, the highest office is a collective decisionmaking body, the council of ministers. Furthermore, although the prime minister is given a dominant role, the president and speaker of parliament are influential personalities as well. This latter characteristic has led some analysts to argue that Lebanon is now ruled by a troika: the president, the premier, and the speaker. By decreasing the prerogatives of the president and increasing those of the prime minister and the speaker, the constitution creates a situation in which effective governing requires some consensus among these three individuals.

One criticism of this political framework must be dealt with here, because it is widespread and yet reflects a deep misunderstanding of how the current system actually works. Some analysts claim that the distribution of the three key political offices among the major sects raises the danger of transforming institutional rivalries into sectarian conflict. It is argued, for instance, that a confrontation between parliament and the prime minister will degenerate into a dispute between Shiites and Sunnis or that a clash between the prime minister and the president will inevitably strain Sunni-Maronite relations. That, however, is not necessarily the case. For the speaker to win a political battle against the prime minister, or for the prime minister to wage one against the president, each needs to be backed by key actors who do not belong to his sect. The speaker will need to enlist the support of Sunni, Maronite, and Druze MPs against the prime minister. Similarly, to have any chance of prevailing over the president, the prime minister will most likely need to rely on the backing of some of his Maronite ministers. Furthermore, prominent politicians who belong to the same sect compete for the same highest office. They therefore have an incentive to reach out to politicians from other sects in order to gather support for their ambitions.

The 1992 Elections

In early 1992, preparations began for elections to be held in the summer. These elections were widely seen as a watershed: the first ones to be held in twenty years and the first ones organized under the new constitution.

The Electoral Law

Prior to the elections, a new electoral law was promulgated, to replace the one that had been in place since 1960. It increased the number of deputies from 99 to 128, divided equally between Christians and Muslims, as shown in Table 5.3:

Table 5.3   Distribution of Seats, 1992–1996 Legislature

Christians	64
Maronites	34
Greek Orthodox	14
Greek Catholics	8
Armenian Orthodox	5
Armenian Catholics	1
Anglicans	1
Others	1
Muslims	64
Shiites	27
Sunnis	27
Druze	8
Alawites	2

It had been agreed at Ta'if that the number of deputies would be 108, not 128. That the higher figure was adopted in 1992 reflected in large part a desire to allow into parliament a larger number of politicians, both those who belonged to the old, pre–civil war elite and those younger leaders who had risen to prominence during and after the hostilities.

The choice of electoral districts was also a contentious issue. At Ta'if, it had been agreed that districts would be based on the *muhafaza*, or governorate. (Lebanon is divided administratively into six *muhafazat:* North Lebanon, Beirut, Mount Lebanon, the Bekaa, Sidon, and Nabatiyeh.) The *muhafaza* was therefore expected to replace the smaller electoral district (*qada*) that had been in use until then. The stated purpose of this change was to undermine sectarianism by eliminating those districts that had a predominantly confessional coloring (for example, those that elected only Maronites or only Shiites). However, the idea of having *muhafaza*-wide constituencies was opposed by many Christian leaders for two reasons. First, they felt that it would allow Muslim voters to determine which Christian candidates would represent their community in parliament. (This is because in no *muhafaza* do Christians constitute a majority.) Second, Christian politicians who owed their influence largely to the fact that they represented a locally influential family feared that, within a *muhafaza*, their ability to win the election might be undermined. Similar considerations explain why Druze leader Walid Jumblatt or the then-powerful speaker of parliament Hussein al-Husseini opposed *muhafaza*-wide electoral districts. Jumblatt, for instance, knew that if Mount Lebanon were to vote as one single *muhafaza*, he would probably lose his seat, as most Christians in Mount Lebanon would support one of his Druze rivals.

To accommodate such objections and to take into account the fact that elections could not be held in those parts of the south occupied by the Israeli army, the electoral law that was ultimately adopted was a compromise. It provided for elections to be held on the basis of the *muhafaza* in the north and Beirut. In the south, the governorates of Sidon and Nabatiyeh were merged into one district. The governorates of Mount Lebanon and the Bekaa, for their part, were split into smaller constituencies—the boundaries of which were drawn so as to favor pro-Syrian candidates and political chieftains whose cooperation was essential to the rebuilding of Lebanon.

The Christian Boycott

Most Christian leaders called for a boycott of the elections, arguing that these should have been postponed until the Syrian authorities redeployed their troops to the Bekaa Valley, in accordance with the Ta'if Accord.[11] Christians also opposed certain provisions in the electoral law. They complained that the subdivision of Mount Lebanon and the Bekaa into smaller electoral districts had been done in a way that favored progovernment, pro-Syrian candidates. In addition, they objected to the selective manner in which the disbanding of the militias had been implemented. The Lebanese Forces (a coalition of Maronite militias) and the militias associated with the Amal, the PSP, and Palestinian groups had all been dissolved. However, Hizballah, backed by both Iran and Syria, remained heavily armed. Some Christian leaders argued that legislative elections should be postponed until Hizballah, too, had been dismantled.

By calling for a boycott, Christian leaders were hoping that they would attract enough international attention and support (particularly from the Vatican, Paris, and Washington) to pressure the Lebanese government into cancelling the elections. That strategy, however, failed. Despite the Christian boycott, the Lebanese government decided to go ahead with the elections, which were held on three consecutive Sundays, beginning on August 23, 1992.

The Results

Primarily because of the Christian boycott but also because a significant proportion of the Muslim electorate decided to stay home, voter turnout was the lowest since independence: a modest 30.34 percent overall, as opposed to figures ranging between 50 and 53.3 percent in the elections conducted between 1960 and 1972. In the district of Jbeil in Mount Lebanon, participation was a mere 6.52 percent, and the two unopposed Maronite candidates received 130 and 41 votes each out of a total of 63,878 voters in the district (El-Khazen 1994: 131). In Mount Lebanon as a whole, only 13.5 percent of voters showed up.

The Christian boycott had two important consequences. First, Christian MPs were elected primarily through the votes of Muslim voters. Therefore, they were not genuinely representative of their sect. Many had pro-Syrian sympathies that were hardly in line with grassroots feelings in their community. Second, in several districts the Christian boycott worked to the advantage of Islamic fundamentalist candidates and contributed to the defeat of moderate Muslim leaders who in the past had relied on Christian votes.

For the first time since Lebanon's independence, Muslim fundamentalists were elected to parliament. Hizballah (the Party of God), which had been formed as a Shiite militia after Israel's 1982 invasion of Lebanon, won 8 seats. Since 4 candidates aligned with Hizballah also won seats, the Hizballah bloc emerged as the largest group within the Chamber. In addition, 4 candidates belonging to two small fundamentalist Sunni movements were elected. The impressive performance of Islamic fundamentalist parties was due not only to the nonparticipation of most Christian voters but also to these parties' ability to build grassroots support through educational, health, and welfare programs.

Table 5.4   Distribution of Seats by Parties, 1992–1996 Legislature

Political Party	Number of Deputies
Hizballah (Party of God)	8
Syrian Social Nationalist Party (SSNP/PPS)	6
Tashnaq (Armenian)	5
Amal	5
Progressive Socialist Party (PSP)	4
al-jama'a al-islamiyya (Sunni fundamentalist group)	3
Baath Party	2
Eight smaller parties with one deputy each	8

As Table 5.4 shows, the total number of parliamentarians elected with party labels was 41, or slightly less than one-third of all candidates (which is roughly similar to pre–civil war trends). All remaining 87 members had run as independents.

From the government's perspective, the election was a qualified success. Despite the Christian boycott, there was no international repudiation of the results of the election. On the other hand, the low turnout, combined with the defeat of several figures closely associated with the ruling team (including President Hrawi's own son), proved that there was limited support for the Syrian-dominated order. Similarly, while at one level the elections had accentuated the divisions in the country, they also had provided for the integration into the formal political system of many politicians who had emerged during and after the civil war. Only 18 of the 128 deputies elected in 1992 belonged to the previous Chamber (the one chosen in 1972). This figure indicates the extent to which the elections had contributed to a much-needed renewal of the political class.

Strengths and Weaknesses of Parliament, 1992–1996

The Chamber elected in 1992 sat for its mandated term of four years. During that time, it was hampered in its work by significant weaknesses. Yet, it also displayed real strengths that justify considering it one of the strongest legislatures in the region.

Constraints on Parliament's Centrality

The greatest constraint on parliament's centrality during its 1992–1996 term was its insufficient representativeness. The absence of credible, prominent

Maronite leaders in its ranks made it difficult for Christians to see the Chamber and its decisions as legitimate. The political autonomy of the legislature was also limited by Syrian influence over most MPs. On issues about which Syria did not care enough to impose its will, parliament was allowed to show real independence and assertiveness. That was not the case for those questions bearing directly on Damascus's interests (most prominently the peace process). Similarly, although the legislature was able to criticize the government, question ministers, oppose some of their policies, and at times extract real concessions from the prime minister and his team, it was clear that it could not bring the cabinet down without Syria's approval.

The Chamber's October 1995 decision to amend Article 49 of the constitution to allow an extension of President Hrawi's mandate showed its readiness to ratify key decisions made in Damascus. Another revealing episode in 1995 was the showdown between parliament and Prime Minister Rafiq Hariri, which led Hariri to threaten to resign. Syrian vice president 'Abd al-Halim Khaddam immediately rushed to Beirut, where he announced that the Hariri government would remain for the duration of President Hrawi's mandate. In so doing, the Syrian leadership demonstrated that the Lebanese government was responsible first and foremost to Damascus's ruling elite—not to the legislature in Beirut, as provided for under the Lebanese constitution.

Constraints on Parliament's Capacity

When the parliament elected in 1992 began to operate, its administrative and technical capacities remained underdeveloped. It lacked a working library and a database on existing and pending legislation as well as on the financial affairs of the country. MPs did not have a professional staff to access and process information. Their ability to legislate and monitor the activities of the executive branch was thus constrained by their inability to draw on the required data and expertise, whether within the Chamber or outside of it. On numerous occasions, the legislature was unable to challenge the Hariri government's draft laws because it lacked the informational and analytical resources that would have allowed it to do so. This was particularly evident in the Chamber's inability to question the often dubious economic projections of the Finance Ministry (Young 1996: 26). The lack of resources also partially accounts for the inability of parliamentarians to put forward concrete counterproposals to accompany their virulent criticisms of the government's successive budgets.

During the 1996 budget debate, for instance, attacks by deputies against the government's financial priorities led to a long and frustrating debate. At the end of the day, however, parliamentarians had little to offer by way of alternative suggestions, and the Chamber as a whole ended up ratifying the final document presented by the government. This episode did great damage to the

Chamber's credibility. In the eyes of the public, it seemed to provide additional proof "that the verbosity of deputies was in inverse proportion to their capacity to substantially modify major government initiatives" (Sassine 1996: 36). Well aware that the legislature's inadequate resources represented a significant impediment to its ability to perform effectively its new constitutional prerogatives, the Chamber's leadership worked assiduously between 1992 and 1996 to strengthen parliament's internal capacity, and significant progress was made in that direction.

The Strengths of Parliament

Despite the weaknesses that have just been examined, the 1992–1996 Chamber performed functions critical to Lebanon's reconstruction. It displayed its importance as an institution of political integration by incorporating in its ranks a large number of previously excluded constituencies, especially from among Shiite Muslims. It is especially noteworthy that Hizballah was allowed to take part in the elections and that it even emerged as the largest party in the new legislature. In this respect, the 1992 elections contributed to Hizballah's transformation from guerrilla organization into mainstream political machine. Islamist deputies in general showed themselves willing to play the parliamentary game. Instead of operating as an antisystem bloc within the Chamber and instead of seeking to unsettle Lebanon, they behaved responsibly and followed the rules of legislative politics. The Chamber thus provided radical forces previously operating on the fringes of the political system with the incentives to work within the existing institutions. Hizballah toned down considerably its former radical rhetoric, largely in an effort not to alienate an electorate on which it knew it had to rely to increase its influence in a consociational system based on power sharing and alliance building. Hizballah's evolution since 1992 thus illustrates this book's argument regarding the moderating effect of legislatures on organizations formerly dedicated to bringing about change through violence and extralegal means.

Capitalizing on its enhanced constitutional powers in the post-Ta'if era, parliament gave expression to public grievances and repeatedly forced the cabinet as well as individual ministers to account for their policies. The government's economic policy was the target of constant criticisms by deputies. Hizballah in particular emerged as one of Hariri's most consistent and effective critics. It assailed the prime minister's multi-billion-dollar reconstruction plan, arguing that it was overambitious and ill conceived. Hizballah used parliamentary debates to seek to embarrass and discredit the government by pointing to the latter's inability to force Israel to withdraw from its self-declared "security zone" in the south. The party also challenged the influence of Amal and Speaker Nabih Berri over the Shiite community, exposing instances of influence peddling and corruption among Amal-affiliated officials and arguing that Berri lacked in his commitment to improving social and economic conditions in the south.

One indication of the Chamber's assertiveness was its repeated refusals to grant the cabinet the right to engage in "delegated legislation." That practice consists of parliament's allowing the cabinet to pass legislation by decree in specific areas and for a set period of time. It is intended to enable the cabinet to take quick action on complex but urgent matters that would take a long time to consider if they were subjected to parliamentary debates. Prior to 1992, governments were often given such delegated power. However, whenever the cabinet of Prime Minister Hariri requested that prerogative between 1992 and 1996, it was rebuffed. Speaker Nabih Berri and other parliamentary figures made it clear that they viewed delegated legislation as an abandonment of their constitutional responsibility.

Moreover, of all parliaments in the history of Lebanon, the 1992–1996 legislature promulgated the greatest number of laws (approximately four hundred). Significantly as well, the ratio of proposed laws (bills proposed by a deputy or group of deputies) to draft laws (presented by the government) increased from 9 percent in 1992–1993 to 20 percent in 1995—both figures being above the world average of 5 percent (Sassine 1996: 35). These statistics point to the Chamber's active role.

Finally, the nature of Syrian influence in Lebanon and the ways in which it plays itself out need to be qualified, for common misperceptions of this phenomenon can seriously distort one's understanding of parliament's current role in the Lebanese political system. One of the provisions of the Ta'if Accord called upon the Syrian armed forces to assist the Lebanese government in disbanding the militias and extending its authority over the entire territory. It was that provision that was invoked in October 1990, when Syrian military intervention helped put down Michel Aoun's attempt to prevent implementation of the Ta'if Accord. Since then, some 35,000 Syrian troops have been stationed in Lebanon, underpinning considerable Syrian influence in the country. Though this Syrian hegemony has not been without benefits—the end of civil hostilities and the rebuilding of government institutions might not have been possible without it—it constantly undermines Lebanese sovereignty. Critical decisions regarding Lebanon are usually made in Damascus, not Beirut. Yet, although the Syrian regime can and does exercise overwhelming power on issues related to the peace process, it frequently has no strong opinions about, or vested interests in, many of the domestic political and socioeconomic issues with which the legislature must deal. As a result, the Chamber's room for maneuver is quite extensive regarding those questions. Syria, furthermore, finds it difficult to accommodate the various political groups active on the Lebanese political stage. Many of the key players frequently described in the U.S. press as "Syria's clients in Lebanon"—Nabih Berri, Rafiq Hariri, and Walid Jumblatt for instance—have sharply different interests and positions on critical issues. The Syrian regime has no strong incentive to side with one of them against the others. In short, Damascus cannot get its way on every single issue, nor does it seek to. In this respect as well, the political autonomy of the Chamber relative to Syria is greater than many commentators have portrayed it to be.

The 1996 Elections

As Lebanon prepared for the parliamentary elections to be held in the summer of 1996, the electoral law remained a contentious issue. As discussed earlier, the 1989 Ta'if Accord had called for elections to take place on the basis of the *muhafaza*. From the government's perspective, the main disadvantage of this system was that implementing it would have threatened the reelection of key members of the ruling coalition, such as Walid Jumblatt. To prevent this from happening, the government issued a new electoral law. According to that law, voting was to take place at the level of the *muhafaza* (or province) in North Lebanon, Beirut, the Bekaa, and South Lebanon. However, the predominantly Christian governorate of Mount Lebanon was divided into six *qadas* (smaller subgovernorate districts): Northern Metn, Kasrawan, Jubayl, Aley, Ba'abda, and the Shuf.

Many, especially Christian leaders, were opposed to this electoral law. One reason was that in the predominantly Christian *muhafaza* of Mount Lebanon, Christians would not be allowed to affect significantly the choice of Muslim deputies, whereas elsewhere in Lebanon the preferences of a primarily Muslim electorate would be the decisive factor in determining which Christian candidates would be elected. The law was challenged by ten MPs and was consequently referred to the Constitutional Council, which declared it unconstitutional. The government responded by adding, as it had done in 1992, the provision that the use of the *qada* as electoral district in Mount Lebanon was to be "for one time only." It then resubmitted the draft law to parliament, where the law passed—but not before political pressures were exercised on parliamentarians to make sure that the law would not again be challenged. The law was eventually issued a mere three days before the elections were held.

The question of participation in the elections led to a split within the mostly Christian opposition. Four opposition figures in exile—head of the National Bloc Party Raymond Eddé, former president Amin Gemayel, former Army commander Michel Aoun, and leader of the National Liberal Party Dory Chamoun—called for a boycott. They urged Lebanese not to take part in what they denounced as a Syrian-controlled process with a Syrian-scripted outcome. However, the larger and more influential opposition within Lebanon decided to participate, even if reluctantly. Christian leaders opposed to a boycott now included former supporters of Michel Aoun as well as such an outspoken opponent of the Syrian-backed government as Albert Mokheiber. (In 1992, Mokheiber had led the call for a boycott, but he had since conceded that this had been a grave political mistake.) Even Maronite patriarch Sfayr, well known for his criticism of the government and its pro-Syrian bent, blasted the electoral law but refrained from supporting a boycott. Eventually, most Christian leaders declared themselves in favor of participation. Contributing to their decision was the advice of international actors sympathetic to Lebanon's Christians: the Vatican as well as the French and U.S. governments. Most important, though, was the realization of the Christian leaders that the boycott of 1992 had had disastrous effects on their community's political influence: It had failed to produce its goal of a Syrian withdrawal from Lebanon and had led to the political marginalization of Christians, weakened the opposition as a whole, and allowed progovernmental figures to dominate the political field.

Voting began in Mount Lebanon on August 18, 1996, and continued on four consecutive Sundays: August 25 in the north, September 1 in Beirut, September 8 in South Lebanon, and September 15 in the Bekaa Valley. Voting was unfortunately marred by numerous irregularities. In some districts, voters had to cast their ballots under the eyes of officials, whereas in others vote buying was widespread. Several Christian opposition candidates, including Albert Mokheiber, cited heavy intimidation and fraud by the government and eventually appealed to the courts against their defeat. The fact that elections were held at all (and on schedule) was nevertheless a sign of renewed internal stability. Furthermore, because of the participation of several outspoken opposition candidates, seats were sometimes hotly contested. In Mount Lebanon, for instance, some 180 candidates competed for 35 seats (25 Christians, 5 Druze, 3 Shiite, and 2 Sunni).

The results were in line with this book's central theme: the trend toward more representative, credible, and capable legislatures in the Arab world. Contributing to this phenomenon was the increase in voter turnout, which rose from 13 percent in 1992 to 44 percent in 1996. Participation was a modest 31 percent in Beirut, but 40 percent in North Lebanon, 45 percent in Mount Lebanon (by contrast with 17 percent in 1992), 48.2 percent in south Lebanon, and a record of 52 percent in the Bekaa Valley. The main reason behind these figures was enhanced participation by the Christian electorate. Consequently, the elections were a major defeat for the Paris-based opposition. They demonstrated that politicians such as Michel Aoun and Amin Gemayel no longer enjoyed much support within Lebanon. These leaders of the "external opposition" were being deserted by a Christian electorate dissatisfied with their inability to present serious alternatives to the existing order. It is significant that throughout the campaign even Christians often derided the leaders of the external opposition by referring to them as the "Champs Elysées" opposition. The increase in voter turnout suggests that most of those who remain unhappy with the Ta'if Accord—or, more often, with the highly uneven manner in which that agreement has been implemented—have come to accept, even if reluctantly, the parameters of the current system. They grudgingly recognize that they must work within that system to change it. According to the framework developed in this book, this new situation should pave the way for an enhanced role for Lebanon's Chamber.

The educational and professional background of the parliamentarians elected in 1996 should also strengthen the Chamber's internal capacity as well as its ability to negotiate with the executive branch. Ninety-two percent of all Lebanese MPs now hold university degrees, and 18 percent even have Ph.D.'s. The 1996 elections thus confirmed the impressive trend toward increasing educational levels for deputies—the number holding university degrees having risen from 51 percent in 1943 to 73 percent in 1972 and 92 percent in 1996.[12] Equally critical is the fact that many of the current parliamentarians are former ministers who bring with them valuable expertise and a keen understanding of how the executive branch operates. This, too, should strengthen the legislature in its dealings with the cabinet.

Politically, the elections resulted in a victory for candidates considered supportive of the outgoing government and its policies. Even in Mount Lebanon, where 450,000 out of 656,000 voters were Christians, 32 out of 35 seats were won by such individuals. In the Shuf, Walid Jumblatt was easily reelected—his list sweeping 7 out of the district's 8 seats.[13] Elsewhere, coalitions brokered or supported by Damascus won decisive victories as well. In particular, both Prime Minister Rafiq Hariri and his archrival, speaker of parliament Nabih Berri, did well. Hariri, who headed a list of 17 candidates in Beirut, had never been directly elected to political office before. His objective in running for his first seat was not only to gain popular legitimacy at the polls but also to establish a strong parliamentary bloc that would allow him to move his reconstruction plan through a Chamber that had often resisted his policies between 1992 and 1996. Most of the candidates on his list were businessmen, many of them political unknowns. Hariri ran an expensive U.S.-style campaign that involved sea parades, air shows, massive advertising, gigantic billboards, paid television programs, close to six thousand full-time staffers, and at least 250 offices across the capital. According to some sources, financing this unprecedented electoral machine—nicknamed "the bulldozer" by newspapers—may have run as high as $30 million. By contrast, a typical campaign was believed to have cost around $400,000, and a number of candidates had to manage with much less: Najah Wakim was reported to have spent less than $200,000 and Samir Franjiyeh less than $100,000. Hariri's efforts paid off. His list won 14 out of the 19 Beirut seats, and supporters of his in the north, Bekaa, and the south also made strong showings that gave him control of a bloc of at least 30 MPs.

Despite his impressive performance, Hariri did not reach two of his main goals: a Chamber virtually free of opposition and, more specifically, one devoid of Muslim fundamentalists. During the campaign, the prime minister had repeatedly described the election battle as one between moderation and extremism, and he had made it clear that he did not want Hizballah to remain a significant force in parliament. He failed to achieve that objective. It is true that Islamist candidates as a whole did not do as well in 1996 as they had in 1992. Sunni fundamentalists in particular lost three of their four seats. However, Hizballah was only partially weakened, as seven of its members and three of its supporters won seats (as opposed to eight and four, respectively, in the outgoing assembly).[14] More generally, even though the opposition could rely on only about eight MPs beyond Hizballah, it was in a stronger position than it had been since 1992. Several opposition MPs, such as Nassib Lahoud, Pierre Daccash, and Salim al-Hoss, were known as articulate, credible, and outspoken individuals. Moreover, some candidates elected on progovernment lists were expected to move into opposition roles later. It was unlikely, therefore, that the Chamber would prove as docile and nearly devoid of internal opposition as it seemed.

In the end, the legislature that emerged was dominated by two large blocs and three smaller ones. The two large blocs were led by Hariri and Berri, the smaller ones by Druze leader Walid Jumblatt, former minister Suleiman Franjiyeh (grandson of the former president who bore the same name), and Hizballah. Each of these blocs had close relations with Syria, but beyond that their interests diverged significantly. Hariri was the dominant figure, but he was not strong enough to dominate parliament; consequently, he would have to negotiate and compromise with other Syrian-backed leaders—particularly Berri—to push his policies through the Chamber. That had already become clear by November 1996, when Hariri, who had just been reappointed prime minister, was beset by mounting opposition in the legislature and when his supporters there won the chairmanship of only two of the seventeen commissions formed by the new Chamber. Meanwhile, Hizballah deputy Mohammed Fneish had been elected head of the Chamber's Committee of Economy, Trade, Industry and Oil—the first time a member of the militant group chaired a parliamentary committee. (Another Hizballah deputy was elected secretary to the chairman of the Planning and Development Committee, and two others joined the Defense Committee.) The road ahead of Hariri, it was clear, would not be a smooth one.

Notes

1. The quorum for a vote of confidence was a simple majority of the Chamber. Since the Chamber had sixty-six members, the quorum was thirty-four. If half of those voting withdrew their confidence, the government had to resign.

2. In addition to its provisions regarding power sharing, the National Pact represented a Muslim-Christian compromise on Lebanon's foreign policy. Christians

agreed not to seek alliances with Western powers, and in return Muslims (especially Sunnis) committed themselves not to try to integrate Lebanon into a larger Arab state. This arrangement was an attempt to provide Christians and Muslims with mutual guarantees. The Christians needed to feel confident that Lebanon would remain an independent country and that Sunni politicians would drop their long-standing call for union with Syria. They also wanted Muslim leaders to promise that they would not try to mobilize external assistance to affect domestic power struggles. The Muslims, for their part, wanted reassurance that the Maronites would abandon their tendency to seek protection from Western powers (France in particular) and that they would respect Lebanon's Arab character.

3. Candidates unable or unwilling to join a list were allowed to compete independently. In general, however, there was a strong tendency among voters to vote for one of the existing lists.

4. This was the case at least until the controversial issue of the Palestinian presence in Lebanon accentuated existing divisions, inflamed sectarian feelings, and radicalized parties such as the Phalange or Camille Chamoun's National Liberal Party.

5. For sources and details, see Baaklini 1976: 238–251.

6. As discussed earlier, the government could declare a particular piece of legislation it would present to the Chamber as urgent. It was then allowed to promulgate that piece of legislation by decree if the Chamber had failed to act on it within forty days.

7. As As'ad AbuKhalil noted, Riadh al-Solh had already promised the elimination of sectarianism in his first speech before the Chamber in October 1943 (AbuKhalil 1993: 58).

8. All ordinary decisions of the council require the approval of a simple majority in it. Important decisions require the approval of a two-thirds majority and must be presented to parliament for approval. Such decisions include declaring a state of emergency, engaging the country in a war, and redistricting the country as well as amending the electoral law, personal and family laws, or naturalization laws. Requiring a two-thirds majority within the cabinet for such decisions is a way of ensuring a degree of consensus in the executive branch before "going to battle" in parliament. Indeed, any measure that has the support of two-thirds of the cabinet is likely to be approved by the legislature, considering that the cabinet's composition should reflect the balance of power within the Chamber.

9. The prime minister has also become more independent from the president, who no longer appoints him or her and can no longer dismiss him or her or his or her ministers.

10. For instance, even before 1990, the prime minister was usually closely involved in setting policy with the president—particularly from the 1960s onward, when the prime minister was often acting as an alter ego to the president and had a de facto veto power over his policies. Similarly, even though the president was not previously constitutionally bound to take his prime minister's advice in nominating the members of the cabinet, he often would do so. Forceful personalities from well-established families—such as Riadh al-Solh or Rashid Karame—exercised as prime ministers powers that far exceeded those that the constitution formally assigned to their office. Yet, prior to 1990, the prime minister's role was essentially a function of political custom. By contrast, the constitution now spells out very clearly the prime minister's prerogatives, which are considerable.

11. The Ta'if Accord provided for the Syrians to assist the Lebanese government in reestablishing its authority (in particular through the disbanding of the militias). However, it also stipulated that Syrian troops would be withdrawn to the Bekaa Valley

in 1992, after which their presence would be renegotiated between Beirut and Damascus.

12. The figures for 1943 and 1972 are from Khalaf 1987: 121.

13. Jumblatt's supporters also took four out of five seats in the nearby Aley district.

14. It took Syrian intervention to save Hizballah from electoral disaster. After the first three rounds of voting—in Mount Lebanon, the north, and Beirut—Hizballah had yet to win one seat. In one of the organization's main strongholds, the Ba'abda district, which includes the Shiite-dominated southern suburbs of Beirut, Hizbollah MP Ali Ammar had been defeated by two moderate Shiite candidates running on Nabih Berri's Amal list. (Ammar undoubtedly received the largest percentage of the Shiite vote, but he lost because Christian and Sunni voters preferred the Shiite candidates on the Amal list.) Even more worrisome to Hizballah was the fact that it seemed bound to lose in its looming electoral confrontation with Amal for the Shiite seats in the predominantly Shiite regions of the south and the Bekaa. Such a prospect, however, was not to the liking of Syria. For its own purposes, Damascus was interested in making sure that Hizballah remained a viable force in Lebanese politics. It thus pressured Berri into having Hizballah run as a junior partner on a joint list with his Amal movement. It was this last-minute Syrian-brokered agreement that enabled Hizballah to pick up seven seats.

6

Morocco

One of Morocco's distinguishing features in the Arab world is the fact that its political system has long included a multiparty legislature. Accustomed to functioning as a forum for the interaction of government and opposition, Morocco's parliament may be better placed than most transitional legislatures to make a significant contribution to political reform in the country. Since the early 1990s, furthermore, Morocco has been engaged in a very significant democratization experiment that revolves in part around an increase in parliament's centrality. The main steps in this process began with the promulgation in 1992 of a new constitution that expanded the powers of parliament and made the cabinet more accountable to it; the organization in 1993 of the first legislative elections since 1984, elections that were freer than in the past; and subsequent attempts by parliament to assert its new constitutional prerogatives. Next came the adoption in September 1996 of a constitutional amendment that restored an earlier upper house (the Chamber of Councilors) and provided for the direct election of all members of the lower house (the Chamber of Representatives); the first direct election on November 14, 1997, of the lower house; and the December 5, 1997, election of the new upper house. The most recent steps have been the monarch's historic appointment in February 1998 of socialist party leader Abderrahmane Youssoufi to serve as prime minister and the formation, a month later, of a coalition government dominated by what had been called until then "the opposition." Each of these developments should be analyzed as part of King Hassan II's attempt to establish the foundations of a more participatory and accountable political system—one in which the monarchy hopes to emerge stronger because it will have been isolated from the vagaries of day-to-day government and placed in the position of arbitrator and guarantor of the rules of the political game.

Parliamentary History Until 1992

Morocco's parliamentary development has occurred in four main phases: 1962–1977, 1977–1992, 1992–1996, and since 1996. In each phase there has been greater agreement on the rules of the political game among the key political actors. Consequently, each period has also witnessed an increasingly important role for the legislature in the political system.

The Failure of Morocco's First Two Experiments with Parliamentary Politics (1963–1977)

Morocco became independent in 1956 but did not adopt a constitution until December 1962. That constitution provided for a legislature composed of two houses: a directly elected Chamber of Representatives and an indirectly elected Chamber of Councilors. The prime minister and all the other members of the cabinet were to be chosen and appointed by the king, but the lower house could force the cabinet to resign through a vote of no-confidence. Parliament was also given a role in reviewing the budget and in areas of lawmaking not reserved for the cabinet or the king. Yet, the dominant institution under this constitution was the monarchy. The king's extensive prerogatives included the right to select and nominate the prime minister and the entire cabinet; the power to dismiss the premier, any other minister, or the whole cabinet (which therefore was responsible to both the king and the Chamber of Representatives); and the authority to dissolve parliament and assume unlimited emergency powers.

Between 1963 and 1977, the kingdom experimented twice with parliamentary politics: from October 1963 until June 1965 and from October 1970 until October 1971. The brief duration of both experiments suggests their ultimate failure. From 1965 to 1970, and then again from 1972 to 1977, Hassan II (who became king after the death of his father, Muhammad V, in 1961) governed without a legislature.

The Chamber of Representatives elected in October 1963 was divided almost equally between two antagonistic blocs: a royalist coalition, represented by the Front for the Defense of Constitutional Institutions (FDIC), and the opposition, led by the Istiqlal and the UNFP (National Union of Popular Forces), whose roots went back to the nationalist movement that had developed under the French protectorate. Created just before the 1963 elections, the FDIC enjoyed only a slight majority (seventy-one seats as opposed to sixty-seven for the UNFP and the Istiqlal). The Istiqlal and the UNFP were therefore in a relatively strong position. They used it to question not only government policies but the very legitimacy of the regime. They were critical of the nature of the 1962 constitution and objected in particular to the monarchy's dominant role over all branches of government. Their ambition was to reduce the monarchy to a purely honorific and symbolic institution. Needless to say, this was not what King Hassan II had in mind.

Considering that key political actors disagreed so sharply on the rules of the political game, it is not surprising that the legislature was unable to operate smoothly. King Hassan was faced with a Chamber of Representatives in which a very large bloc of deputies wanted him to reign but not rule. For his part, he barely tolerated parliament and seemed bent on marginalizing it—drawing the ire of opposition politicians already angered by the weakness of the legislature's constitutional prerogatives. Consequently, parliament was soon paralyzed by ideological disputes between the royalist majority and the opposition. To make things worse, the cabinet could not even count on the undivided support of a parliamentary majority that was internally divided by personal feuds and rivalries. Morocco's first legislature thus achieved little. Quarreling factions and politicians in it could not reach a basic consensus with each other, let alone with the government. Political deadlock prevented legislation from being passed.

When in March 1965 Casablanca was rocked by three days of violent riots that resulted in four hundred deaths and considerable material damage, the king was quick to blame the unrest on the bickering of politicians. He accused them of having spent all their time fighting with each other instead of addressing the problems facing the country. Three months later, he declared a state of emergency and suspended parliament. For the following five years, he assumed full legislative and executive powers and governed by royal decrees (*dahirs*). Morocco's first parliamentary experience had lasted only twenty months.

In 1970, a new constitution was ratified that reduced the power of parliament and the cabinet and gave the king more influence over day-to-day policymaking. In addition, the bicameral legislature established by the 1962 constitution was replaced with a unicameral parliament, only one-third of which was to be directly elected. In short, a less representative parliament was now given even less authority than before.

Although the 1970 constitution was opposed by the Istiqlal and the UNFP, it was approved by an overwhelming 98.7 percent of the electorate, during a referendum marred by fraud and administrative interference. Shortly thereafter, legislative elections were held. Boycotted by the opposition, they resulted in a landslide by "independent" (i.e., royalist) candidates, who won 219 out of the 240 seats. In short, Morocco at the time was still handicapped by major disagreements among key political actors regarding the very nature of the institutional arrangements appropriate for the country. The parties that had developed out of the nationalist movement had not yet reconciled themselves to the monarchy's central role in the political system, and they still harbored the ambition to reduce the king to a mere figurehead. In this context, Hassan II resorted to heavy-handed tactics in order to assert the monarchy's supremacy.

As it turned out, Morocco's second parliamentary experience was even briefer than the first one. On July 10, 1971, a coup attempt put an end to it. Still, in an effort to revive political life, the king promulgated a third constitution in March 1972. The new document made limited but nevertheless significant concessions to the long-standing demands of the opposition. For one, two-thirds of parliament's members were now to be elected by direct universal suffrage. In addition, the responsibilities of the cabinet and the premier were somewhat expanded. However, another coup attempt in August 1972 and continuing political tensions led the king to postpone parliamentary elections for several years. Not until 1977 would these elections take place.

Resumption and Consolidation of Parliamentary Politics (1977–1992)

In 1974, Spain announced its intention to withdraw from the Western Sahara, which it had held since 1884. King Hassan immediately reasserted Morocco's historic claim to this phosphate-rich territory. Algeria's opposition to Moroccan designs and the World Court's rejection of Morocco's claim in October 1975 had no impact on King Hassan's determination to annex the Western Sahara. In November 1975, he organized the so-called Green March, during which an estimated 350,000 unarmed Moroccan civilians entered the disputed territory.

The Western Sahara issue produced a climate of unprecedented national unity. All the main political forces in the country—including the Istiqlal and the new socialist party, the Socialist Union of Popular Forces (USFP—which had been created in 1972 as a breakaway from the UNFP)—agreed that the former Spanish colony should be "reintegrated" into Morocco. The king was able to exploit this nationalist fervor to consolidate popular support for the monarchy and move toward a resumption of parliamentary activity. As the ideological polarization of the 1960s and early 1970s gave way to a new national consensus, the king felt confident that he could open up the political arena. In 1974–1975, he began to consult actively with the leaders of the main opposition parties. Both the Istiqlal and the USFP progressively came out of their isolation and were permitted to resume their activities and criticism of certain governmental policies. In 1974, the Communist Party, renamed Party of Progress and Socialism (PPS), was legalized. Within a few months, some political prisoners were released and many controls over the press lifted. In 1975, Hassan II announced that the "restoration" of democracy was now one of his primary objectives. In 1976, local and provincial elections were held, and the much-awaited parliamentary elections finally took place in 1977.

The elections again resulted in the victory of independent (i.e., pro-palace) candidates, who received 140 out of 264 seats.[1] The Istiqlal gained 49 seats, the USFP 16, and the PPS 1. Shortly after the election, the Istiqlal accepted an invitation to participate in government—a major victory for King

Hassan. Though clearly dominated by progovernment forces, parliament became the scene of acrimonious debates, particularly over the government's economic policies.

In May 1980, a referendum approved a constitutional amendment extending parliament's term from four to six years. Elections initially scheduled for 1981 were thus pushed back until 1983. Because of a serious economic crisis and mounting social unrest, in 1983 King Hassan decided to postpone those elections by one more year. When elections were finally held in 1984, they yielded a legislature dominated by a centrist coalition in line with the policy preferences of the palace.[2] With only forty-one seats, the Istiqlal had suffered a setback. Nonetheless, the USFP had doubled its representation, reaching thirty-six seats. This was a clear indication that the regime was willing to tolerate greater dissent in the new legislature.

Parliamentary debates rapidly centered on the implementation of the Structural Adjustment Program (SAP) adopted in 1983. The Istiqlal, which opposed the drastic economic reforms initiated by the government, left the cabinet in 1985. Parliament, dominated as it was by progovernment forces, was prompt to pass the legislation needed to carry out Morocco's neoliberal economic restructuring. However, the Chamber of Representatives provided a forum for lively debates, during which the opposition voiced its strong disapproval of the SAP. Nor could the cabinet count on the unconditional support of parliament. This was shown in 1989, when the Chamber forced important modifications of the privatization bill introduced by the government.

In 1990, Hassan II extended parliament's term for two years, on the ground that elections should not interfere with the forthcoming referendum in the Western Sahara. During that 1990–1992 period the legislature began to assert itself. In May 1990, a no-confidence motion was considered (and defeated) in the Chamber. In parliament as elsewhere, the opposition displayed greater confidence and more forcefulness in voicing criticism of the cabinet's policies and in pressing for greater governmental accountability and transparency. In December 1990, violent riots in Fez and other cities rocked the country. The kingdom also experienced strikes and other manifestations of labor unrest in 1990, 1991, and 1992. It was in this context that King Hassan submitted a new constitution to a popular referendum.

Parliament's Enhanced Role Under the 1992 Constitution

All Moroccan constitutions since 1962 have tilted the balance of power firmly toward the executive branch. The 1992 constitution was no exception. However, it expanded parliament's prerogatives far beyond what they had been until then, thus ushering in a new stage in Morocco's legislative development.

The 1992 constitution granted parliament, for the first time, the authority to endorse or reject a new government after it had been appointed by the king. It stated that, once appointed by the monarch, the prime minister must present his or her program to parliament. This presentation is followed by a debate in the plenary and then by a vote over the government's program. If the vote is negative, the entire cabinet must resign. To compel governments to submit to a vote of confidence is an important innovation that highlights the cabinet's responsibility to the legislature.

The 1992 constitution also mandated that ministers answer the questions of parliamentarians within twenty days of the submission of these questions. This new provision was significant, considering that previously most of the questions asked by parliamentarians had remained unanswered by the government.[3] The constitution thereby improved the effectiveness of one of the major means—the interrogation of ministers—through which members of Parliament (MPs) can exercise some oversight over the executive branch. Similarly, the 1992 constitution provided for quicker promulgation of laws after their adoption by the legislature. In Morocco, a law passed by parliament takes effect only after it is issued by royal decree (*dahir*). Previous constitutions had not set any limit on the time that could lapse between the passing of a law by parliament and its promulgation by the king, a situation that resulted in lengthy delays. Such delays tarnished parliament's public image by underscoring the fact that, even in the area of lawmaking, the legislature's powers were strictly circumscribed. By contrast, the 1992 constitution stated that the king must promulgate a law passed by parliament no more than thirty days after parliament had forwarded that law to the government. This provision eliminates the monarch's ability to "sit on" a law that has been adopted by parliament.

Parliament was also empowered to create commissions of investigation, which had been a long-standing request of opposition parties. Although these commissions have no specific authority (they are merely intended to provide parliament with information) and are only temporary (their mission ends with the submission of their report to the legislature), they provide yet another avenue for parliamentary control over the executive.[4] In addition, although under the 1992 constitution the king retained the power to dissolve parliament, his declaring a state of emergency no longer automatically entailed the disbanding of the legislature. The new constitution thus opened up the possibility of parliament's remaining in session and making its voice heard even after a state of national emergency has been proclaimed.

Finally, the 1992 constitution provided for a Constitutional Council, the main function of which is to decide on challenges to the constitutionality of laws. After consulting with the parliamentary groups, the Chamber's president appoints four of the Council's nine members. (The other five, including the Council's president, are appointed by the king. All members serve six-year terms.) The new document also made it easy for parliament to seize that

Council: To do so only requires a request by the Chamber's president or one-quarter of its members. (The king and the prime minister also can seize the Council.)

The 1993–1997 Legislature

In June and September of 1993, elections were held for the first legislature to operate under the 1992 constitution. Here we review the 1993–1997 legislature.

Strengths of the 1993–1997 Chamber

The legislature elected in 1993 featured the strongest opposition since 1963–1965. With 106 seats (out of 333) between their two parliamentary groups, the USFP and the Istiqlal formed a powerful front that the government could not ignore. More active and lively parliamentary debates stimulated the media to increase coverage of the Chamber's activities, which in turn prompted some nongovernmental organizations (NGOs) and special interest groups to try to further their agenda by seeking to improve their access to parliament. The parliament elected in 1993 was also energized by the arrival of a whole new cohort of deputies, since 249 of its members (or close to 75 percent) had never sat in the Chamber before 1993. For the first time, two women had been elected—Badia Skalli (USFP, Casablanca) and Latifa Smires-Bennani (Istiqlal, Fez). They were among 33 women who had run in 1993, as opposed to the mere 15 who had contested the 1984 elections.[5]

Unlike any other Arab legislature, Morocco's parliament also awards significant resources to political parties, thus recognizing the contributions that parties can make to a well-functioning legislature. Political parties represented by at least twelve members are allowed to form a parliamentary group. The Chamber elected in 1993 initially featured eight such groups. Each parliamentary group is headed by a chairperson, who is not necessarily the leader of the party; in fact, in the 1993–1997 legislature, all parliamentary groups had decided to keep the two positions separate, thereby emphasizing the distinctiveness of the parliamentary wing of these parties.

Parliamentary groups play a critical role in the Moroccan parliament. They constitute the main forum in which deputies affiliated with a specific political party coordinate their positions on the issues debated in the plenary and in committees. MPs usually meet with their respective parliamentary groups to determine their parties' position on a bill and to give instructions to those of their members who belong to the committee in which that bill will be discussed. In addition, the right to ask oral questions during plenary sessions is a privilege conferred not on individual MPs but on political parties. As a result, the larger the parliamentary group, the greater the number of oral questions it can ask.

Parliamentary groups are not only represented (according to their size) in the Chamber's decisionmaking bodies, but they also receive a substantial share of the resources at the disposal of parliament. For instance, whereas in the United States the professional staff of Congress is allocated to committees, in Morocco it is given to parliamentary groups.[6] This facilitates the process of democratization and strengthens the parliamentary institution in two respects. First, it provides political parties with incentives to play a constructive role. For instance, as long as political parties have a say in setting parliament's agenda and internal rules, they are less likely to opt out of the parliamentary game. Second, by involving political parties in all aspects of parliamentary life and by making staff and resources available to them, the legislature helps parties become more effective. This enhances prospects for the consolidation of a viable multiparty system, which itself is a prerequisite of a well-functioning democracy.

Yet another strength of the Moroccan legislature by the mid-1990s was the growing vitality of parliamentary debates. Questions asked of government ministers would routinely raise highly sensitive topics that previously were not discussed in the Chamber. Increasingly, calls for broader political participation or for the defense of human rights were mounted from within the legislature. Parliamentary debates had also become noteworthy for the opposition parties' heated critiques of the government's economic strategy. At the request of the king, the oral questions session, held every Wednesday afternoon, was now broadcast live on Moroccan television from 3:00 to 6:00 P.M. One incident witnessed by the authors during one of these sessions deserves to be described here, for it illustrates both the new freedoms enjoyed by the Chamber and their limits.

On May 18, 1994, during the oral questions session held that afternoon, an opposition deputy asked a question related to the status of political prisoners. Only a few years earlier, no parliamentarian would have dared to publicly raise such a controversial issue. That a deputy was now doing so during a session that was being broadcast live on television underlined the broadening of public discourse in the kingdom. But the limits of Morocco's new freedoms were also highlighted when the broadcast was interrupted just as the deputy was asking his question. There followed a very heated exchange—which was not shown on television—between the deputy and the minister of interior, Driss Basri, during which the latter appeared to make barely veiled threats.

A week later, Fathallah Oualalou, then head of the parliamentary group of the USFP, began the oral questions period by protesting vehemently the sudden interruption of the broadcast of the May 18 session. Oualalou noted that the action had been in direct contradiction with the directives issued by the king himself. (Oualalou was thereby skillfully invoking on his side the authority of the monarch as a guarantor of the fairness of the political process.) He added that, contrary to a promise made shortly after the incident, the question and its follow-up had not been shown on television the following day. He concluded by complaining that oral questions sessions, scheduled to begin at 3:00 P.M., were systematically being delayed by at least thirty minutes, thus preventing the live broadcast of several questions, since television coverage stopped at 6:00 P.M.

He was followed by an Istiqlal deputy who elaborated on the same theme and observed that the most sensitive questions were usually scheduled for after 6:00 P.M. and therefore were not shown on television. That deputy argued that television coverage of parliamentary proceedings was slowly being undermined by governmental interference and obstruction. Shortly after this intervention, all the deputies of the opposition stood up and left the room for ten minutes to protest formally against the practices that two of their colleagues had just highlighted. Significantly, television cameras remained fixed on the podium and the new speaker and did not show the opposition leaving the room.

This episode sheds light on the dynamic of parliamentary politics in a country that is negotiating a transition toward a more democratic political system. The live broadcast of the oral questions sessions and the fact that a deputy had dared raise a question on a sensitive human rights issue had shown how far Morocco had gone toward expanding participation and freedom of speech. At the same time, the interruption of the broadcast and the veiled threats directed by the minister of interior had highlighted the limits of democratization, the continuing unwillingness of certain elements in the regime to tolerate the discussion in public of certain topics, and the persistence of practices—in this case, intimidation and ultimate government control over the media—inherited from the authoritarian era.

The events described above also illustrate one important component of transitions toward more democratic political systems, that is, the negotiation of new rules of the game. Regime and opposition alike realize that the system is becoming more open. They are aware that the rules of the game are being liberalized, yet neither knows exactly what the new rules will end up being. The regime appears confident that it can control the pace at which, and the extent to which, the rules are being altered. It is orchestrating reforms on the assumption that these reforms will ultimately strengthen its position. The opposition, for its part, believes that its bargaining power is increasing with every concession made by the regime. It hopes that, in the long run, the small and incremental changes that are being implemented will amount to a significant shift in the balance of power between state and society.

As the political system becomes more democratic, the regime wants to make sure that the new, far less restrictive limits on freedom of expression and political behavior are not constantly pushed back by the opposition. To do so, the incumbent elite must emphasize the existence of certain "red lines" that the opposition should not cross. This explains the interruption of the broadcast and the veiled threats from the interior minister. For its part, the opposition is aware that demands for drastic political changes could prove destabilizing and backfire. It also knows that, at this stage of the game, the regime retains the upper hand and can roll back reforms as fast as it implemented them. This explains why the opposition is willing to content itself with incremental changes and why it is preoccupied with keeping the game going. It is significant that although opposition deputies exited the premises of parliament to protest the regime's interruption of the broadcast, they were back within ten minutes. Thus, just as the regime goes out of its way to keep alive the dialogue with the opposition, the latter is careful not to burn its bridges with the regime or to put excessive pressure on it, for fear that doing so might provoke a government crackdown that in turn would erase any gain the opposition might have made and may yet make in the future.

Every time the regime makes a concession, however, the opposition seeks to determine how far it can stretch the new rules, thus trying to negotiate ever more liberal ones. This is how one should interpret the opposition's decision to seize the opportunity offered by television broadcasting to raise a highly controversial and sensitive issue. Had the television censors let the deputy ask his question live, the opposition would have succeeded in stretching the new rules to the point of turning them into even more tolerant ones. (The regime's hope was that the opposition would refrain from using its new freedoms to raise issues, such as political prisoners, that at the time remained very controversial.) By pulling the plug on the television broadcast, the censors denied the opposition a clear-cut victory.

They were unable, however, to silence the opposition altogether. First, in the days that followed, opposition newspapers were able to exploit the incident. Second, a week later, as we saw, the opposition was once again indirectly bargaining with the regime by arguing that the broadcast interruption meant that the government had reneged on its commitment to broadcast oral questions. By walking out of the Chamber, the opposition intended to display in a dramatic fashion its discontent at what it claimed was the regime's failure to abide by its earlier promise. For his part, the minister of interior could contend that the original question had been a deliberate provocation that justified a firm response. Such disagreements over what the rules of the game really are at any given point of the transition (and, therefore, over what is "fair game" versus what amounts to a violation of the new rules) are typical of polities undergoing a transition through negotiation. At least, that is the case until the new rules have been formalized and agreed upon by all key actors. As argued in Part One, that is precisely what the transition is ultimately about.

Finally, Morocco's parliament in the mid-1990s was also characterized by its relatively well developed internal capacity, especially by regional standards. Since the 1980s, parliament had endeavored to facilitate interactions and communications among representatives of the various political groups represented in the institution. As discussed earlier, it had institutionalized the practice of providing those groups with professional staff in order to enable them to contribute more effectively to the performance of parliamentary functions. It had also succeeded in establishing the principle that parliamentary staff should be remunerated more generously than comparable staff elsewhere in the governmental administration.

In addition, the premises in which parliamentarians worked were also adequate. The Chamber was housed in an impressive building. Its plenary hall was decorous and spacious. Committees had their own rooms, and parliamentary groups had space in which to conduct their business. The 1993 Chamber also included the best-educated group of politicians ever to sit in Morocco's parliament, as 202 out of 333 (almost 61 percent) held a university degree, and 91 (or 27 percent) were high school graduates. Schoolteachers and university professors alone represented 21 percent of all MPs.[7]

On the eve of the 1996 constitutional amendment, the Chamber was also engaged in a major internal reorganization effort aimed at making the institution more effective. In 1993, the Office of the Secretary General of the Chamber had issued a report presenting the results of a comprehensive self-examination. This document identified organizational and procedural flaws and proposed ways to remedy them, based in part on the study of the organizational charts and internal operations of more than one hundred parliaments around the world. The existence of such a thorough study was a clear indication that the Moroccan authorities were aware of the need to improve the organization, procedures, and overall capacity of their legislature and that they were determined to see this process through. Indeed, efforts at internal reorganization proceeded apace during 1994 and 1995.

Weaknesses of the 1993–1997 Chamber

In the mid-1990s, the credibility and public image of the Moroccan parliament were still undermined by an electoral law that remained widely contested. At the time, the Chamber had 333 members, who served a six-year term. Two-thirds (222) of these deputies were elected directly and one-third (111) indirectly. Direct elections took place in single-member districts. There was only one round, and the candidate who received the most votes was the winner. Indirect elections were organized a few months later (direct elections had been held on June 25, 1993, and indirect ones on September 17, 1993) through five electoral colleges. The most important one was that formed by the 22,282 members (in 1993) of the country's 1,544 local councils, who elected 69 out of the 111 indirectly elected deputies.[8] There was only one round of voting, and votes were for individual candidates.[9] The remaining 42 deputies were chosen as follows: Fifteen were selected by the members (544 in 1993) of the Chambers of Agriculture, 10 by the members (678 in 1993) of the Chambers of Commerce and Industry, 7 by the Chambers of Crafts (402 members in 1993), and 10 by representatives of salaried employees (this feature explaining the presence of some trade union representatives in Parliament). All were chosen through electoral lists that were awarded seats in proportion to the number of votes they received.

The opposition had long opposed the selection of one-third of parliament's members through an indirect election, requesting instead that all MPs be directly elected. However, the palace and its allies had opposed such a change. This was understandable, since the indirect election of one-third of parliament provided a built-in conservative bias. After all, the Chambers of Agriculture (heavily influenced by rural notables), the Chambers of Commerce and Industry (dominated by urban industrialists), and the Chambers of Crafts leaned by nature toward the parties of the right and center. Similarly, local councils have historically been dominated by politicians close to the regime. The latter are better equipped to deliver goods and services and hence enjoy a clear advantage over their competitors, since local elections are dominated by issues of service delivery. In addition, vote rigging, vote buying, administrative interference, and pressures on candidates and electors alike are most common during local elections, and these practices benefit disproportionately (though not exclusively) centrist and right-wing candidates.

The indirect election of one-third of parliament thus allowed the regime to "correct" the results of the direct elections. The "correction" would take place in several areas. The first was the balance between the majority and the opposition. Indirect elections would allow conservative and centrist parties to make up for a poor performance in the direct vote. This is what happened in September 1993, when these parties received about 70 percent of the votes against 15 percent for the opposition. This outcome eliminated the possibility that the Istiqlal and the USFP might control enough seats in the Chamber to claim the right to form a government by themselves.

Another correction concerned the balance within each camp, because indirect elections allowed the regime to make sure that no political party—whether progovernment or opposition—would become either too strong or too weak in the Chamber. One should not forget that Morocco's pluralism remains to a large extent orchestrated from above, by a king who has proven a master at playing parties and ambitious politicians against each other. For Hassan II to be able to play this role, the political arena must include a multiplicity of parties, but none of them must be too strong. Indirect elections were very useful for achieving this result. In 1984, for instance, they had enabled the Istiqlal to regain some of the ground it had lost to the USFP in the direct elections held three weeks earlier. This very much suited the king, who did not want to be faced with an opposition in which the socialist USFP would be too strong and the Istiqlal (which historically had been easier for Hassan II to deal with) too weak. Similarly, during the September 1993 indirect elections, administrative interference was rumored to have contributed to the surprising performance of the PPS, which had won four seats (as many as the far more influential USFP). Many observers saw in this outcome a reward for the conciliatory tone that the PPS had adopted toward the regime since 1992. For instance, the PPS had been the only party in the opposition bloc to call for a "yes" vote in the referendum on the 1992 constitution, an action that had strained its relations with the USFP, the Istiqlal, and the leftist Organization of Democratic and Popular Action (OADP). From the regime's perspective, furthermore, a stronger PPS could prove a useful counterweight to the USFP and Istiqlal. The unexpected, strong performance of the Constitutional Union in the indirect election of September 1993 was also noteworthy in rescuing from potential oblivion a party that had fared disastrously in June.

Saving the regime's so-called barons was another form of correction. Candidates who were closely identified with the palace but who had been defeated during the direct elections were often "saved" in the indirect elections. Typically, various forms of pressures and incentives would "convince" potential rivals not to present their candidacies. If necessary, electoral fraud was used (usually as a last resort). Thus, politicians who had been denied access to the Chamber in the direct elections would nevertheless secure that very same access through the indirect elections held a few weeks later.

Ultimately, the third of the Chamber that was indirectly elected was the single most important factor shaping Morocco's parliamentary map. It ensured that conservative and centrist parties would always hold a majority in the Chamber and that no party in that same Chamber would ever become too powerful.

Growing Pains of a Legislature in Transition

To conclude this discussion of the 1993–1997 Chamber, it should be noted that as the legislature assumed a more prominent and visible role, public criticism of its shortcomings also became sharper. Between 1994 and 1996, media coverage of parliament repeatedly complained about the lack of focus of parliamentary debates and their tendency to degenerate into shouting matches between ministers and opposition deputies.[10] One factor contributing to this situation was the fact that the cabinet was composed primarily of technocrats who lacked political experience. These individuals did not evoke any strong feelings of loyalty or respect in the Chamber, even among the parties that made up the cabinet's parliamentary majority. Furthermore, they rarely displayed the skills, attitudes, and outlook conducive to fruitful, professional interaction with the Chamber. They repeatedly showed themselves impatient with parliamentary criticisms of their performance and were sometimes downright contemptuous of the legislative branch. Many deputies, too, were still in the process of developing a better understanding of the role and limitations of the legislature in Morocco's evolving political system.

One incident may be cited to illustrate these problems, which are typical of transitional legislatures. On April 26, 1995, opposition deputies confronted the justice minister regarding a highly publicized scandal involving the Algemene Bank and the Goodyear firm, a joint venture between Goodyear USA, which holds 55 percent of the stock, and Moroccan entrepreneurs. That scandal had led to a trial that had been extensively covered by the press. In its wake, several prominent and well-connected individuals had been sent to prison and denied temporary release. Within days of the verdict, however, these very same individuals were out of jail. The opposition was incensed, seeing this as a clear indication of hidden interference in the judicial process. During the oral questions session of parliament, opposition deputies called the justice minister to account for what had happened. What began as a normal exercise of parliamentary prerogatives, however, soon deteriorated into highly personal verbal attacks against the minister. Undocumented allegations were made, and hidden motives were assumed. Before long, what should have been an effort to reconstruct a sequence of events and identify potential irregularities had become an exchange of insults, an opportunity to settle old scores and historical disputes, and an exercise in public posturing. For his part, the minister of justice showed himself incapable of dealing with opposition criticism, invoking at one point such arguments as his personal qualifications ("I teach law at the university") and the fact that he "was not minister at the beginning of this affair."[11]

This incident—and many similar ones—damaged the public image of the legislature and left observers skeptical about the effectiveness of parliamentary oversight of the executive. It certainly was not a coincidence that, three weeks after this highly publicized episode, the king gave a speech in which he denounced what he referred to as "the parliamentary circus" and called for a profound modification of the way the Chamber was conducting its business.

The September 1996 Constitutional Amendment

The 1996 constitutional amendment—announced by the king on August 20 and approved overwhelmingly by referendum on September 13—ushered in a new era in Morocco's parliamentary development. It introduced two key innovations. The first was the direct election of all the members of the Chamber of Representatives, the long-standing request of opposition parties. This change removed a major source of contention between the regime and the opposition. Furthermore, by making it easier for the parties that developed out of the nationalist movement to win a majority in the lower house, this change opened the door to the long-announced but also long-delayed *al-*

ternance (alternation of power, i.e., the formation of a cabinet headed by what had been the opposition).

The second modification brought about by the 1996 constitutional amendment was the reestablishment of an upper house, the Chamber of Councilors. Such an upper house was not without precedent. The kingdom's first constitution (that of 1962) had also provided for a bicameral system (replaced by a unicameral system in the constitutions of 1970, 1972, and 1992). This upper house is designed to articulate the concerns and interests of the very same institutions that used to be represented through the indirect election of one-third of the Chamber of Representatives, that is, local councils and professional associations.

Parliament in the New System

Understanding the significance of the 1996 constitutional amendment requires familiarity with the composition, mode of election, and prerogatives of each house under the new system. The Chamber of Representatives is now composed of 325 members elected for five-year terms by direct suffrage. The Chamber of Councilors consists of 270 members elected for nine years. Three-fifths of them (162 members) are chosen by regional electoral colleges composed of representatives of local councils. An additional 81 members are selected by regional colleges of delegates of professional chambers, and the remaining 27 members are selected by a national college made up of representatives of salaried employees. One-third of the upper house is up for reelection every third year.

The Chamber of Representatives' prerogatives are somewhat more extensive than those of the Chamber of Councilors. For instance, once a prime minister has been selected, he or she must present his or her cabinet and program to both houses. However, only the Chamber of Representatives is then empowered to vote on the cabinet's program. Similarly, although both houses can force the cabinet to resign through a vote of no-confidence, it is much easier for the Chamber of Representatives to do so. To begin with, a no-confidence motion must receive the signatures of at least one-third of the members of the Chamber of Councilors before the upper house can vote on it. By contrast, only a quarter of the members of the Chamber of Representatives need to sign a motion of no-confidence before a vote can take place on it in the lower house. Furthermore, for the motion to pass and force the resignation of the cabinet, a two-thirds majority is needed in the Chamber of Councilors but only a simple majority in the Chamber of Representatives.

The above notwithstanding, the prerogatives of the upper house are far more extensive than is the case in most bicameral systems. This characteristic is reflected in seven key attributes of the Chamber of Councilors. First, it is one of only three such houses in the world to have the power to force the cabinet to resign through a vote of no-confidence (the other two countries are Italy and

South Africa). Second, it can initiate laws just as easily as the Chamber of Representatives. Third, it can pass a warning motion (*motion d'avertissement*)—a provision without precedent in Morocco's constitutional history. Whenever a warning motion receives the signatures of at least one-third of the members of the Chamber of Councilors (that is, ninety members), a vote on this motion must take place within three days. The motion is considered passed whenever it receives a simple majority in the Chamber. The president of the Chamber then sends the text of the motion to the prime minister. Within six days of receiving that text, the prime minister must address the Chamber of Councilors to clarify the position of his or her government regarding the issues raised in the warning motion. Following the prime minister's address, a debate must take place within the Chamber of Councilors. That debate, however, cannot be followed by a vote. Fourth, the upper house—like the king and the Chamber of Representatives—is empowered to create commissions of investigation. As in the case of the lower house, the support of one-half of the members of the Chamber of Councilors is required for a commission to be established.[12] Fifth, following presentation of the cabinet and its program by the prime minister–designate, the Chamber of Councilors is empowered to debate that program. (As mentioned above, however, only the Chamber of Representatives can vote on the government's program.) Sixth, just like the lower house, the upper house devotes one of its weekly sessions to the oral questions that its members have for the government. Finally, a bill does not become law until it has been adopted in similar terms by both houses.

What the 1996 constitutional amendment did not change, of course, was parliament's subordinate relationship to the monarchy. First, parliament may only legislate in certain clearly delineated areas, described in the constitution.[13] By contrast, the king's lawmaking authority knows no functional boundaries. Second, should the king disagree with a law passed by parliament, or should he want modifications made to it, he can refuse to promulgate it and can return it to the legislature, along with his comments. Unless the law is then adopted or rejected by a two-thirds majority in both houses, the king may decree that the issue will be decided through a popular referendum. These provisions make it extremely difficult for parliament to pass a law with which the monarch disagrees. Third, the king is still constitutionally empowered to dissolve parliament and rule by decree, after proclaiming a "state of exception." The fact that this happened on two occasions (1965 and 1971) under the present monarch gives this provision added deterrent power. Finally, the independence of the legislative branch is weakened by the king's ability to set the date of parliamentary elections. As discussed earlier, elections were postponed in 1983 (for one year) and in 1990 (for three years). In both cases, the extension was decided upon at a time of domestic unrest and is believed to have worked to the advantage of progovernment parties. Successive delays can also help the king keep political forces off balance.

Political Significance of the 1996 Constitutional Reform

The 1996 constitutional amendment highlighted the role of the legislative institution as a focus of Morocco's democratization process. Because the amendment was supported by a very large majority of political forces, including the main parties on the left, it represented a decisive step in the consolidation of a broad national consensus on the country's institutions. In that respect, it enhanced prospects for further democratization. Since the essential rules of the game are no longer contested by key political actors, the king has become freer to make concessions that give more influence and visibility to representative institutions. The fact that the USFP, the Istiqlal, and the PPS all campaigned actively in favor of the ratification of the amendment demonstrated that these parties no longer question the central political role of the monarchy. In this context, the king is understandably better disposed toward political reforms than he was two or three decades ago, when these same political forces questioned his very legitimacy. Dealing from a position of strength, he can now afford compromises.

In several other respects as well, the amendment strengthened the monarchical institution and established new safeguards against sudden disruptions of the political system. For instance, the creation of an upper house endowed with very significant prerogatives (including, as we saw, the power to pass a no-confidence vote in the government) creates a powerful brake on the ability of the now directly elected lower house to introduce radical socioeconomic or political changes. As shown earlier, the Chamber of Councilors will articulate the concerns of those constituencies that used to be represented through the indirect election of one-third of the unicameral parliament that existed prior to 1997. The senate, therefore, will have a conservative makeup and will act as a restraint on the capacity of the cabinet or the lower house to push for legislation or policies that might be opposed by the monarchy or by local and professional elites and that could constitute a threat to their position.

The Chamber of Councilors' central purpose is therefore to reassure powerful political forces that might feel threatened by the process of democratization. Because they wield considerable social influence and control significant economic resources, these forces need to be appeased if democratization is to succeed. To provide such reassurance is the reason why upper houses were initially created in most of today's democracies, and Morocco seems to be following that pattern.

In Morocco's case, therefore, the establishment of a bicameral system—in which two chambers are given almost equal prerogatives but are likely to be controlled by rival political alliances—will enhance the king's position as ultimate referee. The creation of a Chamber of Councilors that balances the power of the lower house should help the monarchy further extricate itself from involvement in day-to-day politics. It also reduces the regime's need to engage in the kinds of electoral manipulations that were previously necessary to ensure a compliant Chamber of Representatives. As a result, the regime's overall legitimacy and its claim to operate according to the rule of law should be enhanced, and the king's assertion that he operates above electoral and party politics should become more credible. In short, the 1996 constitutional amendment represents yet another manifestation of King Hassan's effort to combine day-to-day political maneuvering with long-term institutional restructuring so as to allow the monarchy to survive into the twenty-first century as a credible, legitimate, and powerful institution.

The November-December 1997 Elections

The parliamentary elections of November and December 1997 were the first test of Morocco's new constitutional framework. Elections to the Chamber of Representatives took place on November 14, 1997, and the members of the new upper house were chosen on December 5, 1997. The period leading up to the vote was marked by intense negotiations designed to ensure that the elections would be transparent and fair. These negotiations took place at the urging of King Hassan, who thereby once again emphasized his role as arbitrator among the forces competing in the Moroccan political arena. They culminated on February 28, 1997, when Minister of the Interior Driss Basri sat down with representatives of the eleven political parties represented in the legislature elected in 1993 to sign a "code of honor" (*mithaq sharaf*, also referred to in the French-language Moroccan press as Charte d'honneur or Déclaration commune). The purpose of this document was to reflect the consensus of all key actors regarding the conditions under which the forthcoming elections should be held. The government committed itself to refraining from interfering in the electoral process and to undertaking legal proceedings against state employees shown to have engaged in fraud or administrative pressures. In return, political parties promised not to question electoral results—and therefore the legitimacy of parliament's makeup—unless substantial evidence of organized fraud and irregularities was uncovered. They also agreed to mobilize their members and newspapers in order to ensure that the vote would proceed smoothly.

Following the adoption of this electoral charter, a commission was established to guarantee its proper implementation and help resolve electoral disputes. This National Commission for the Supervision of the Electoral Process (Commission nationale de suivi des élections) was composed of government representatives, the leaders of the political parties represented in parliament, and magistrates. Similar commissions were established at the level of the province and the governorate (*préfecture*). In addition, a new electoral law, a new political party law, and a new law regulating the work of the media and access to them by the political parties were enacted.

When elections to the Chamber of Representatives were finally held on November 14, 1997, 3,319 candidates belonging to sixteen political parties competed for the house's 325 seats. Only 69 of these candidates were women—a very small increase from 33 in 1993, 15 in 1984, and 8 in 1977. Despite the host of preparatory meetings designed to ensure a free and fair ballot, the elections were marred by vote buying and by government interference and manipulation—leading most observers to conclude that the results were largely orchestrated from the top. Ultimately, the parties that won the most seats were the left-leaning USFP (57), the conservative Constitutional Union (50), the centrist National Rally of Independents (RNI; 46), the conservative, Berber-dominated Popular Movement (40), a new left-of-center party known as the Movement of Social Democrats (MDS; 32), and the Istiqlal (32—a poor showing that led to major soul-searching and finger-pointing within the party). The opposition bloc as a whole won 102 seats, the progovernment bloc 100 seats, and a group of centrist parties 97 seats. With no bloc having a majority, King Hassan was under no political pressure to appoint a prime minister from one political tendency or the other (constitutionally, of course, the king is under no obligation to appoint a prime minister to reflect the legislature's political composition).

Three weeks later, on December 5, 1997, elections were held for the new Chamber of Councilors. They were the culmination of a series of nationwide ballots held earlier in the year: local elections (June 13), elections to the professional chambers (July 25), and elections of representatives of wage earners (September 26 and October 3). As provided for in the new electoral code, representatives of local councils elected 162 of the Chamber of Councilors' 270 members; Chambers of Agriculture elected another 33; the Chambers of Crafts 21; the Chambers of Commerce, Industry, and Services 24; and the Chambers of Fishermen 3. Representatives of wage earners chose the upper house's remaining 27 members. As had been expected, a bloc of centrist parties (RNI, MDS, and Popular National Movement [MNP]) won the largest number of seats (90), followed by conservative parties (the so called Wifaq, which obtained 76 seats). What was then referred to as "the opposition" (a group of left-leaning parties) won a total of only 60 seats. The new upper house would therefore have the centrist-conservative orientation that it had been expected to display.

Parliament in the New Political and Institutional Context

By 1998, Morocco's new system of representative institutions was in place. On January 6, the lower house chose Abdelwahed Radi (USFP) as its president. The following day, the upper house selected Mohamed Jallal Essaïd (Constitutional Union) to serve as Radi's counterpart. These two elections provided the new parliament with a credible and respected leadership. Radi, who had belonged to all legislatures since 1963, was known as a pragmatic and open-minded politician who excelled at consensus building. He seemed determined to enhance the image of the lower house by professionalizing its budget and staff, cutting back on MPs' various perks, and introducing several measures to improve the coherence of parliamentary work. A former minister, Radi was familiar with the functioning of the executive branch, which was seen as an asset as the lower house dealt with the executive. Mohamed Jallal Essaïd, for his part, was expected to provide much needed experience at the head of the new upper house, since he had served as president of the Chamber of Representatives from 1993 until 1997.

Still, numerous obstacles hindered parliament's ability to discharge its functions. For one thing, two houses with almost 600 members and 400 staff people were forced to operate in a building that had been planned for one single chamber of about 300 MPs, with only one plenary hall and 118 offices. Fortunately, a new building adjacent to the current one was being prepared for the new upper house. In the meantime, however, MPs and their staff were being forced to work in difficult conditions. More significant in the long run was the resistance that Radi encountered when he tried to push through measures designed to enhance the efficiency of the lower house. His attempt to increase from twelve to twenty the number of deputies required to create a parliamentary group failed. Consequently, the lower house ended up with ten parliamentary groups, which would undoubtedly slow it down and reduce its effectiveness. The upper house, for its part, was still looking for its role in the political system, especially after the appointment as prime minister of socialist leader Abderrahmane Youssoufi, who hailed from a political bloc rival to the majority found in the Chamber of Councilors.

Conclusion

Political developments in Morocco between 1996 and 1998 represented the maturation of a process of democratization that revolves to a large extent on enhancing the centrality of the legislature in the political system. Parliament thus has become one of the instruments through which King Hassan is seeking to "reinvent" the monarchy and redesign the political system in light of changing social, economic, and political conditions. In this context, the democratic opening that began in the late 1980s and gained momentum in the early 1990s reached yet another stage between 1996 and 1998. Building on the enhanced legitimacy of the monarchy and the more positive image that Morocco has gained internationally, King Hassan took the lead in forging a national consensus on fundamental and sweeping changes in the political system. Having defined his role as ultimate referee and protector of the agreements reached among the various forces competing in the Moroccan political arena, the king laid the foundation of a new order capable of accommodating the legitimate needs of the main political constituencies and interests in the country. This ongoing political transformation represents one of the most encouraging and thus far successful attempts at gradual democratization in the Arab world.

Notes

1. One year later, these so-called independents were organized into a new party, called the National Rally of Independents (RNI).

2. With 215 out of 306 seats, four center-right parties (the Constitutional Union, the RNI, the Popular Movement, and the National Democratic Party [PND]) held a very comfortable majority.

3. The percentage of unanswered questions was particularly high for those addressed to the Ministry of Interior and Information, which presumably were on the more sensitive subjects (including civil liberties, human rights, and governmental control over information). Furthermore, even when questions were answered, the answer sometimes came months—and in some instances a couple of years—after the question had been asked.

4. Commissions of investigation had been formed in the past (for instance, to look into the December 1990 riots in Fez), but this always happened at the initiative of the king, since parliament had no constitutional mandate to create such commissions.

5. These figures are drawn from *Majlis an-Nuwab al-Maghribi* (The Moroccan parliament) (Rabat: Moroccan parliament, 1994).

6. In the mid-1990s, the size of the staff allocated to parliamentary groups ranged from six for the smallest group (the PPS) to thirteen for the largest (the Constitutional Union). Parliamentary groups select their staff in one of three ways: (1) from outside state institutions (this can become a way to reward party loyalists), (2) from the central administration (for instance, by requesting that a technocrat currently working in a ministry but affiliated to the party be detached to the parliamentary group of that party), and (3) from the parliamentary administration itself (which presents the advantage of providing parliamentary groups with individuals who are familiar with the inner workings of parliament and who may enjoy the confidence and goodwill of the parliamentary staff).

7. *Majlis an-Nuwab al-Maghribi.*

8. In 1993, these sixty-nine seats were divided as follows: Local councilors (*conseillers communaux*) in fifty-one of Morocco's sixty provinces and urban prefectures were given the right to elect one deputy each, and those in the remaining nine provinces or urban prefectures (Rabat, Béni-Mellal, El Jadida, El-Kelaa es-Sraghna, Kénitra, Oujda, Safi, Settat, and Taroudant) selected two deputies each.

9. In the fifty-one provinces and urban prefectures that elected a deputy each, the candidate who had received a plurality of votes was elected. In the nine provinces and urban prefectures that chose two deputies each, the first two candidates with the most votes were elected.

10. For instance, the Moroccan weekly *Maroc-Hebdo* devoted much of its May 5, 1995, issue to an analysis of what it described on its front page as "the Great Circus," referring to the oral questions sessions of the Chamber.

11. See Hachimi Idrissi, "Le Grand cirque," *Maroc-Hebdo*, May 5, 1995, p. 6.

12. Commissions of investigation cannot be formed if the events that they would be investigating are already the subject of legal proceedings.

13. The government can thus oppose legislative initiatives that it believes lie outside parliament's domain (in which case the issue will be decided by the Constitutional Council).

7

Jordan

Since 1989, Jordan has been engaged in a gradual democratization experiment that in many respects is reminiscent of Morocco's. Jordan's experiment, too, is led by a monarch who has sought to broaden participation and create new bases of legitimacy for the throne by, among other means, increasing the influence of parliament in the country's political system. This effort has met with significant success, albeit not as much as in Morocco's case, for reasons that have to do primarily with Jordan's embroilment in the Arab-Israeli dispute. Thus, although Morocco's democratization process gathered steam between 1996 and 1998, Jordan's suffered from the failure of the Jordanian-Israeli October 1994 peace treaty to deliver on several of its promises. Consequently, the November 4, 1997, elections to Jordan's lower house took place amid a crisis between the palace and a coalition of Islamist, leftist, and nationalist opposition parties.

This crisis had been precipitated by a number of divisive issues, among which the most prominent was the apparent breakdown of the Arab-Israeli "peace process" following the May 29, 1996, Israeli elections. These historic elections had resulted in the return of the Likud party to power and the formation of a hard-line coalition government headed by Binyamin Netanyahu. When under that government the peace process turned sour, King Hussein was faced with growing domestic criticisms of Jordan's continued efforts to normalize relations with the Jewish state. To combat critics in the press and the legislature, the king engineered the adoption of a new, highly restrictive press law, and he ignored the opposition's call for a change in the controversial electoral law that had been adopted in 1993. As a result, the November 1997 elections were boycotted by most Islamic and leftist political parties. The low voter turnout (56 percent of registered voters and 46 percent of all eligible voters) showed that disillusionment with the political and economic situation in the country was widespread.

133

Nevertheless, the elections took place as scheduled and were deemed by most observers to have been relatively free and fair. Furthermore, the confrontation between the government and the opposition was a peaceful one. None of the political parties went so far as to criticize the legitimacy of the monarchy. Those who boycotted the election did not seek to disrupt the electoral process and behaved as a "loyal opposition." The king, for his part, did not respond to criticisms of his policies in the sensitive area of national security and foreign affairs as he might have done in the past—that is, by canceling the elections and/or suspending the legislature. He even paid tribute to the Muslim Brotherhood's "honorable stands" in politics. These developments demonstrate that Jordan has now institutionalized parliamentary elections as a normal and regular part of the political process. Thus, despite the tense political situation prevailing in the Hashemite kingdom in 1998, and despite the widespread perception that the democratization process has suffered serious setbacks since the October 1994 signing of the peace treaty with Israel, Jordan remains engaged in the difficult attempt to develop more democratic and participatory institutions.

The Roots of Parliamentary Politics in Jordan (1922–1946)

Jordan's ongoing attempt at legislative development is not as much of a novelty as it may seem, for there are precedents in the country's history. Although the central feature of Jordan's political system has always been the supremacy of the monarchy, consultative councils or elected legislatures have long been an important part of the kingdom's political landscape.

Jordan is a relatively new country. Created by Britain in 1922, it was carved out of the ruins of the Ottoman Empire. From its establishment until independence in 1946, the country, then known as Transjordan, was a British mandate. It was ruled by Emir Abdallah, the second son of Sharif Hussein (the leader of the Arab revolt against the Ottomans during World War I). Abdallah was originally from the Hijaz, in today's Saudi Arabia. Grandfather of Jordan's current ruler, King Hussein, he had been installed on the throne of Transjordan by the British.

Almost from the moment Transjordan came into existence, there were demands for the establishment of some sort of representative body. For years, those demands were successfully resisted by the British, who feared that an elected assembly might challenge their control over the country's affairs. In 1923, for instance, Abdallah took concrete steps toward the convening of an elected assembly, but the idea was quickly abandoned as a result of British pressures (Abu Jaber 1972: 93). The country that invented parliamentary government, it turned out, was far more opposed to creating a representative body than a tribal leader born and raised in the Arabian Peninsula. Abdallah indeed knew that, being an outsider to the country over which he now ruled, he needed to legitimize his rule. He understood that one of the ways to do so was through a representative assembly in which the leaders of Transjordan's major tribes and families would be able to articulate their concerns.

At the end of the 1920s, the British grudgingly came to the conclusion that an elected assembly might serve three useful purposes. First, it would allow them to claim that they were fulfilling their international obligations. After all, under the agreement that they had signed with the League of Nations, they were committed to promoting Transjordan's capacity for self-government. Second, a representative assembly would improve the image of the Jordanian regime, both at home and abroad, by providing it with an aura of constitution-ality. Third, having an elected assembly ratify the recently signed Anglo-Tran-sjordanian agreement would help Britain legitimize its presence in the country (Robins 1991: 185).

Plans were thus made for the election of what came to be known as the Legislative Assembly (LA), although precautions were taken to ensure that it would be subordinated to the executive branch and, through it, to the palace and the British resident-general. This approach is reflected in the 1928 Or-ganic Law, which defined the prerogatives of the LA and the modalities of its election: Members of the Executive Council (the cabinet) would continue to be chosen and appointed by the emir and were not made accountable to the LA; the emir was given the power to convene, adjourn, suspend, or dismiss the LA at will; all bills adopted by the LA had to be ratified by the emir and the British resident-general; all six member of the Executive Council were ex officio members of the twenty-two-member LA; and the head of the Execu-tive Council would also chair the LA and thus be in a position to shape its agenda and the course of its debates. (A modern equivalent of this would be for a prime minister to be ex officio speaker of the lower house.) In addition, through a system of quotas, the electoral law ensured that the Christian and Circassian minorities, which were seen as natural allies of the palace, would be overrepresented in the LA. The law gave the minorities five of the sixteen elected seats (two to the Circassians and three to the Christians). As a result, Circassians had a seat for every 5,000 inhabitants and Christians a seat for every 7,000 inhabitants, whereas Muslims had one seat for every 27,000 in-habitants (Khatib 1975: 158).

Despite these measures, the first LA, elected in April 1929, turned out to be quite assertive and critical of the executive branch—to the surprise of those who had concocted the provisions designed to ensure its docility. It so often embarrassed the government that the emir finally decided to disband the LA on February 9, 1931.[1] By then, the LA had become the focus of widespread demands that it be made more representative and influential. It was thus seen as a credible institution, capable of providing an effective counterweight to the executive. In 1928, for instance, a national conference brought together 150 notables, tribal leaders, and intellectuals who adopted resolutions protesting the electoral law and the LA's lack of power. Their grievances were formally conveyed to the emir, the British resident-general, and the League of Nations. Similar conferences were held in 1929, 1930, 1932, and 1933 (Abu Jaber 1972: 94–95).

In short, the LA's very limitations triggered a debate over the need for more representative institutions. That by itself was a considerable achievement. Although this debate had few, if any, immediate effects, it paved the way for the adoption of a fairly liberal constitution in 1952. In the meantime, the election of five LAs between 1929 and 1946 served as a valuable apprenticeship with the practice of representative government. These LAs performed functions vital to Jordan's political development. First, they helped legitimize the new regime by providing a channel through which different constituencies—from the tribal populations of the south to the middle-class professionals living in the northern towns—could express their political demands. Second, they contributed to national integration by facilitating interaction among politicians from various regions. Third, by reserving a number of seats for minorities, LAs gave these minorities a stake in the new country and made them feel like full-fledged participants in it. Fourth, LAs played a role in the struggle for independence by agitating for a reexamination of the 1928 agreement with Britain. Finally, successive assemblies pushed for the Transjordanization of the administration. Through the 1920s, the bureaucracy had remained dominated by Palestinians and Syrians, owing in part to the low literacy rates that prevailed among Transjordanians. In this context, successive LAs made the Transjordanization of the administration one of their main demands, and they were relatively successful in bringing this goal about. They thus made it possible for the indigenous population to gain experience in governmental affairs and thereby prepared the country for self-government (Khatib 1975: 136–173).

Jordan's Difficult Search for Representative Government (1946–1988)

From independence in 1946 to the onset of the democratization experiment in 1989, Jordan's experience with parliamentary politics went through four distinct phases. The first (1947–1955) witnessed momentous changes: the adoption of the first constitution of independent Transjordan in 1947; the creation of Israel and the first Arab-Israeli war in 1948; Transjordan's annexation of the West Bank in 1950; the assassination of King Abdallah in July 1951; the adoption of a new, more liberal constitution in 1952; and the ascent of King Hussein to the throne in May 1953. During this eventful period, the kingdom's successive rulers—Abdallah (1946–1951), Talal (1951–1952), and

Hussein (1952–present)—endeavored to establish the foundations of a political order designed to ensure the dominance of the monarchy while allowing an elected parliament to play a meaningful role in the political system.

The second phase lasted only seven months. It began with the parliamentary elections of October 1956, which were the freest that Jordan had ever known, and ended with a political crackdown by King Hussein in April 1957. Although very brief, this period deserves to be singled out for three reasons. First, parliament asserted itself and succeeded in holding the cabinet responsible. Not until the 1990s would an elected assembly wield as much power in Jordan. Second, the ultimate failure of this experiment in parliamentary politics contains several important lessons. Third, it also explains, in part, why King Hussein remained for so long unwilling to allow parliament to play the role to which the 1952 constitution entitled it.

The third phase stretched from the 1957 crackdown to the convening of the National Consultative Council (NCC) in 1978. During this period the legislature played a much reduced role in the political process. Indeed, there were times during those two decades when the king ruled without a parliament. Nevertheless, although it was forced to operate under great constraints, parliament, when in session, was able to assert itself on numerous occasions. Finally, the fourth phase began with the convening of the NCC in 1978 and ended with Amman's renunciation of its claim to the West Bank a decade later. This was a period of transition that paved the way for the resurgence of parliamentary politics after 1989.

Getting Started (1947–1955)

The constitution of 1947, which replaced the 1928 Organic Law, provided for a bicameral legislature (Majlis al-Umma) composed of an elected Chamber of Deputies (the lower house, Majlis al-Nuwwab) and an appointed Assembly of Notables (the upper house, Majlis al-A'yan). According to the constitution and the electoral law that was passed shortly after the constitution was ratified, the Chamber would have 20 members. 12 Muslims, 4 Christians, 2 representatives of the tribes, and 2 representatives of the Circassian and Chechen communities. These members were to be chosen for four-year terms, through elections held in nine districts. Only Jordanian male citizens were allowed to vote. The Assembly, or senate, would have ten seats (one-half the number of seats in the lower house). Senate members were to be chosen by the king from among "individuals who held the confidence of the people," as the constitution had put it (Abu Jaber 1972: 97–98).

The constitution and the electoral law reflected a desire to make the legislature a docile one. For instance, the appointed senate was intended to act as a conservative counterweight to the elected Chamber and was meant to enhance royal influence over the legislative branch as a whole. It is also revealing that 40 percent of the seats (eight out of twenty) in the lower house were reserved for representatives of religious and ethnic minorities. This quota, which was considerably higher than these minorities' share of Transjordan's population, worked to the advantage of the regime since, as mentioned earlier, members of the minorities were usually supportive of the palace.

Even more decisive were constitutional provisions limiting the power of the legislature in relation to the executive branch and the monarchy. One such provision made the cabinet responsible only to the monarch, not to parliament. The constitution, moreover, gave the king the power to choose the speaker of the lower house, which added to the palace's influence over the legislative agenda and parliamentary debates. The constitution also stressed the king's exclusive responsibility for concluding treaties with foreign powers (Abu Jaber 1972: 98). The regime's basic foreign policy orientations—in particular Jordan's relationship with Britain—were thus sheltered from parliamentary interference. Finally, the cabinet could adopt the budget even if the lower house had refused to pass it. "The power of the purse," a traditional prerogative of parliaments, was thereby denied to the Jordanian legislature.

Although these provisions succeeded in producing a parliament dominated by notables, tribal leaders, and members of the landed and commercial elite, they failed to make it subservient to the executive branch. From the moment the first lower house convened, several of its members criticized those elements in the constitution and the electoral law that undermined the authority and representativeness of the legislature. They complained that the constitution had given to the cabinet prerogatives that should have belonged to parliament. They went so far as to request that the government be made responsible to the lower house and not the king. Such demands, which called into question the very nature of the political system, were voiced repeatedly in the Chamber of Deputies (Robins 1991: 187). In short, even at this very early stage of Jordan's history as an independent country, the legislature was already trying to assert itself.

It was at this juncture that the first Arab-Israeli war broke out, shortly after Israel was created on May 15, 1948. During the war, Transjordan gained control over the West Bank and East Jerusalem. In 1950, King Abdallah formally annexed them, at which point Transjordan became known as Jordan.

Upon annexing the West Bank, the king granted Jordanian citizenship to its Palestinian population. To underscore the Hashemite regime's equal commitment to native Transjordanians and Palestinians, the two banks of the Jordan River were given equal representation in the lower house.[2] A new electoral law was passed that increased the membership of the lower house to 40 (20 members for the West Bank and 20 for the East Bank) and that of the upper house to 20. Shortly afterward, in April 1950, new elections took place.

The new Chamber was bound to be more assertive than its predecessor, since it now included representatives of the Palestinian population of the West Bank, which was more educated and politicized than that of the East Bank.

Indeed, three opposition parties—the National Socialist Party (NSP), the Baath, and the Communist Party—won fourteen of the lower house's forty seats (Abu Jaber 1972: 99). Several deputies elected in West Bank constituencies thus added their voices to those East Bankers who had long been urging that the government be made more responsible to the legislature. In May 1951, the lower house refused to pass the budget, which prompted Abdallah to dissolve it. New elections were held, which actually slightly increased the opposition's strength in parliament.

It was against this background that King Abdallah was assassinated in July 1951 and that his son Talal ascended the throne. Talal's reign was short, but it was under it that Jordan's current constitution was promulgated in January 1952. This constitution was far more liberal than that of 1946. Although it would be amended in 1974, 1976, and 1984, its main provisions remain in force today.

The 1952 constitution was a landmark in Jordan's legislative history. For the first time, it made the cabinet responsible to an assembly elected by the people. In addition, it introduced several other modifications that enhanced very substantially the authority of the legislature:

- The prime minister was still chosen and appointed by the king, but he or she and the cabinet now had to secure a vote of confidence from the lower house before they could formally assume their functions. Prior to that vote, the prime minister had to present his or her program to the Chamber. Even after being invested, the government could be forced to resign by a two-thirds majority in the Chamber.
- Ministers could be impeached by the lower house.
- No bill originating in the executive branch could become law without being submitted to the Chamber, which had the power to amend or reject it. Furthermore, although the king could veto legislation adopted by parliament within six months of its passing, deputies could override this veto with a two-thirds majority.
- The lower house was granted new authority over foreign affairs, including the power to ratify treaties. This represented a substantial encroachment on what until then had been considered the king's "reserved domain."
- The 1952 constitution also eliminated several provisions that previously had enabled the executive branch to control the legislature's agenda.

In August 1952, Talal, who suffered from acute schizophrenia, was asked to abdicate in favor of his son Hussein. Hussein was not yet eighteen and therefore, under the constitution, he could not be crowned king. Thus, a regency council directed the country's affairs until May 1953, when Hussein finally ascended the throne.

From the beginning of his reign, Hussein was under considerable domestic and international pressure. Since the addition of the West Bank to the kingdom in 1950, a majority of the country's population was of Palestinian origin. Many, if not most, of these Palestinian-Jordanians were unwilling citizens of the state. They opposed the institution of the monarchy and did not recognize Jordanian sovereignty over the West Bank, which many of them still considered Palestinian territory. They espoused various Arab nationalist and "progressive" ideologies ranging from communism to Nasserism through Baathism. The East Bank itself featured a young and radicalized intelligentsia, the political expression of which was the NSP (*al-hizb al-watani al-ishtiraki*). These *muthaqqafun* (intellectuals) were highly critical of the Jordanian regime's pro-Western policies and of its generally conservative orientation. To complicate Hussein's task even more, outside powers were interfering in the kingdom's domestic politics. The Jordanian Baath party was actually run from Damascus. Other groups, in particular the Arab Nationalist Movement (*harakat al-qawmiyyin al-'arab*), were professing total allegiance to Gamal Abdel Nasser's government in Cairo (Dann 1989: 16).

Caught in the middle of powerful domestic and external pressures, and at a time when Arab monarchies in general seemed condemned to be swept aside by history, King Hussein's margin of maneuver was limited indeed. It is not surprising that a former British foreign minister (Anthony Nutting) could declare that "however much one may admire the courage of this lonely young king, it is difficult to avoid the conclusion that his days are numbered" (Dann 1989: vii). What we will now show is that in such a divisive context—one in which there was no agreement on the rules of the game (indeed, no agreement on such basic issues as the proper role of the monarchy in the political system or on whether Jordan had a legitimate claim to the West Bank)—the legislature could not be expected to discharge its functions effectively.

The Fifth Chamber and the Nabulsi Episode (October 1956–April 1957)

The parliamentary elections of October 21, 1956, were a watershed in Jordan's modern political history. By the standards that had prevailed until then, these elections were remarkably fair. Not until 1989 would an election be as free from governmental interference. And not until 1993 would political parties again be allowed to take part in an electoral contest.

The October 1956 elections resulted in a strong showing for the pan-Arab NSP led by Sulayman Nabulsi, who was well known for his admiration of Egyptian president Gamal Abdel Nasser. With 11 out of 40 seats, the NSP emerged as the party with the most representatives in the Chamber. Baathists and Communists won 2 and 3 seats respectively. Other candidates sympathetic to leftist and pan-Arab ideas won 4 seats. Thus, "progressive" and Arab nationalist elements controlled 20 seats, or one-half of the Chamber. This was in sharp contrast with the results two years earlier, when parliamentary elections had returned a very loyalist Chamber. For the first time in Jordan's history, the assembly was divided equally between, on the one hand, leftists, Nasserites, and other Arab nationalists who owed little or no loyalty to the Hashemite kingdom and the throne and, on the other hand, an amalgam of conservative and pro-monarchy forces.[3]

Faced with the ascendancy of pan-Arab and nationalist feelings, King Hussein decided to try to ride the nationalist and progressive wave, instead of resisting it. This was a classic example of "If you can't beat them, join them." Thus, on October 27, he appointed Nabulsi—the leader of the largest party in parliament—as prime minister. The new premier immediately formed a government that represented a coalition of leftist and pan-Arab forces.

Under the leadership of its speaker, Hikmat al-Masri, himself a member of the NSP, the Chamber developed a strong agenda for itself. It abolished the Anglo-Jordanian Treaty in February 1957, ratified the Arab Union between Iraq and Jordan, and asserted itself on a number of legislative matters. Most important, it succeeded in holding the cabinet accountable. To some observers, it seemed to be moving Jordan toward a constitutional monarchy with a representative, accountable parliamentary system.

By early April 1957, however, the Nabulsi government was engaged in a showdown with the monarchy. Some of its members had suggested publicly that the king should become a mere figurehead or that he should resign and the monarchy be abolished. Defying the king, the cabinet had even dismissed several of his protégés who occupied key positions in the state bureaucracy. Particularly symbolic had been the forced retirement of the director of security, Bahjat Tabara, a close adviser to the monarch (Dann 1989: 52). At about the same time, King Hussein was faced with a coup attempt by military figures, which he successfully deflected.

On April 10, the king decided that it was time to stand up to what seemed like a frontal attack on the monarchy. His first move was to fire Nabulsi. At first, however, he was careful not to cut his bridges to nationalist and leftist opinion. Instead, he formed a cabinet that he thought would be acceptable to "progressive forces" and would refrain from challenging the monarchy's authority. It quickly became clear that this was like an attempt to square the circle, particularly as another coup attempt was unveiled. Hussein's patience finally snapped as a result of the holding of a Patriotic Congress in Nablus on April 22. This gathering brought together leftist forces that still constituted the backbone of the coalition behind the new cabinet. Well represented were the NSP, the Baath, the Communist Party, and the Arab Nationalist Movement.

The Patriotic Congress issued a "proclamation to the people" that challenged not only the king's authority but also the very existence of Jordan as a separate entity. It called for Jordan's merger into a "federation" with Syria and

Egypt, "unity between the people and the army" (a barely disguised invitation to a military coup), and a general strike and demonstrations against the government. The proclamation bore the signatures of seventy-seven participants, twenty-three of whom were members of the Chamber. Particularly worrisome to the regime was the fact that these resolutions were coauthored by the NSP, the main force in the cabinet and the lower house (Dann 1989: 61).

Hussein understood that he was fighting for his throne, and his response was swift. No longer would he try to appease "progressive opinion" by making concessions to it. Instead, on April 25, he launched a massive crackdown. Martial law was imposed, and all political parties were banned. Several hundred people were arrested (including Nabulsi). Five weeklies were shut down. The largest cities—Amman, Nablus, Irbid, Jerusalem, Ramallah—as well as the main refugee camps were put under curfew. Most of the municipal councils in the West Bank were disbanded, and military courts were set up (Dann 1989: 64).

Although the king allowed the legislature to complete its term, he did so only after expelling nine deputies and forcing six others to resign their seats. In by-elections, those fifteen vacant seats were filled by supporters of the monarchy (Abu Jaber 1972: 108). This action ensured that the legislature would be far more compliant and would no longer provide a power base for politicians who opposed the very legitimacy of the country's institutions and borders.

The Nabulsi interlude and the failure of the king's first attempt to elevate the importance of parliament in the political system contain important lessons. It is clear in retrospect that the experiment was doomed from the outset, because it did not feature one of the essential prerequisites of a properly functioning legislature: the existence of a "loyal opposition," which opposes the government of the day but accepts the legitimacy of the system and its institutions. Instead, regime and opposition could not even agree on what the identity of the country was, on what its proper geographical boundaries ought to be, or on whether it should exist at all! Leftist and pan-Arab forces saw it as their duty to bring down a regime that they considered illegitimate. King Hussein, for his part, was determined not to see the monarchy disappear or be reduced to a merely symbolic institution. He wanted not only to reign but to rule and felt very strongly that there were certain issues that belonged to his "reserved domain," a claim the opposition was unwilling to accept. In such a polarized and confrontational atmosphere, differences could only be resolved through a showdown, with one key player (in this instance the monarchy) eliminating another (the leftist–pan-Arab nationalist alliance).

The Eclipse of Parliament (1957–1978)

Following the ban on political parties, Communists, Baathists, and Arab nationalists either went underground or languished in jails.[4] Meanwhile, King Hussein consolidated his control over the political system. In this context, the representativeness and authority of the legislature were greatly reduced. Elections were often marred by administrative interference.[5] Opposition candidates and their supporters were frequently intimidated or harassed. In addition, the electoral law was altered to favor the government. Through these and other tactics, the regime by and large succeeded in neutralizing the legislature. And when all measures failed and the Chamber still adopted a defiant attitude, it was dissolved or suspended. This was the case when, in April 1963, the lower house denied a vote of confidence to the new government. The king responded by disbanding the Chamber and calling for new elections.

The ninth Chamber was elected in April 1967. Two months later, the six-day war broke out, during which Jordan lost the West Bank to Israel. This situation created a serious predicament for the lower house, since half of its members came from the West Bank. Clearly, no new parliamentary elections could take place in a territory that was now under Israeli control. Thus, when the Chamber's term expired in March 1971, the monarch invoked a constitutional provision that allowed him to extend it. The official rationale was that new elections would be postponed until the West Bank could be returned to Jordanian sovereignty.

In 1974, however, King Hussein was faced with yet another dilemma when an Arab League summit held in Rabat adopted a resolution that declared the Palestine Liberation Organization (PLO) to be the sole representative of the Palestinian people, thus implicitly denying the Jordanian monarch the right to speak for West Bank Palestinians. Although he had been opposed to the resolution, King Hussein had felt compelled to accept it.[6] But in his eyes, as in those of most native Jordanians, the resolution also implied that, since West Bank Palestinians were represented by the PLO, they should not at the same time be represented in the Jordanian parliament, where at that time they accounted for half the members of both houses. Thus, on November 24, 1974, the king issued a decree dissolving both the Assembly and the Chamber. Instead of setting the date for new elections, he decided to rule without a parliament. By then, however, Jordan's tradition of representative government had become so rooted that calls were heard almost immediately for the establishment of an institution that would provide popular input into the policymaking process. It was in response to these demands that the king created the NCC.

A Period of Transition (1978–1988)

The decree establishing the NCC in 1978 stated that its sixty members would all be appointed by the monarch and that it would be dissolved automatically when a new Chamber would be elected. The NCC was given a very limited mandate, defined primarily as providing the Council of Ministers with advisory opinions on specific bills and policies, upon request by the prime minister. The NCC thus had no independent authority. It could not approve, amend, or reject a bill and could not pass motions of no-confidence against the cabinet (Hooglund 1991: 190). In addition, when King Hussein finally selected the NCC's members, he did not call on any resident of the West Bank. Still, he made sure to include several Jordanians of Palestinian origin, to show that he remained attentive to the concerns of that important component of its population (Gubser 1988: 103).

The NCC sat from 1978 until 1983. Despite its limited representativeness and power, it proved to be a valuable institution. Its members took their responsibilities seriously and endeavored to make the most of their prerogatives (Khoury 1981: 435). The NCC facilitated contacts between the bureaucracy and the population. It provided a forum in which important bills and policies were debated. It also allowed for the expression of opinions that otherwise might not have received as much attention as they did. In short, it carried out several of the functions normally performed by legislatures. The questions with which it dealt were often sensitive ones, including civil liberties and the future of the West Bank. Discussion of these issues in the council ensured a wider reporting of different views about them in the press (Khoury 1981: 435–436). Accordingly, the NCC contributed to the emergence of a more informed citizenry.

In 1984, King Hussein finally recalled parliament. His decision reflected both domestic and foreign policy considerations. It was an attempt to assuage growing internal discontent with the lack of democracy in the country as well as to revive the Jordanian monarchy's claim to speak on behalf of West Bank Palestinians.

In the lower house, the six West Bank seats that had become vacant since 1967 were filled by means of an internal election: Members of parliament (MPs) chose six West Bankers to join their ranks. On the East Bank, however, elections were held to fill the seats of the eight parliamentarians who had died since the 1967 elections. These elections were historic in that Jordanian women could exercise for the first time the right to vote they had been granted in 1974.

By and large, the elections were fair, and their outcome contained a few surprises (Robins 1991: 192–193). For instance, several candidates who had run on a religious platform were elected, whereas those defeated included notables from prominent families closely connected to the palace. With the benefit of hindsight, it is possible to read in these results a harbinger of the November 1989 elections, in which the Muslim Brotherhood would produce an unexpectedly strong showing. In another prelude to the 1990s, the new Islamist members of the lower house combined with a handful of other deputies to form a parliamentary group that immediately proceeded to criticize the cabinet on such issues as corruption, human rights, abuses of authority by government officials, and the excessive powers of the secret police.

Within four years of reconvening parliament, King Hussein was forced to deal with the ramifications of the Palestinian uprising, or intifada, which had erupted in the Israeli-occupied territories in December 1987. The monarch was quick to realize that the intifada had dealt a final, lethal blow to the pro-Jordanian Palestinian notables who had been his main allies in the West Bank. The king also had grown tired of fruitless efforts to develop with PLO leader Yasir Arafat a common position on the peace process. Accordingly, in July 1988, the king decided to cut administrative and legal ties between Jordan and the Israeli-occupied West Bank. Having done so, he no longer could keep a parliament in which half the members came from the West Bank, and he therefore dissolved the legislature. A few months later, he announced that legislative elections would be postponed to an undetermined date. Before convening a new parliament, the Hashemite ruler wanted to wait until the outcome of ongoing peace initiatives had become clearer.

Lessons from Four Decades of Legislative Development in the Hashemite Kingdom

This brief examination of Jordan's parliamentary experience from 1946 through 1988 provides ample evidence to support several of the claims made in this book. First, it points to the existence of a legislative tradition that has been neglected or downplayed by scholars. The constitution of 1952—which as was shown gave parliament very significant powers—remained in place throughout the entire period. Certainly, the legislature often led a precarious existence, and it was disbanded on several occasions. But that is no more significant than the fact that it was restored every time after it was dissolved. Whenever the legislature was not functioning, voices called for its reconvening or for the establishment of some other form of representative institution. This suggests that years of parliamentary experience had had a profound impact on the country's political culture, causing Jordanians to take it for granted that there should be an institution capable of overseeing the executive branch and providing popular input into the policymaking process. Thus, the much-acclaimed assertion of parliament after 1989 did not take place in a historical vacuum but had deep roots in the country's history.

The preceding analysis also highlights the importance of several factors to the success of a parliamentary experiment. One is the need for the key players to reach a consensus on the basic parameters of political life. Only when that has taken place can parliament perform the functions with which it has been entrusted. For instance, the sharp decline in parliament's influence after the 1957 crackdown was largely due to the inability of the monarchy and the pan-Arab nationalist opposition to agree on fundamental issues, including institutional framework and party laws. (Disagreements centered on the amount of power that the monarchy was entitled to exercise and on whether political parties could have foreign connections.)

Another factor that hindered Jordan's legislative development was the regional context in which the country operated throughout these four decades. Because Jordanian politics revolved primarily around issues of war, peace, and regime survival, King Hussein was hardly in a position to tolerate a parliament critical of his policies or those of the government. The stakes were simply too high. During the 1950s, the monarch was threatened by radical nationalists who wanted to overthrow him and merge Jordan into a broader pan-Arab entity. In 1967, the country experienced the traumatic loss of the West Bank and East Jerusalem to Israel. Three years later, the regime was engaged in a deadly struggle with Palestinian guerrilla organizations that had created a state within the state and made no secret of their ambition to eliminate the Jordanian monarchy. The 1973 war with Israel, followed by the Arab League summit in Rabat a year later, presented the Hashemite regime with yet new dilemmas. Finally, during the 1980s, the Likud party's "Jordan is Palestine" rhetoric, combined with renewed diplomatic efforts toward Arab-Israeli peace, forced the king to navigate in difficult waters. In short, parliament was never given a chance to operate within the realm of "normal politics," that is, distributional issues. Instead, it acted in an environment dominated by national security questions that threatened the country's very survival. Such a context is rarely conducive to legislative development—let alone in a country in which the basic rules of the game were not yet agreed upon.

Yet, one must also account for the surprising resiliency of the parliamentary institution. What in particular explains the willingness of all key actors to take part in parliamentary politics? Why did not more players boycott the game on the ground that the legislature (or the National Consultative Council, between 1978 and 1983) did not have enough power or had been disbanded too frequently by the king? To answer these questions, one must consider several characteristics of political life in Jordan throughout the period under consideration.

One particularly important factor was King Hussein's sustained effort to keep the regime's political actions within the framework of the law. Even when he felt that the constitution was placing undue constraints on him, the monarch did not disregard it. In 1976, for instance, he decided to postpone parliamentary elections for an indefinite period. Under the 1952 constitution, however, he was not allowed to do so. It is significant, in this context, that he decided not to ignore the constitution but to have it amended through a process that would provide a measure of legitimacy for the change he sought. He called for an extraordinary session of the parliament that he had dismissed two years earlier. Within twenty-four hours, parliament adopted the amendment desired by the king, at which point it was disbanded again. Analysts have frequently dismissed such processes as constitutional disguises for authoritarian rule. This interpretation, however, fails to capture what is significant about the kind of episode described above: an authoritarian regime making a deliberate effort not to disregard existing constitutional norms, preferring instead to see them altered by an elected assembly that can provide the seal of popular endorsement of the modifications sought by the ruling elite. This conscious effort to keep the state's behavior within the rule of law is one of the features that most clearly differentiated Jordan from the single party and military regimes found elsewhere in the region, few of which ever bothered to maintain even the appearances of constitutionality. It also helps explain why much of the opposition accepted the necessity of working within the confines of the law and why in particular it decided not to boycott the game of parliamentary politics.

King Hussein's attempt not to exclude any significant group from power for a prolonged period also had a positive impact on political development in Jordan. For instance, in his selection of prime ministers, ministers, senators, and senior government officials, the king consistently endeavored to maintain a certain diversity of representation (among regions, between Palestinians and East Bankers, and among tribes). Even those who conspired against the regime were usually given the opportunity to repent, and several of them ended up serving the monarchy. In fact, the king is well known for his propensity to pardon former enemies and offer them government posts. By preventing the emergence of permanent losers and winners, this wise policy made political actors more willing to compromise and more likely to accept the system, which in turn contributed to the resiliency of the legislative institution.

Parliamentary Politics Since 1989

After it was reconvened in late 1989, Jordan's legislature quickly asserted itself. Its growing influence and visibility seemed all the more remarkable given that the Jordanian regime was forced to operate within the difficult domestic and regional environment created by Iraq's invasion of Kuwait (August 2, 1990) and the consequences of the Gulf War (January-February 1991). In an earlier era, such external shocks would have led the government to restrict parliament's freedom of maneuver. But in the early 1990s, the opposite process took place. In this section, we examine the factors that led to this parliamentary resurgence, then turn to an analysis of the more difficult period that began in 1996, when the Oslo peace process began to unravel. Special attention is paid to the elections of 1989, 1993, and 1997 as well as to their significance to Jordan's legislative development. We conclude by highlighting the limitations of Jordan's legislature as the twentieth century draws to a close.

The Reconvening of Parliament

In April 1989, five days of rioting rocked the kingdom. Although the disturbances were triggered by a sudden increase in the price of gasoline, cigarettes, and other basic commodities (a decision implemented in the context of an austerity program negotiated with the International Monetary Fund—IMF), they also reflected a broader economic and political crisis.

The collapse of oil prices in the mid-1980s had led to an economic recession in Jordan. In the decade following the 1973 oil boom, the kingdom had been a major recipient of economic aid from the Gulf states, and its economy had been pulled by remittances from Jordanian workers in the Gulf. Much of this windfall disappeared in the mid- to late 1980s, creating popular discontent that was intensified when the government of Prime Minister Zaid al-Rifa'i introduced austerity measures in the fall of 1988.

There was also growing resentment at the lack of political freedoms and the absence of mechanisms to hold the government accountable. The accountability issue had become particularly sensitive in the wake of revelations about the wide scope of corruption among well-known government figures. The use of public office for private gain seemed even more unacceptable at a time when belt-tightening measures were being imposed on the population. Thus, the public was eager for institutional checks on potential abuses of power and authority by state officials.

It is not surprising, in this context, that the absence of a parliament should have emerged as an important grievance. From 1967 until 1988, the Israeli occupation of the West Bank had provided the regime with a convenient excuse for not holding general elections. However, that justification had evaporated in July 1988, when King Hussein had announced the severing of administrative and political ties between Jordan and the West Bank. At that point, Jordanians had expected that new parliamentary elections would soon be held on the East Bank. When it became clear that this expectation was not to be fulfilled, and when instead the population experienced the increasingly heavy-handed government of Prime Minister al-Rifa'i, Jordanians became increasingly frustrated with the political direction in which their country was headed.

It is against this background that the April 1989 riots must be understood. The upheaval demonstrated the extent to which society had become alienated from the state. Particularly worrisome to the regime was the fact that the uprising had been carried out mostly by native Jordanians, not Jordanians of Palestinian origin, and that it had broken out not in the capital, but in the southern town of Ma'an, traditionally a stronghold of pro-Hashemite feelings. From Ma'an, rioting had spread to Karak and other provincial cities and had involved bedouin constituencies long regarded as bedrocks of support for the Hashemite monarchy.

The king responded to this challenge quickly and decisively. Immediately after the riots, he fired Prime Minister Rifa'i and declared his intention to democratize political life in the kingdom. Publicly, he downplayed the economic roots of the unrest, preferring to read into the protests growing popular demands for political participation (Freij and Robinson 1996: 9). As part of his political reform program, he announced that the first parliamentary elections in twenty-two years would soon take place.

These elections were intended to achieve five main goals. The first was to provide tangible proof of the king's new commitment to democratization and to satisfy at least part of the demand for political liberalization. Second, King Hussein was gambling that the elections would improve his personal standing and help restore popular support for the regime after its image and self-confidence had been shaken by the uprising. Third, a parliament exercising close oversight over the executive branch could operate as a check on incompetence, mismanagement, or corruption by government officials. Fourth, by moving ahead with elections that would involve only East Bank constituencies, the monarch was hoping to demonstrate to Israel, the United States, the PLO, and Palestinian-Jordanians that his decision to sever ties with the West Bank was irreversible. Fifth, and perhaps most important, parliament was expected to provide a peaceful outlet for the expression of grievances regarding governmental corruption and economic austerity. By reviving the legislature as a forum through which popular complaints could be articulated and at least partially satisfied, a new explosion of popular anger might be avoided. Related to this was an attempt to deal with the rise of Islamic fundamentalism in the kingdom. In the 1980s, various Islamic groups—foremost among them the Muslim Brotherhood (MB)—had benefited from the growing discontent with deteriorating economic conditions, corruption in high places, and the lack of political reform. King Hussein apparently decided that a political opening might provide a venue for containing the Islamist challenge. This approach—which contrasts sharply with that adopted in Tunisia after 1989, Algeria after 1992, and Egypt since the early 1990s—would remain a characteristic of the regime's strategy toward political Islam.

The 1989 Elections

The elections held in November 1989 suffered from three main restrictions. First, political parties were banned, as they had been since 1957. Second, electoral districting discriminated against urban areas and in favor of rural ones, where support for the throne was strongest. Finally, minorities were still given a fixed share of seats that was disproportionate to their share of the population. For instance, Christians had nine seats reserved for them in the eighty-seat parliament, even though they made up no more than 5 percent of the population.

Nevertheless, these elections were the freest in Jordan's history. The government had just lifted most restrictions on the press. It had begun to dismantle the martial law provisions that had been in place since the 1967 war and had returned confiscated passports to political dissidents. This was also the first time women were allowed to vote in a *general* election. Twelve of them contested seats, but none was elected. Finally, although the ban on political parties forced all candidates to stand as independents, their ideological orientations—which stretched from Islamic fundamentalism to Baathism and communism—were well known.

Most important, the campaign was very lively. Professional associations and private clubs organized debates among the various candidates. These debates were often heated and followed by strikingly frank questions that focused on such sensitive issues as government corruption, economic mismanagement, civil rights abuses, and the excessive powers of the security and intelligence services. The government interfered very little in the campaign, and the opinions of the candidates were widely reported by the press.

The outcome of the election came as a surprise to many observers. The well-organized MB, which since 1957 had been unaffected by the ban on political parties because of its official status as a charitable organization, captured 22 seats, making it the largest bloc in the new parliament. In addition, independent Islamist candidates won another 12 seats. Thus, Islamic fundamentalists controlled 34 seats altogether.

There was much controversy over whether the Islamists' showing was an accurate reflection of their strength in society. On the one hand, the underrepresentation of urban areas had hurt Islamist candidates, since it was in the country's largest cities that these candidates had done best.[7] On the other hand, political Islam had clearly benefited from the provision in the electoral law that gave voters as many votes as the number of seats allotted to their district. In a district with four seats, for instance, individuals could vote for four different candidates. In practice, it meant that they would usually cast their first vote for the candidate they felt could best defend their interests. Usually, that person was someone with a direct connection to their family or tribe. Having done so, however, they still had three more votes, which they could use to support a more ideological candidate, such an an Islamist. In short, the law enabled individuals to vote both their interest and their heart and did not force them to choose between "service" or "tribal" candidates on the one hand and candidates representing a party or an ideology on the other hand.

This may also explain why the secular left did relatively well. Defined here as candidates known for their communist, Baathist, Arab nationalist, or pro-Palestinian sympathies, the left had captured a dozen seats. The rest (thirty-four seats) went to two main types of politicians. The first consisted of "tribal" or "traditionalist" candidates, who were the regime's strongest backers. The second represented modernist constituencies, such as professionals and businesspeople whose moderate and pragmatic outlook had led them to reject both the Islamists' and the left's message. Although generally supportive of the regime, they were inclined to be more ideologically oriented than the tribal candidates, and more critical of the government and some of its policies.

An Active and Vocal Legislature (1989–1993)

The new legislature quickly demonstrated that it would be no rubber stamp. Shortly after the election, the king appointed Mudar Badran as prime minister. As discussed earlier, under the 1952 constitution the prime minister must present his or her cabinet and program to the lower house and win a vote of confidence there. Unfortunately for Badran, there was considerable opposition to his appointment among the new MPs. Badran had once been in charge of Jordan's secret police, the General Intelligence Department, and the enemies he had made at the time included many of those who had just been elected to parliament. Badran also had been prime minister for most of the period between 1976 and 1984, and many new MPs blamed his policies at the time for the country's economic woes in the late 1980s.

When Badran realized that parliament's endorsement was far from secure, he was forced to engage in difficult negotiations with the Islamist bloc. During these, he made several concessions to the demands of the MB, including a commitment to tighten the laws regulating the distribution and public consumption of alcohol. He also promised to establish a new Islamic teacher-training college and to create an Islamic Law Studies Department in one of the universities. Even then, his cabinet received the necessary vote of confidence only after a grueling parliamentary debate that lasted three days and undermined his personal prestige and authority.

From the moment it first met, the new assembly debated such sensitive topics as corruption, economic reform, and civil liberties. Its proceedings were widely reported in the press, providing the citizenry with an opportunity to witness heated exchanges on public policy. Several MPs affiliated with the MB criticized the structural adjustment program sponsored by the IMF. A Committee on Public Freedoms was formed to investigate alleged violations of civil liberties. That committee launched highly publicized inquiries into corruption by government officials. Former prime minister Zaid al-Rifa'i, who had been forced to resign as a result of the April 1989 riots, was one of the committee's main targets, and he narrowly escaped parliamentary indictment for misuse of public funds.

The driving force behind parliament's assertiveness was the MB, which had formed the largest bloc in the House. The MB was often supported by independent Islamists and therefore could rely on more than 40 percent of all MPs. On many issues, Islamist MPs could also count on the backing of the left. That was the case, for instance, when the MB sponsored resolutions critical of the economic reform program. Similarly, when they pressed for investigations into alleged instances of corruption and abuses of power by governmental officials, Islamist MPs were sometimes joined not only by the left but also by some independents and centrists.

Another factor that allowed Islamists to muster support from other blocs in parliament was the reluctance of many deputies to antagonize the MB. As discussed earlier, the electoral law in place at the time gave each voter as many votes as the number of seats allotted to his or her district. In the next election, followers of the MB were clearly expected to heed the advice of the movement's leadership in deciding how to use their "extra votes" (the ones left after they had voted for the MB candidate). That is why many non-Islamist MPs who had been elected as centrists or independents were unwilling to oppose the MB. They remembered that in 1989 the MB had helped several independent candidates win closely contested races, and they wanted to ensure its support or at least neutrality in their bid for reelection. As a result, on several close votes, they either voted with the MB (even when they did not support its position) or they stayed home, to avoid being on the record as having voted against a resolution or a bill introduced by the Islamists.

Shortly after Iraq's invasion of Kuwait on August 2, 1990, widespread popular criticism of U.S. policy in the Gulf put pressure on King Hussein to move from his initially neutral stance to a decidedly pro-Iraqi position. As opposition to the U.S.-led military buildup in the Gulf continued to grow across Jordan throughout autumn, the new legislature became a rallying point for condemnation of the Western coalition against Saddam Hussein. On this issue again, the MB joined forces with pan-Arab and leftist deputies. In December 1990, it even managed to have one of its members—Abd al-Latif Arabiyyat, who holds a Ph.D. from Texas A&M—elected speaker of parliament. On January 1, 1991, seven Islamists (five affiliated with the MB and two independents) were appointed ministers.[8] Throughout the crisis, King Hussein's willingness to allow the Islamists to express themselves in parliament, and his acceptance of their entry into the cabinet, played an instrumental role in the stability of the regime at a difficult historical juncture. Had the Islamists not been provided with official recognition and institutional outlets for their outspoken criticisms of the U.S. military intervention in Iraq and Kuwait, they might have expressed their positions in a much more disruptive fashion.

Still, Islamists remained in the cabinet for less than six months. On June 9, 1991, the king appointed Tahir al-Masri to replace Mudar Badran as prime minister. Al-Masri formed a new cabinet, from which the Islamists were excluded. The MB's strong opposition to al-Masri did not prevent his confirmation, although the vote hardly represented an overwhelming endorsement of the new prime minister: It was 47 for, 37 against, and 1 abstention (Piro 1992: 40–42). Shortly thereafter, the relations between parliament and the executive branch deteriorated, especially when it became clear that the cabinet supported U.S.-led efforts to promote peace between Israel and Arab countries.

For all its power in the lower house, the MB proved unable to prevent Jordan from joining the U.S.-sponsored peace process. By November 1991, King Hussein had become determined to curb relentless parliamentary attacks on the Jordanian government's support for a comprehensive settlement of the Arab-Israeli dispute. One way in which he attempted to do so was by appointing his cousin, Zayd Bin Shaker, as prime minister, in replacement of al-Masri. Because of his status as a relative of the king, Bin Shaker could not as easily be criticized as his predecessor. The MB knew that; therefore, even though it continued to oppose Jordan's participation in the peace talks, it refrained from provoking a showdown with the regime on this issue.

The regime also decided to rein in those parliamentarians who, in its eyes, were going too far in their crusade against corruption and the peace process. During the summer of 1992, two such Islamist MPs, Laith Shbailat and Ya'qub Qarsh, were arrested on charges of illegal possession of weapons and a link to an underground terrorist Islamic organization financed by Iran and intent on overthrowing the regime. Shbailat was a popular deputy from an upper-middle-class constituency in West Amman. A member of parliament since 1984, he had been elected in 1989 with the highest number of votes in the entire country. One of twelve independent Islamists, he was also popular among independents, leftists, and pan-Arab nationalists. Between 1990 and 1992, he had made a name for himself as an outspoken critic of government corruption and the excesses of Jordan's internal security services. He had headed the lower house's committee investigating several incidents of official corruption, including some involving former prime minister al-Rifa'i.

Many in Jordan suspected that the charges against Shbailat had been trumped up by the regime, to neutralize someone who had made a nuisance of himself to a large segment of the political and bureaucratic establishment. The lack of compelling evidence put forward by the accusation during the trial provided further support for this interpretation. On November 10, 1992, the State Security Court sentenced Shbailat and Qarsh to twenty years of hard labor. Demands for a retrial were immediately heard across the political spectrum. Within forty-eight hours, the king settled the question by decreeing a general amnesty that led to the release of the two MPs. The entire incident, however, had not been a futile exercise. It had reminded politicians, and parliamentarians in particular, that their new freedom to criticize, investigate, and oversee the executive branch should not be abused.

The regime's attempt to curb parliament or intimidate its members should not be overstated. On the contrary, what stands out in retrospect is its effort to make the assembly a credible, visible, and influential institution, actively involved in all the areas with which a legislature normally concerns itself. From the moment it reconvened in 1989, the lower house was allowed to become a forum for the expression of a wide spectrum of political opinions, some of which were very much at odds with the official policies of the government. It asserted its prerogative to oversee the executive branch by launching numerous investigations into government corruption and mismanagement. Many of the scandals it uncovered or publicized involved individuals in high places, some of whom were very close to the palace. The Assembly also contributed to lawmaking. During the meetings of parliamentary committees, cabinet ministers were pressed to explain their proposed legislation and to support it with evidence. Changes suggested by committee members were often incorporated into the bills proposed by the cabinet.

In a clear indication that the regime was forced to take the legislature's opinion seriously, several of the main parliamentary blocs were represented in successive cabinets nominated by the king. The Assembly's influence on the composition of cabinets was also displayed when it managed to derail the formation of a new government under prime minister–designate Tahir al-Masri. Most important, the Assembly was able to debate all the key issues facing the country: economic reform, the Gulf War, and peace negotiations with Israel as well as other regional and international issues in which Jordan had an interest. Although the resolutions that it adopted during these debates were not binding, they were known to reflect general public sentiment and thus imposed certain political limitations on the cabinet and perhaps even the king.

Three key factors enabled the 1989–1993 legislature to play an active role in the political system. The first was the regime's need for an institution that could act as a safety valve for the expression of public discontent. The April 1989 riots had highlighted the necessity of creating or reviving such an institution. By providing a channel through which criticisms of Western policies could be expressed, parliament also performed a very important function during the Gulf crisis. As mentioned earlier, had it not played that role, the widespread popular opposition to the U.S.-led coalition against Saddam Hussein might have taken the form of antiregime activities. Furthermore, parliamentary resolutions against U.S. actions in the Gulf made it easier for King Hussein to provide the West with justifications for his pro-Iraqi tilt. The monarch could claim that his stance was merely reflecting the views of his people's elected representatives. How could Washington argue with that while still claiming to support the expansion of democracy around the globe?

A second important factor that enabled parliament to become more assertive was the king's policy to further distance himself from cabinet decisions. King Hussein made it clear that he would retain ultimate power to intervene in any area of policymaking he deemed appropriate. However, continuing a trend that can be traced back to the 1970s, he allowed the prime minister and his cabinet to make more of their own decisions. Like Morocco's King Hassan, he realized that the monarchy had little to gain from becoming involved in routine matters of government. Accordingly, he granted the prime minister and his cabinet greater responsibilities and autonomy, putting them in a situation where they could take credit for policy successes but where they would also have to face the consequences of their failures. This strategy was designed to strengthen the monarchy by sheltering it from direct criticism of governmental policies. It also explains the successive changes of prime ministers and cabinets, which were responses to internal criticisms and dissatisfaction. The cabinet was now expected to act as a shock absorber, and its members became expendable in times of crisis.[9]

The king's policy of further distancing himself from the day-to-day decisions of the government had a profound effect on the legislature. Criticism of the cabinet could no longer automatically be interpreted as attacks on the monarch or the regime. This in turn spurred the assembly to become far more assertive in its oversight of governmental policies and the actions of specific ministers. MPs now knew they could blast the government without being accused of challenging the monarchy. Indeed, parliamentarians opposing a particular policy or decision of the cabinet often found themselves appealing to the king as an impartial arbitrator. This feature is one that makes countries such as Jordan and Morocco more likely to accommodate a greater role for parliament than is the case in one-party systems, where any criticism of senior government officials is almost always interpreted as an attack against the head of state and the regime.

Finally, the third decisive factor that allowed parliament to become more visible and influential was the greater degree of consensus over the rules of the political game. It will be remembered that in the mid-1950s an earlier attempt to elevate the legislature's role in the political system had failed owing to the inability of key political actors to agree on ground rules for solving political differences. Several players questioned the legitimacy of the monarchy and the regime's basic domestic and foreign policy orientations. Some refused to accept the very borders of the country and were willing to let themselves be used by outside forces bent on destabilizing the kingdom. In such a polarized and unstable context, parliament could hardly be expected to discharge its functions

By contrast, in the early 1990s, Jordan's major political forces were able to agree on the basic parameters of political life in the kingdom. The legitimacy of the monarchy was no longer questioned, and all key players were now willing to operate within the existing constitutional framework. This consensus was officially displayed and reasserted when the so-called National Charter was adopted in June 1991. The document had been drafted by an appointed royal commission of sixty members, representing the entire political spectrum, from the Muslim Brotherhood through the Communists. It amounted to a contract through which the country's various political forces agreed to abide by certain ground rules of the game. In particular, it spelled out the conditions under which political parties would be legalized. They would have to commit themselves to the principles of democracy, pluralism, and respect for the constitution. They would not be allowed to receive funding from abroad, be linked to foreign groups, or seek to organize within the military and the security forces. They also would have to recognize the supremacy of the monarchy.

The signing of the National Charter by all the major political forces in the country, including the MB, paved the way for further democratization measures. In April 1992, martial law (which had been in place since the 1967 war) was abolished, and in September the ban on political parties was lifted. The new law regulating the operation of political parties allowed any party without connections to external interests to organize and contest elections. Several parties immediately appeared, the most important of which was the Islamic Action Front (IAF), which represented the MB. With the main political actors committed to working within the system, the regime found it possible to increase the legislature's autonomy and responsibilities. That, in turn, decreased pressures on the Islamists to seek a nonparliamentary outlet for their opposition to policies such as peace with Israel and helped the political system meet the challenge of political Islam without resort to violence and bloodshed (unlike the events in Algeria and Egypt).

The 1993 Elections

The November 1993 elections differed in several important ways from those held in 1989. Since September 1992, several political parties had been legalized. More important, King Hussein was now under great pressure to reconcile his commitment to expand democracy with his desire to move as quickly as possible toward peace with Israel. A parliament dominated by Islamists and leftists was clearly an outcome that he wanted to avoid, considering the opposition of such forces to making peace with Israel. Consequently, the monarch moved to have the electoral law rewritten so that it would diminish the strength of Islamists and leftists while benefiting progovernment and independent candidates. The strategy was implemented in three stages (Stevens 1994: 13–14). First, King Hussein issued a decree dissolving parliament on August 4, 1993, three months before the end of its term. Shortly thereafter, a date was set for a new national election (November 8, 1993). Finally, on August 17, 1993, the government issued an important amendment to the electoral law, introducing a one-person, one-vote formula.

As discussed earlier, according to the electoral law under which the 1989 parliament had been elected, each person could vote for as many candidates as there were seats in his or her district. Thus, voters had from two to nine votes, depending on the district in which they lived. By contrast, the new electoral law granted each person only one vote, giving a clear advantage to those candidates who could best deliver services while creating a major hurdle for "ideological" candidates such as lefists and Islamists. Politicians who were expected to do well under the new system included tribal leaders, who could fall back on family solidarities for support, as well as candidates who had access to independent resources and government patronage. In short, the new electoral law favored influential, generally conservative families that were the bedrocks of support for the monarchy.

Predictably, the IAF and leftist groups denounced the way in which the new electoral law had been adopted. They argued that it should have been discussed and ratified by parliament before taking effect. They also emphasized that it had done nothing to redress what they saw as the two major flaws of the previous electoral law: the quota system for minorities and a gerrymandering that underrepresented urban areas, where the opposition tended to do well, while favoring the hinterland, where support for the regime was strongest. They even threatened to boycott the forthcoming elections but chose not to do so following a royal speech that called upon all forces to take part in the contest.

In the end, 536 candidates competed for the lower house's eighty seats. Approximately 90 percent of them campaigned as independents. The rest were affiliated with one of the fifteen parties in the race, the most important of which was the IAF. The low percentage of candidates running on party labels reflected both a realization that the election would be decided on bread-and-butter issues and the population's growing disenchantment with ideological politics. Significantly, even candidates who belonged to political parties often ran as independents. Meanwhile, those who ran as party candidates gave less emphasis to their party's ideology than to their personal ability to deliver services. And whenever possible, they tried to mobilize the electorate less by publicizing a specific platform or program than by seeking to activate tribal, ethnic, or family-based solidarities. This was true even of several of the IAF candidates (Stevens 1994: 26).

That the campaign was far more subdued than the one held in 1989 was due mostly to three factors. First, it was very short, so parties and candidates had little time to organize and advertise their platforms. Second, most of the candidates were independents who focused on local, concrete issues as opposed to ideological ones. Finally, administrative interference was greater than in 1989, owing to the government's fears that the election might polarize the country between supporters and opponents of peace with Israel. The IAF claimed that government employees who were known IAF activists were being transferred away from their home districts in order to prevent them from campaigning for the party (Stevens 1994: 55). Initially, the government also imposed a ban on public rallies, before the decision was declared unconstitutional. Candidates opposed to peace with Israel clearly felt that their freedom of maneuver was being far more circumscribed than it had been in 1989.

The elections resulted in a victory for traditionalist and middle-of-the-road candidates closely associated with the palace. Liberals and center-left candidates also did reasonably well. By contrast, Islamist and leftist candidates suffered a setback. Overall, the elections produced a far more centrist, moderate, pragmatic, and "mainstream" parliament than the one that had been elected in 1989. They significantly shifted power back to Jordan's traditionalist-conservative-tribal elite, which had been on the defensive since the onset of the democratization experiment in 1989. Another significant development was the election of the first woman ever to serve in the Jordanian parliament: forty-four-year-old Tujan Faisal, a feminist and former television program host, who took one of the three seats earmarked for Circassians in Amman's relatively liberal Third District.[10]

The main result, however, was the relatively weak showing of the IAF, which captured only 16 seats, as opposed to 22 for the MB in 1989. Meanwhile, independent Islamists received a mere 2 seats, instead of the 12 they had won four years earlier. Particularly significant was the failure of three leading IAF figures to win seats: former house speaker Abd al-Latif Arabiyyat, ex–Muslim Brotherhood spokesman Ibrahim Khreisat, and hard-line fundamentalist Mohamed Abu-Fares. The poor performance of the Islamist faction was compounded by the low scores realized by the left and by the defeat of most of the incumbent Christian MPs. This was significant because, in the previous parliament, these candidates had voted with the MB on a number of issues, such as the peace process.

Several factors explain the decline of the Islamist faction. One was the change in the electoral law. (It should be stressed here that the new electoral law did not so much discriminate against the Islamists as reflect their real strength better than the one that had been in force in 1989.) Another reason was widespread disappointment with the Islamists' performance between 1989 and 1993. Many Jordanians, including those who had voted Islamist in 1989, were unimpressed with what the seven Islamist ministers had done during their six months in the cabinet. Instead of addressing real problems, they had engaged in such controversial actions as separating men and women in ministries or limiting women's involvement in the running of these ministries. The minister of education had even forbidden fathers from attending their own daughters' basketball games, on the ground that it would lead them to see other girls "immodestly dressed." The MB had to face another obstacle in the November 1993 elections: After four years in the legislature, Islamist deputies no longer looked very different from other lawmakers. Several had been implicated in scandals. Most had behaved just like other parliamentarians. As a result, it had become difficult for the MB to argue that it offered an alternative to the existing order or that, if given a chance, it would "govern differently."

Even more damaging to the MB and its allies was the fact that they had failed to take advantage of their significant control over the legislative agenda to push through real changes. Instead of concentrating on solving concrete problems, they had focused on trying to implement their conservative social agenda. Most Jordanians, however, were either uninterested in that agenda or frightened by it, and they saw it as a diversion from the real issues facing the country. In short, Islamist candidates in 1993 were punished for the failure of previous Islamist MPs to bring about real change, for their focus on the wrong issues, and for the corruption or incompetence displayed by many of them. In light of the previous four years, the slogan "Islam is the solution" sounded hollow and so did the promise that, if elected, MB candidates would bring greater integrity into government.

Finally, the IAF was also handicapped by internal divisions as well as by tactical blunders. For instance, in several constituencies, it split the vote of its own supporters by presenting more than one candidate. Furthermore, the campaign of its candidates focused on the peace process, whereas most Jordanians were actually preoccupied with domestic issues and had come to feel that peace with Israel should be given a chance. In short, the discourse of the IAF had been overtaken by events and contradicted by much of what Islamist deputies had done between 1989 and 1993.

All of this being said, the extent of the IAF's weak performance should not be exaggerated. With sixteen seats, the IAF remained the strongest political party in parliament. Furthermore, IAF candidates won the greatest number of votes in four of Amman's six electoral districts. In short, the IAF was bound to remain a significant force in the lower house, as it quickly demonstrated.

The 1993–1997 Legislature

Shortly after parliament's opening day, the members of the lower house organized themselves into six parliamentary blocs, in accordance with their respective political orientations and positions regarding the fundamental issues facing Jordanian society.[11] The opposition was represented by two blocs: the Islamic Action Front (sixteen seats) and the smaller Democratic Progressive Coalition, a loose coalition of left and left-of-center parties (seven seats). Some independents and centrists created the Independent Bloc. Most other lawmakers joined one of three blocs, all of which included individuals broadly supportive of the regime's policies: the National Action Front, which soon grew to include twenty MPs;[12] the National Bloc, which brought together the Jordanian National Alliance Party (four seats) and the centrist Al-Yaqatha party (two seats); and the twelve-member National Democratic Coalition. A member of that bloc, Saad Hayel Srour, was elected speaker, defeating the Islamist-backed candidate Abdul Razzaq Tbeishat by a vote of forty-six to forty-one.[13] With the exception of the IAF, these blocs lacked cohesion and therefore rarely voted as single units. Nevertheless, they did represent the main political forces in the country: Islamists, leftists, tribal conservatives, and centrists (the latter breaking into modernist and traditionalist wings).

In the wake of the elections, several commentators referred to the new legislature as a "yes parliament." It soon became clear that they were mistaken. Although the elections had indeed yielded a more conservative, traditional, and pro-monarchy legislature that was largely supportive of the government's policies, they had not produced a rubber-stamp parliament. The IAF remained a force to be reckoned with in a lower house that also included a significant number of Baathists, leftists, and pan-Arabists. Liberal and centrist candidates also showed themselves to be quite vocal. Even MPs frequently described as representing the "tribal" or "traditionalist" vote did not want to be taken for granted by the regime and were quick to assert their prerogatives.

This was shown during the confidence debate over the new cabinet appointed immediately after the election. After presenting his cabinet and program to the lower house, prime minister–designate Abdel Salam al-Majali faced unexpected questioning and criticism by lawmakers. Eventually, his government was confirmed by a one-vote majority (41 in favor, 29 against, 9 abstentions, and 1 absent). Furthermore, this slim majority was secured only after intense pressure was placed on some deputies to endorse a government that was known to have the blessing of the king.

At least two main factors account for parliament's unexpected combativeness. First, many centrist, independent, and traditionalist candidates were determined to prove that they would not let their proregime leanings translate into systematic support for the government. Instead, they wanted to reassure their constituents that they would actively stand up for their interests. Second, the new MPs also wanted the government to take their opinions into account, and several had hoped to become ministers. Consequently, many felt offended when al-Majali decided not to include any deputies in his government.

When parliament met for its second regular annual session in November 1994, its agenda was dominated by the peace treaty that Jordan had just signed with Israel on October 26. That treaty had far-reaching implications for the kingdom, since it had not only ended a forty-six-year state of war but had also called for close cooperation between the two neighbors. Islamists and some leftist MPs used parliamentary debates to denounce the recognition of the Jewish state. Their opposition was to no avail. In the end, the peace treaty was ratified by a comfortable fifty-five to twenty-four vote. Parliament's endorsement was instrumental in legitimizing King Hussein's policy toward Israel. Had parliament not existed, it would have been far more difficult for the regime to argue that the normalization of relations with Israel had broad support from the electorate.

It had been expected that by the end of parliament's second regular annual session (March 1995), the lower house would have repealed laws banning economic dealings with Israelis. New legislation in this area was needed to enable Jordan to comply with the provisions of the peace treaty with Israel. By boycotting parliament's debate of the issue, however, Islamist and leftist lawmakers were able to block the presentation of the draft amendments to the legislature. In their absence, a quorum could not be met, and no action was taken.

The opposition's victory was nevertheless short-lived. Within weeks, King Hussein received a memo, signed by forty-five members of the lower house, in which he was asked to convene an extraordinary meeting of the legislature, in order to amend the laws forbidding commercial relations with Israelis. By early May 1995, the monarch had called parliament to a special three-month session, by issuing a royal decree that also spelled out the draft laws and amendments that lawmakers should consider.[14] When the session was held, Islamist MPs did their utmost to prevent the adoption of new legislation. They tried to boycott parliamentary sessions and held numerous demonstrations and sit-ins outside parliament. Despite their opposition, the laws providing for an economic boycott of Israel were eventually repealed by a wide margin (fifty-one to nineteen). However, parliament did not content itself with ratifying the draft laws that had been submitted to it. Instead, lawmakers made their own mark by including several amendments to prevent excessive Israeli investment in Jordanian companies and real estate. The laws that were eventually passed specify that non-Jordanians are allowed to buy land in Jordan only if Jordanians have reciprocal rights to buy land in their country and if the deal has been approved by the Jordanian government and publicized in local newspapers. This legislation was eventually approved by the upper house by a thirty to three vote.

In 1995 and 1996, parliament passed important legislation to attract foreign investment, by allowing non-Jordanians to own more than 50 percent of businesses in Jordan and to fully repatriate capital and profits. In addition, a series of laws revamped the taxation system by reducing sales and income taxes as well as taxes on the profits of corporations. The lower house also strengthened the protection of copyrights and intellectual property while taking important steps toward the privatization of the energy and telecommunications sectors. This flurry of legislation significantly altered economic life in the kingdom, making it a much friendlier place for both domestic and foreign investment.

Although economic issues dominated the legislature's agenda in 1995 and 1996, political controversies were never far from the surface. There was much concern in Jordan at the time that because of its determination to normalize relations with Israel the government had restricted public liberties and clamped down on dissident voices. Such claims were repeatedly made in parliament, mostly by the Islamist and leftist opposition. For instance, in mid-September 1995, on the last day of parliament's extraordinary session, the lower house's Public Freedoms and Citizens' Rights Committee came out with a report accusing the government of curtailing personal and group freedoms by engaging in arbitrary arrests, banning certain public meetings, and punishing opponents of peace with Israel by replacing their regular passports with two-year temporary passports. During the same period, the Islamist opposition asked for a vote of no-confidence in the justice minister, whom it accused of having tried to intimidate twenty-three senior judges who had complained of poor working conditions and benefits. These parliamentary attacks on the cabinet made it clear that even this supposedly conservative legislature was determined to force the government to account for its actions.

Indicative of the assembly's political clout was the composition of the cabinet that took office in February 1996. Led by a two-term member of parliament, Abd al-Karim Kabariti, this new government included more members of the legislature than any previous cabinet: twenty-two out of thirty-one ministers, five more than in the previous cabinet. All the leading parliamentary blocs, with the exception of the IAF, were represented in Kabariti's cabinet. It seemed, therefore, that in addition to its new prerogatives and increased autonomy, parliament was also emerging as a very significant channel for recruitment into the governmental elite.

In selecting prime ministers or asking them to resign, the king also appeared to give careful attention to whether they enjoyed or might develop a good working relationship with the legislature. For instance, it is believed that one of the reasons the monarch asked then–prime minister al-Majali to step down in January 1995 was the premier's confrontational attitude toward the lower house, which had created much resentment and hostility toward the cabinet among legislators. Significantly, when Zayd Bin Shaker was nominated to replace al-Majali, he went out of his way to signal that he would refrain from using the heavy-handed tactics that his predecessor had employed toward the legislature. In forming his cabinet, he consulted widely with the major parliamentary blocs, including the IAF. Eventually, his government included seventeen members from the lower house. Similarly, the king's February 1996 appointment of Kabariti as prime minister may have been motivated, in part, by the new premier's potential for developing a good working relationship with parliament. Kabariti had served in the lower house since 1989 and knew the institution well. He was also a close friend and business partner of the speaker of the lower house, Saad Hayel Srour, and a son-in-law of senate speaker Ahmad al-Lawzi.

During Kabariti's term, however, relations between the government and parliament actually deteriorated. The reason lay mostly in Kabariti's determination to push through an unpopular agenda. To begin with, Kabariti implemented economic reforms required under an agreement with the IMF and without which Jordan would not become eligible for favorable credit and new grants. In order to comply with the provisions of that agreement, the government lifted its subsidies on wheat on August 13, 1996. Bread prices immediately doubled, leading residents of the southern town of Karak to take to the streets. Riots ensued that lasted two days. When the police proved unable to cope with the unrest, the army had to be sent in, and a curfew was imposed. By then, however, the demonstrations had spread to other towns, including Ma'an and al-Tafilah. It was not until several days later that the situation was brought under control. But by then the government had been badly shaken, and in the lower house opposition to its economic reforms had become even stronger.

Kabariti's foreign policy also contributed to the legislature's growing alienation from the government. The prime minister ignored strong parliamentary opposition to his policies of isolating Iraq and aligning himself with U.S. goals in the region. Most important, he pushed forward with the normalization of relations with the Jewish state, in spite of Israel's refusal to deliver on its side of the agreements it had signed with the Palestinians. Sensing that his prime minister was running out of political capital, the king dismissed him in March 1997. He replaced him with Abdel Salam al-Majali, who proceeded to form a cabinet made up primarily of technocrats. Two months later, a royal decree imposed tough restrictions on the press, prohibiting in particular any "news, views and analysis" that "disparage the king or royal family, the armed forces, and heads of friendly states" (the latter provision being clearly intended to muzzle criticisms of Israel and the Jordanian-Israeli peace treaty). Also included in the new law was an amendment banning articles "which include false information or rumors that lead to harming the general interest, government institutions, or its workers." In addition, a very high minimum capital requirement was set for any weekly publication, and fines for breaking the new press laws were raised fifteenfold.

Significantly, the royal decree on the press allowed the regime to bypass parliament altogether, leading to accusations that the authorities were now bent on marginalizing the legislature. By the fall of 1997, the new press law had led to the closure of a dozen weekly newspapers.

The November 1997 Elections

Opposition to the "single vote" election law, the normalization of ties with Israel, and the new press law created the most important crisis between government and opposition since the reconvening of parliament in 1989. Consequently, the November 1997 elections were marred by a boycott by ten opposition parties, including the IAF. Also boycotting the race were nearly one hundred prominent Jordanians, including two former prime ministers.

Despite the IAF's boycott, however, four leading members of the MB ran as independents, as did other Islamists and a number of leftists and Arab nationalists. Thus, voters could still choose among individuals representing a variety of ideological orientations. The number of candidates (561) was also close to that in the 1993 elections, suggesting that the boycott had failed to deter many politicians from entering the contest.

The electoral process was marked by certain irregularities, although the government seemed genuinely committed to preventing fraud and in several cases prosecuted candidates who had violated the rules. More worrisome was abundant evidence that the authorities were unwilling to tolerate public criticism of Israeli policies or Jordan's peace treaty with the Jewish state. On numerous occasions, for instance, election placards critical of Israel or "the peace process" were removed by the security services.

The elections' main results came as no surprise. As in 1993, most of the victors were tribal notables well disposed toward the palace. They had usually campaigned on local issues and shied away from the controversial questions of peace with Israel and economic reforms. Still, not all those elected could be described as solidly behind government policies. About 7 independent Islamists and 8 leftists had won seats, and at least another 3 new members of the lower house were seen as moderately to strongly critical of the cabinet's orientations. Political parties, though, had fared disastrously, winning only 5 seats. Particularly striking was the poor showing of the much-touted National Constitutional Party (NCP), led by Abdelhadi Majali, a brother of the prime minister. Founded in early 1997 through a merger of eight centrist parties, the NCP had aimed to establish itself as Jordan's dominant party. Its platform was based mainly on support for the peace process and economic reforms. Although analysts had expected the NCP to win at least fifteen seats, only two of its members were elected. Finally, none of the seventeen women in the race won, although several—including prominent opposition figure Tujan Faisal (who lost the seat she had won in 1993 to a former Information Ministry official)—secured far more votes than most male candidates.

On November 21, less than three weeks after the election to the lower house, King Hussein issued a decree appointing the forty members of the upper house. Among those selected were three former prime ministers (including Kabariti), the person who was prime minister at the time, four other members of the cabinet, and three women. The senate, however, contained no Islamists.

Parliament's Persistent Weaknesses

As this chapter has shown, the Jordanian democratic experiment is predicated on a central role for the legislature. Parliament now features more prominently in the calculations of the country's most important players. Since 1989, it has become a more credible, representative, and influential institution. Still, serious constitutional, political, and internal hurdles continue to prevent it from enjoying the prerogatives and from performing the range of functions that are appropriate for a legislature in a democratic system. In this final section, we highlight these weaknesses, some of which affect parliament's centrality, others its capacity.

With respect to centrality, the Jordanian legislature can still function only within the constitutional and political space granted and tolerated by the king. The monarch appoints the forty members of the senate and selects its president. This is a very important prerogative, considering that even after bills have been adopted by the lower house, they cannot become law until they have been approved by the senate. The king can suspend parliament, dissolve it, and shorten or extend its term as he sees fit. He exerts considerable influence on the legislative agenda. Most important, he can veto any bill passed by parliament. In short, at least for the time being, the legislature remains heavily dependent on royal will. The monarch's ability to dictate the rules of the parliamentary game was displayed dramatically in August 1993, when he dismissed the legislature three months before the end of its term and had the electoral law rewritten in a way that was bound to reduce the influence of the Islamist and leftist opposition in the lower house. The new law then served as the basis for the next parliamentary elections, even though it had not been ratified by parliament.

Insufficient confidence in the electoral process constitutes yet another variable that continues to undermine the credibility and legitimacy of parliament and therefore its centrality in the political system. The electoral law remains very controversial, especially because it still discriminates so heavily against urban areas, and therefore against Jordanians of Palestinian origins. For instance, both the predominantly bedouin Tufeila district in the south and Amman's second district, the population of which is predominantly poor and of Palestinian origin, have three seats in parliament. The former, however, had only about 27,000 eligible voters in 1997, whereas the latter had almost 120,000. Similarly, Amman and Zarqa, where nearly half of Jordan's population lives, have only a quarter of the seats in the lower house. Unless progress is made toward redressing these imbalances, the feeling will persist that parliament is not representative enough of the country's real political makeup.

Another limit on the representativeness of the lower house elected in November 1997 stems from the boycott by the IAF. Even though some Islamists ran as independents and were elected, the Islamists' presence in parliament does not reflect their influence in the country. More generally, the opposition boycott hurt the credibility of the parliamentary institution. The absence of women in the current lower house represents another significant setback.

The extent to which parliament is seen as an institution that genuinely reflects public opinion also continues to suffer from low voter turnout. Participation was a mere 41 percent of eligible voters in the 1989 election, 45 percent in 1993, and 44 percent in 1997. In 1997, the turnout in Amman and

Zarqa, the country's two largest cities, was barely 35 percent. Such dangerous apathy demonstrates the electorate's skepticism toward the parliamentary process. Most Jordanians still do not believe that the makeup of the legislature has a real impact on their lives. They do not yet see parliament as the primary arena for political contestation and governance. Worrisome as well is the fact that participation among Jordanians of Palestinian origin was about half the national average in both the 1993 and 1997 elections. This, in turn, helps explain why deputies of Palestinian origin represent only about 20 percent of the lower house's membership. This limited involvement of Jordanian-Palestinians in the legislature's work must be corrected if parliament is to play a more central role in the political system.

Finally, parliamentary sessions are still too short, since they average only five months a year (November to March). As a result, for seven months of the year there is no legislature to act as a check on the government. Parliament's overall influence would clearly be enhanced if the constitution were amended in a way that significantly increased the length of its annual session.

Insofar as capacity is concerned, three main internal constraints continue to hinder the Jordanian parliament's ability to discharge its functions: the absence of a bill-drafting capacity, an underdeveloped committee system, and the lack of staff and technical support.

As the number of bills that the cabinet sends to the assembly for consideration and approval continues to increase, the absence of a genuine bill-drafting capability within the lower house has become a serious hurdle. It significantly reduces the assembly's ability to initiate legislation and its capacity to introduce significant changes to bills sponsored by the executive branch.

The lower house's committee system also remains underdeveloped. Committee members have few resources with which to study or elaborate the bills they receive. Their research and staff support is so inadequate that they are hard-pressed to ask informed and meaningful questions to the ministers who come to them to present the cabinet's proposed legislation. During committee proceedings, members are often forced to rely on outdated reports or on information supplied by the executive branch. This in part explains why debates in committees are usually dominated by ministers, as is the outcome. Furthermore, rewards for hardworking committee members are virtually nonexistent. They receive neither extra compensation nor political credit for their contributions to committee deliberations. Any attempt to strengthen the public policy role of parliament must address the needs of committee members for information, research, staff support, and financial and political rewards.

However, the single most important internal constraint that parliament faces is the insufficiency of staff and technical support for MPs. Because of the lack of space, personnel, communications equipment, and institutionalized links to governmental agencies, legislators are hard-pressed to meet their constituents' needs for information and contacts with officials. They often cannot even answer adequately their constituents' questions about specific government programs. Unless these deficiencies are redressed, the Assembly's ability to provide constituency services will remain limited.

Not only is parliament's support structure underdeveloped, but also it has been asked to serve both the senate and the lower house. This is inadequate, because these two institutions have different orientations and missions. The needs of an elected body representing the country's various districts and ethnic and religious groups are different from those of the senate, an elitist institution whose members are all appointed by the king. In the future, the lower house and the senate each ought to have its own specialized staff and research facilities.

Finally, the mode of selection and promotion of the legislative staff is inadequate. The staff is usually appointed and promoted by the executive branch. Certainly, that takes place in coordination with the secretary-general of parliament but with little input from MPs and the leaders of the various parliamentary groups. As a result, the staff's loyalty to the institution and to lawmakers is far less developed than it should be. Furthermore, there are still many senior staff members whose appointments go back to the pre-1989 era (when the overwhelming majority of current MPs did not yet belong to the legislature). This creates yet another barrier between the staff and the individuals they are supposed to serve. In addition, the institution also does not provide enough opportunities for the staff to develop their skills or acquire new ones. Finally, once tenured, a staff member will retain his or her job until he or she retires or chooses to transfer. This limits the accountability of parliamentary employees to lawmakers and in many instances discourages performance. These serious staff-related problems must be addressed and resolved if Jordan's parliament is to continue to develop its role in the political system.

Notes

1. The straw that broke the camel's back was the LA's refusal to approve the government's request for financing the Desert Patrol (Abu Jaber 1972: 95).

2. The East Bank was still favored under that system, since it elected half of the Chamber of Deputies, even though close to two-thirds of Jordan's population at the time lived on the West Bank. Furthermore, East Bank constituencies were delineated in such a way as to give a clear advantage to native Transjordanians over residents of Palestinian origins.

3. Apparently, King Hussein had not expected the opposition to do as well as it did. He may have believed that his March 1, 1956, dismissal of Lt. Gen. John Bagot Glubb ("Glubb Pasha") had provided him with the pan-Arab credentials that would allow his supporters to contain the appeal of leftist parties.

4. The only organized political force that was allowed to operate in the country was the Muslim Brotherhood (MB), which was defined not as a party but as a "charita-

ble association." This special status, plus the tacit support of the king who for years relied on it as a counterweight to leftist and pan-Arab groups, explains why the MB was able to develop a large grassroots following. This, in turn, goes a long way toward explaining its strong showing in the 1989 parliamentary elections.

5. The extent of electoral fraud varied from one election to another. The elections of 1962 and 1967, for instance, were much freer than that held in 1961.

6. The king could afford neither to antagonize Jordanians of Palestinian origins (who represented more than half of the population) nor to go against what had become a new "Arab consensus" (the notion that the PLO was the sole legitimate representative of the Palestinian people). To do so would have left him dangerously isolated, both domestically and in inter-Arab politics.

7. In Amman, for instance, Islamists had won fourteen of the eighteen seats allotted to Muslim candidates. Similarly, in Irbid, the five largest numbers of votes had gone to Islamists.

8. The five members of the MB in the cabinet were given the following ministries: health, justice, education, Islamic affairs and social development, and Islamic endowments. The two independent Islamists received the portfolios of agriculture and of transportation and communication.

9. By reshuffling the cabinet, the king could also indicate domestic and foreign policy reorientations. For instance, the bringing of seven Islamists into the government on January 1, 1991, and the appointment of al-Masri as prime minister six months later reflected the king's effort to adjust to a rapidly changing domestic and regional environment. On several such occasions, cabinets were changed to enable Jordan to position itself to undertake foreign policy initiatives or to respond to the initiatives of other international and regional actors.

10. The other two women running in 1993 failed to win. In 1989, twelve women had stood as candidates, but none had been successful. In 1993, two women (Leila Sharaf and Na'ila Rushdan) were also appointed to the forty-member senate.

11. The following description draws on Stevens (1994: 27).

12. The most important party within the National Action Front was Al-Ahd, headed by Abdelhadi Majali, leader of the prominent Majali family in southern Jordan.

13. Srour was a former minister who twice had been elected to represent his northern bedouin district in the lower house. Tbeishat was an independent Islamist, whom the IAF had decided to support after withdrawing its own candidate. The IAF suffered another blow when its candidate for the position of first deputy speaker lost to National Action Front leader Abdelhadi Majali.

14. The Jordanian constitution specifies that parliament is free to debate any subject it finds fit during a regular session but that it is the king's prerogative and responsibility to identify which topics should be discussed during extraordinary sessions.

8

Kuwait

Kuwait's long experience with parliamentary politics sets this emirate apart from its neighbors in the Gulf. Since achieving independence from the United Kingdom in June 1961, Kuwait has been without a legislature for only two relatively brief periods: 1976 to 1981 and 1986 to 1992. Furthermore, since it was reestablished in 1992, the Kuwaiti parliament has proven to be one of the most assertive in the Arab world. As of this writing, Kuwait still has the only elected legislature in the Gulf region.

The roots of Kuwait's parliamentary experience go deep into the country's past. As early as 1938, when Kuwait was still a British protectorate, a fourteen-member National Legislative Council (Majlis al-Umma al-Tashri'i) was established to act as a check on the power of the ruling al-Sabah family. The Council came about as a result of two decades of pressure by the country's leading merchant families. Although it was short-lived (the emir disbanded it six months after its establishment), its memory inspired an entire generation of Kuwaiti reformers during the 1940s and 1950s.

In November 1962—less than eighteen months after achieving independence—Kuwait adopted a constitution that provided for a unique blend of hereditary rule and representative government. Although the constitution stipulated that the ruler of Kuwait should be a male descendant of Mubarak al-Sabah (Kuwait's ruler at the turn of the century) and made it clear that this emir would not be accountable to any elected body, it also provided for a fifty-member elected National Assembly (NA) endowed with genuine powers and influence over the political system.

In the years that followed the first legislative elections in January 1963, the NA repeatedly asserted its constitutional prerogatives against an executive branch reluctant to share power. This assertiveness largely explains why Kuwait's parliamentary experience has been a tormented one. On two occasions—first in 1976 and then again a decade later—the vigorous criticisms of

169

government policies emanating from the NA convinced the emir to suspend it, leaving the government in sole control of the country's affairs. It is very significant, however, that in both instances the regime eventually decided to reconvene the assembly, the first time in 1981 and the second in 1992. As this chapter will show, this suggests that the NA had performed important political functions that no other body had been able to assume after it had been dissolved.

When in session, the NA has been consistently the central arena for the airing of competing views over the rules that should govern political life. It has been in the NA that the ruling family, its allies, and the opposition have tested each other and have succeeded or failed in hammering out the necessary compromises. Parliamentary debates have often been acrimonious and widely reported in the press. On numerous occasions, the NA has been able to act as an effective check on the cabinet. Consequently, parliament has been the one institution in which the defining struggle that has driven political life in the emirate has played itself out most clearly: the tug-of-war pitting a ruling family jealous of its prerogatives against a broad array of political forces pushing for greater governmental accountability and more political participation. The legislature's ability to play that role was a by-product in part of the country's constitution, which gave it significant oversight powers over the cabinet, and in part of the relatively free political atmosphere that has prevailed in the emirate.

By all accounts, Kuwait has been one of the most politically open and tolerant polities in the Arab world. Except during short periods of governmental crackdowns, it has displayed a very lively, diverse, and independent-minded press. Rarely have Kuwaitis hesitated to speak out against their government, and civil liberties have been better respected in the emirate than in most other Arab countries. This state of affairs has allowed the legislature to exercise real political influence. The freedom of maneuver enjoyed by the legislature, in turn, has contributed to the relative pluralism and tolerance that have made Kuwait the freest polity in the Gulf.

Iraq's devastating occupation of Kuwait, which lasted from August 2, 1990, until February 28, 1991, had a profound effect on politics in the emirate. It radically changed the nature of the relationship between rulers and ruled and the balance of power between advocates and opponents of political reform. After much hesitation, and despite the ambivalence of many members of the ruling family toward democratization, the emir called for parliamentary elections in October 1992. The elections resulted in a strong showing by opposition and independent candidates, who captured thirty-five of the assembly's fifty seats.

The new legislature moved quickly to address the most important and sensitive issues facing the country, including security matters, economic reform, the management of the country's overseas investments, and the need for political reform. Parliamentary debates included acrimonious exchanges between prodemocracy activists, Islamists, and the tribal allies of the ruling family. Still, the parliament was careful not to repeat the mistakes that had led to its dissolution in both 1976 and 1986. Although assertive, it refrained from engaging in the kind of excessive rhetoric that might have prompted a crack-down by the ruling family. In short, the opposition endeavored not to let its push for greater democracy disrupt the country's new stability or its recon-struction effort. This pragmatism, combined with the ruling family's greater willingness to make concessions, allowed parliament to become more effec-tive. The elections held on October 7, 1996, as well as developments since then, have confirmed these trends.

Roots of Kuwait's Parliamentary Experience

Until the turn of the century, political life in Kuwait was driven by an infor-mal but close alliance between the ruling al-Sabah family and a group of elite merchant families. This alliance rested on a division of labor between the rul-ing family and the merchants: The al-Sabah controlled political and military matters while the merchants dominated the economic life of the country. In return for the right to make money and for the protection and security that the ruling family provided, the merchants accepted the political supremacy of the al-Sabah, and even supported them financially. It was understood, however, that the emir would always consult with the merchants on matters of impor-tance to them. The merchants' political influence stemmed from the ruler's economic dependence on them, whether through taxes and customs dues or through the loans that prominent merchants frequently extended to him. At the time, most of the revenues the ruler needed to perform his political and military functions were derived from the taxes he levied on the pearl diving, fishing, and boatbuilding activities that the merchants controlled. The mer-chants' political leverage was always evident after the death of an emir, since they were consulted during the process of selecting the next ruler from among the leading contenders in the al-Sabah family. Typically, the act sealing the succession consisted of a gathering of leading merchants acclaiming the nom-inee chosen by the al-Sabah (Khalaf 1984: 245).

The al-Sabah also maintained close ties to the many nomadic tribes that lived in the desert outside of the then town of Kuwait. And because the loyalty of these tribes was essential to the emirate's security, their leaders, too, expected to be consulted on issues involving their interests. Overall, therefore, the al-Sabah were not absolute rulers. Their power was constrained by tribal customs, Islamic law, the centuries-old practice of *shura* (consultation), and the influence of prominent merchant families. To maintain the support of merchant and tribal elites, they needed to consult widely before making critical decisions.

Although this political formula proved stable for many decades, it was disrupted in the late nineteenth century by two developments. First, the al-Sabah acquired substantial date groves in southern Iraq, where they began to engage in commercial activities that made them more financially independent of the merchants (Zahlan 1989: 26). Consequently, the political leverage that the merchants had enjoyed until then was reduced. A second, ultimately decisive, event was the arrival of the British. In 1899, Kuwait's ruler, Mubarak al-Sabah—known in Kuwaiti historiography as Mubarak the Great—signed a treaty with Britain that essentially turned Kuwait into a British protectorate. In doing so, the emir was trying to protect Kuwait from attempts by the Ottoman authorities to reassert their control over his country, which was nominally part of the Ottoman Empire. Thus, by surrendering to Britain control over Kuwait's defense and foreign policies, Mubarak al-Sabah made sure that the al-Sabah, protected by British power, would retain control over domestic matters, free from Ottoman interference. Only by turning to the British, Mubarak al-Sabah reasoned, could Kuwait protect its internal autonomy from the threat posed by such a powerful regional power as the Ottoman Empire.

Soon, however, the British presence in Kuwait fundamentally transformed the emirate's political dynamic. Bolstered by Britain's political and financial support, Mubarak al-Sabah—who ruled from 1896 until 1915—progressively distanced himself from the country's economic elite. He began to act more independently of Kuwait's merchants, making key decisions without consulting with them. He also started to tax them more heavily, in part to raise the revenues necessary to centralize power in his own hands and in part to break their economic power (Aarts 1994: 17–22).

As the emir disregarded the previous implied consensus, which was that he would not govern without the tacit support of the leading merchant families, his relations with the country's economic elite turned sour. Some merchants became so disillusioned that they left Kuwait for neighboring Bahrain. From then on, the tension between the ruling family and the merchants would be the single most important force driving Kuwaiti politics.

In 1918, during Jabir al-Sabah's rule (1915–1917), some prominent merchants began to call for the establishment of an elected consultative council, or *majlis*, as a way of checking the ruler's power and preventing abuses of authority by his agents. Although their calls were ignored by the ruling family, including Emir Salim al-Sabah (1917–1921), the issue remained on the public agenda. When the emir died in 1921, the merchants were quick to inform the ruling family that they would support whichever of the three candidates for the succession would express a willingness to establish an advisory council. Ahmad Jabir al-Sabah accepted that condition, and shortly after he became the new emir he formed a twelve-member advisory council. However, the new emir was president of the council, and he never formally convened it. Instead, he ruled in the same authoritarian manner as his predecessors (Zahlan 1989: 27; Tétreault 1991: 575).

Nevertheless, the merchants did not give up. Throughout the 1920s, they persisted in calling for the council to meet. And by the late 1930s, new conditions were making it increasingly difficult for the emir to ignore their demands. In the first place, Kuwait was now beset by a serious economic crisis fueled by a Saudi economic blockade and by the collapse of the pearl industry that until then had been the dominant economic activity in the emirate. Second, Kuwait's educated population was becoming more aware of political developments in the region. It was following with particular interest the turmoil in Palestine, where tensions were rising between Jews and Arabs and between Arabs and the British. At a time when Britain's image in the region was being tainted by its support for Zionist aspirations in Palestine, Kuwait's ruling family became hard-pressed to defend its close association with the British. In addition, the growing appeal of Arab nationalism in neighboring Iraq was being echoed in Kuwait.

The political activism spurred by this combination of social mobilization and economic crisis was compounded by the emir's increasingly heavy-handed tactics, which were causing him to become more and more isolated. The British came to feel that it might be wise to distance themselves from him (Tétreault 1991: 576). There was even dissent within the ruling family, and the emir's cousin, Crown Prince Abdallah al-Salim al-Sabah, joined the call for reforms. With the emir on the defensive, the merchants took the lead in demanding that he consult with them to find answers to Kuwait's growing economic problems. Ultimately, they were able to tap popular dissatisfaction to force him to recognize the National Legislative Council (Majlis al-Umma al-Tashri'i), which they already had elected from among their ranks. All fourteen members of this council belonged to prominent Kuwaiti families. The council was presided over by Abdallah al-Salim al-Sabah.

This council accomplished much over the time of its very short existence (June through December 1938). Its most important act was to draw up a Basic Law, consisting of five articles. That document, which the emir reluctantly approved on July 2, 1938, is sometimes called Kuwait's first constitution. It stipulated that the nation is the source of all authority and that it should be represented by an elected assembly authorized to legislate on all matters of concern to the country, including security, foreign policy, the budget, and social policy (particularly in the areas of education, health, and housing). Such an assertion of prerogatives by the newly formed council represented a considerable reduction in the power of the emir. Furthermore, Article Three of the new Basic Law stated that internal concessions, leases, and monopolies, as well as all agreements and treaties with foreign powers, could not be considered legal and binding unless approved by the assembly. This article was

aimed at the British and the oil companies. By that time, the latter had become aware of Kuwait's oil deposits and felt confident that they could convince the emir to grant them more concessions. Predictably, neither the
British nor the oil companies welcomed what they saw as the council's attempt to interfere with their interests. In the months that followed the adoption of the Basic Law, the council passed far-reaching legislation. It revamped
the tax and the judicial systems, launched important construction projects, expanded educational facilities, and introduced public health regulations.

In December 1938, however, the council may have overreached when it
requested that it, rather than the emir, should decide how the money that
Kuwait received from the oil companies should be allocated. The emir responded by disbanding the assembly. When the members of the council resisted, the ruler resorted to force (Crystal 1992: 19–20). The British did not
interfere. Although initially they had seen some benefit in the establishment
of an assembly that would put some checks on the emir's increasingly arbitrary power, they had withdrawn support for the council after it had shown its
determination to exercise oversight over the granting of concessions to oil
companies and the signing of agreements with foreign powers. Ultimately, the
council's speaker was executed for calling for the overthrow of the regime.
The remaining members either fled or were arrested. Even then, however, a
number of consultative committees, appointed by the emir, came into being
and remained in place until Kuwait gained independence on June 19, 1961.

The key development before Kuwait achieved independence, however,
was the spectacular increase in oil revenues, which jumped from $760,000 in
1946 to $169 million in 1953 (Zahlan 1989: 30). This oil bonanza drastically
altered the nature of the relationship between state and society. It enabled the
former to launch social programs and create government-related jobs, which
in turn helped it depoliticize the population. In effect, large segments of the
population were bought off by the state and turned into grateful beneficiaries
of its largesse. As a result, demands for political participation and governmental accountability became less pronounced. Furthermore, unlike taxes, which
had to be levied from the local population (the merchants in particular), oil
revenues accrued directly to the ruler, freeing him from his long-standing financial dependence on the country's economic elite.

Since the ruler no longer had to rely on the merchants for revenues, the
trading families lost much of the political leverage that they traditionally had
been able to exercise in return for their taxes. Thus, their political power fell
sharply, the more so since they struck an implicit bargain with the state: They
would for the most part withdraw from politics if the ruling family were to
guarantee them economic prosperity. It did so through a variety of means: by
directing to them a sizable share of the oil wealth through government contracts, by making sure that the state's expanding role in the economy did not
come at the expense of the private sector,[1] by protecting Kuwait's economic

elite from competition by foreign firms,[2] and through a land purchase program whereby the government bought at high prices large tracts of land
mostly owned by merchants and then sold that same land back at low prices,
again mostly to members of the leading trading families (Crystal 1992: 74).

The development of the oil industry therefore enabled the regime to convince the merchants to adopt a lower political profile. This was particularly important considering that the trading families had historically played a leading
role in pressing for greater governmental accountability. Nevertheless, demands for formal political participation lingered well into the 1950s. Although
the country's economic elite became less politically active, new social strata
filled the vacuum. The intelligentsia (the members of which were often the
sons and daughters of prominent merchants) was growing in size and was feeling the pull of Arab nationalism and Nasserism. Ahmad al-Khatib, a physician
and Arab nationalist leader who would remain a leading figure in Kuwaiti politics through the 1990s, led the call for the establishment of a parliament.

Parliament in the 1962 Constitution

Within days of Kuwait's becoming independent on June 19, 1961, Emir Abdallah al-Salim al-Sabah issued a decree calling for the election of a Constituent
Assembly (al-Majlis al-Ta'sisi) entrusted with drafting a constitution. Kuwait
was divided into ten districts that would each elect two representatives to the
Assembly. The vote, which was open to all Kuwaiti males over twenty-one,
was direct and by secret ballot. It took place on December 30, 1961, and was
by and large free: It is significant, for instance, that opposition leader Ahmad
al-Khatib was elected and became vice chairman of the Assembly. Similarly,
the Assembly's chairman, Thnayyan al-Ghanim, had been a major figure in the
1938 movement and had spent several years afterward in jail (Ghabra 1991:
201). The fourteen members of the Council of Ministers were added to that Assembly, thus nominally raising its total membership to thirty-four. Three members of the Council had run successfully for the Assembly, so the actual number was thirty-one. (Although the ministers were allowed to participate in the
Assembly's deliberations, only elected members could vote.)

On November 8, 1962, the Constituent Assembly forwarded to the emir a
proposed constitution, which he signed unaltered three days later. This constitution created a unique, hybrid political system, characterized by the mixing
of two different traditions: hereditary rule and representative government.

As far as Kuwait's being defined as a hereditary emirate is concerned, the
constitution stipulates that the country's head of state must be chosen by the
ruling family from among the male descendants of Mubarak the Great. Under
normal circumstances, the emir cannot be forced to step down. He selects and
appoints the prime minister (who by convention has always been the crown

prince) as well as the entire cabinet.[3] Since the cabinet is responsible for day-to-day policymaking, the emir's ability to select all the ministers without having his choices ratified by a popular vote underscores his power.

Side by side with these features, however, the constitution also provides for a fifty-member National Assembly. Elected every four years, the NA is endowed with significant constitutional prerogatives. It is in charge of passing the country's laws. Although the emir can veto legislation approved by the NA by refusing to sign it, parliament can override the emir's veto by a two-thirds vote.[4] The NA is given particular authority in matters related to the budget and foreign affairs. Under the constitution, the NA must debate the budget and approve all government expenditures. It must ratify treaties related to war and peace, alliances, the use of natural resources, and financial obligations. The NA is allowed to discuss any issue it deems appropriate, including the cabinet's policies and actions. To that end, Kuwaiti legislators are granted numerous constitutional protections against arrest or prosecution by the government. No member of parliament (MP) can be prosecuted unless the NA has suspended his immunity.

Any MP can request specific information from a minister, and the answer must be forthcoming within a week. If unsatisfied by the government's explanation, MPs can express their objections and ask for clarification. At the initiative of only five of its members, the legislature can even call for a general debate on the issue. Although the NA cannot pass a vote of no-confidence in the cabinet, it can do so for ministers individually. Parliament's ability to request the resignation of ministers is in part a by-product of its ability to question them and investigate their conduct.[5] Upon the request of ten of its members, the NA can ask that a specific minister be interpellated.[6] Finally, although the emir is empowered to designate his successor, his choice has to be ratified by the NA through a majority vote.

The question emerges as to why Emir Abdallah al-Salim Al-Sabah approved a constitution that gave so much power to an elected parliament. It is true that the restrictive electoral law adopted in November 1962 was bound to limit parliament's ability to serve as a vehicle for popular participation in decisionmaking. The right to vote was restricted to male citizens over the age of twenty-one, whose families had lived in Kuwait since at least 1920. Women were excluded, and so were male Kuwaiti citizens whose parents or grandparents had arrived in Kuwait only after 1920. But even though it was to be elected by a small percentage of the emirate's total population, the National Assembly had been given significant powers by the new constitution. Four reasons can be put forward to explain this.

First, Emir Abdallah al-Salim al-Sabah was well known for his liberal tendencies. (As crown prince, he had chaired Kuwait's first legislative assembly in 1938 before it was dissolved by the emir.) Second, he correctly perceived the importance of having an elected parliament to provide avenues for political expression. By the 1960s, Kuwait had a very significant and politicized intelligentsia. The merchants, although not as active as two decades earlier, also remained a powerful force. The emir understood that the ruling family could not deny this middle class a voice in public affairs; otherwise, dissent might take the form of antiregime activities. In this context, parliament could work as a shock absorber—providing the opposition with a way of letting off steam. It also would help legitimize the rule of the al-Sabah, by giving the seal of popular consent to it.

The third reason is that the decision to create representative institutions was heavily influenced by long-standing Iraqi claims to Kuwait. Within days of Kuwait's becoming independent, Iraq threatened to invade the country (on the ground that, under the Ottoman Empire, Kuwait had been part of the *wilaya* of Basra). Against this backdrop, a constitution that conferred significant prerogatives upon an elected parliament was intended to help muster domestic support in the face of a serious regional threat. Kuwaitis, it was hoped, would realize that the relative political freedoms they enjoyed under the new constitution would likely disappear under Iraqi rule, and they therefore would rally around the regime (which they indeed proceeded to do).

The fourth and most important reason was that Emir Abdallah al-Salim was wise enough to understand that a representative assembly would foster national integration, establish Kuwait as a nation-state, and legitimize the rule of the al-Sabah. One is reminded here of Bertrand De Jouvenel's and A. F. Pollard's insights into the reasons that had driven the King of England to convene a parliament.

> A parliament is needed to take any decision of importance. The reason is not that the King is not entitled to take decisions of importance without parliament, but that he is under the practical necessity of convoking this assembly because it consists of the men whose goodwill and entire support are necessary to the success of any plan whatsoever. (De Jouvenel 1957: 176)

> Parliament was the means of making the English nation and the English state. There was an England centuries before there was a Parliament, but that England was little more than a geographical expression. It was hardly a nation, still less a state. Prior to the establishment and working of Parliament, England was an organization of feudal forces involving local and class associations, but not national association. (Pollard 1964: 4–9)

This same logic applies to Kuwait. Without an elected assembly to embody the nation and reflect a measure of popular consent to his rule, the emir of Kuwait (or for that matter King Abdallah of Transjordan) could hardly claim that he governed a country. At the most, he was first among equals presiding over a collection of tribes and extended families. An assembly made up of representatives of the people was as critical to the making of Kuwait and to the legitimacy of the al-Sabah as it had been to the making of England and the consolidation of its monarchy in an earlier era.

Parliamentary Politics up to the Iraqi Invasion

The elections to Kuwait's first National Assembly took place on January 29, 1963. Additional elections were held in 1967, 1971, and 1975, but in 1976 the emir suspended parliament. He reopened it following elections in 1981 but dissolved it once again in 1986. As its disbanding on two occasions in a decade suggests, Kuwait's parliament has had a turbulent history. Nevertheless, throughout the period under review, it helped make the emirate "the closest thing to democracy between Israel and India" (Graz 1992: 89). Then as today, it functioned as the central arena in which the defining issue in Kuwaiti politics—how democratic should the emirate be?—played itself out.

The First Phase (1963–1976)

From the moment it convened, parliament quickly asserted itself. Close examination of its proceedings from 1963 to 1976 shows a lively National Assembly actively participating in the formulation of public policies. The members appeared to be extremely well informed about the issues. They also showed themselves to be very resourceful, often unearthing critical information not made public by the government. Legislative debates were usually vivid. Outside observers who witnessed them were repeatedly struck by their honesty, openness, and frankness. Attendance was high, since the National Assembly's internal rules penalized unauthorized absences and since parliament could not meet unless a majority of its members were present.

Although parties were illegal, the political preferences of candidates to parliament were well known. Therefore, after joining the legislature, new MPs would usually attach themselves to one of several political blocs. From 1963 to 1976, three main blocs could be discerned. The first consisted of tribal supporters of the ruling family. During the 1960s, the regime granted citizenship to large numbers of bedouins and offered them various advantages—low-income housing, social services, and jobs in the bureaucracy and the army. In effect, the government used material incentives to turn tribes into political allies. As a result, representatives of these tribes became the backbone of support for the ruling family in parliament. Members of Kuwait's business oligarchy formed a second important bloc in parliament. Although this bloc was not homogenous, it included primarily independent and moderate reformist elements intent on pressing the government to become more accountable and to open up the political process. The third and most vocal group consisted of deputies with pan-Arab and leftist sympathies. Led by the articulate Dr. Ahmad al-Khatib, this bloc served as a mouthpiece for the aspirations of many intellectuals, university professors, and professionals. It mounted fierce criticisms of government policies and Kuwait's social and political order. It energetically pushed its agenda for internal reforms and advocated support for the Palestinian cause and "antiimperialist" forces in the region. Its members openly sympathized with Egyptian president Gamal Abdel Nasser's call for nonalignment, Arab unity, and economic justice.

Because of the diversity of political and social forces represented in it, parliament provided an avenue through which bedouins, intellectuals, professionals, and the business community were all able to express themselves on issues ranging from the annual budget to women's rights and the proper role of religion in politics and society (Crystal 1992: 100). Through their questioning of government policies or the actions of individual ministers, MPs were able to hold the cabinet accountable (even though criticisms of the prerogatives and legitimacy of the royal family remained beyond the pale). By publicizing instances of corruption, anticonstitutional behavior, misuse of public funds, violation of due process, and abuse of authority, the NA operated as a vital check on arbitrary rule. In addition to initiating and passing laws, it weighed heavily on the government's foreign policy choices. For instance, pressure from the Arab nationalist opposition in the NA induced the government to express support for the Palestinian cause.

That pressure also explains why the emirate consistently refrained from policies that could be characterized as being too pro-Western and why it repeatedly sought to distance itself from British and U.S. positions in the region. Similarly, many of the most important debates in the Assembly revolved around oil policy and had a critical impact on it. In the early 1970s, opposition members played an instrumental role in the radicalization of the government's oil policy. Parliamentary pressures convinced the government to put a ceiling on the country's oil production in 1972 and to nationalize the Kuwait Oil Company two years later.

Because legislative debates were widely reported in the press, the NA also performed an important educational function. It gave the public a better understanding of domestic and foreign policy issues, regional developments, and the policies of the superpowers in the region. It raised issues that subsequently made their way into newspapers and daily conversations. In many instances, had parliament not existed, these issues would not have become part of the national political agenda. For similar reasons, parliament contributed to a vibrant associational life. Kuwaiti associations—particularly those with Arab nationalist leanings—looked to the National Assembly for inspiration and information.

Most important—and as a by-product of the functions that have just been examined—the Kuwaiti National Assembly played a vital legitimizing function. Paradoxically, through the very act of circumscribing the authority of the al-Sabah and the cabinet, the parliament helped the former legitimize their rule by projecting the image of a polity that was far more open and participatory than most others in the Arab world. This characteristic highlights the double-edged nature of legislatures in family-based regimes such as Kuwait. On the one hand, an outspoken assembly curtails the freedom of maneuver of the ruling family. On the other hand, such an assembly is also essential to the long-term political survival of that family, because it provides a controlled forum for the expression of dissent. By forcing the cabinet and individual ministers to provide justifications for their policies and actions, Kuwait's legislature also helped limit corruption and incompetence in government. Without parliament's relentless striving to bring a measure of governmental accountability, Kuwait would likely have experienced more nepotism, mismanagement of public resources, and abuses of power and authority.

Parliament's First Dissolution (1976)

In August 1976, the emir suddenly disbanded the legislature elected a year earlier. In justifying his decision, he claimed that the deadlock between parliament and the cabinet had led to governmental immobilism. He blamed this situation on the National Assembly, contending that it had been far too slow in acting on important pieces of legislation and that it had abused its authority through devices such as the interrogation of ministers and the passing of motions of no-confidence in the ministers. Such arguments only captured part of the emir's motives. In reality, the shutdown of parliament could be explained by two features of the NA's behavior in 1975–1976.

To begin with, the leftist and Arab nationalist opposition in the NA no longer merely sought to scrutinize the work of the cabinet; it now extended its ambitions to overseeing the performance and the expenditures of the ruling family. This was seen by the al-Sabah as a violation of the previous, tacit understanding between the regime and the opposition. According to that implicit compact, the opposition would refrain from directly criticizing the ruling family and would not seek to use parliament to assert control over the al-Sabah's expenditures.

The second basic reason for the disbanding of the NA in 1976 was the civil war in Lebanon and the resolutions that parliament adopted toward this issue. The ruling family was understandably disturbed by the possibility that what was happening in Lebanon might be repeated in Kuwait. After all, many observers believed that Lebanon's civil war had been made possible, in part, by that country's liberal democratic atmosphere, which they viewed as having been abused by certain groups to encourage civil strife. To the extent that Kuwait presented many of the same features as pre–civil war Lebanon—including a free press and an active parliament—might the freedom of expression that Kuwaitis enjoyed not result in the same fragmentation that was leading Lebanon to chaos? This concern was all the more pronounced considering that Kuwait's pan-Arab and leftist groups were developing ties to external actors and were receiving strong support from Palestinians and other alien Arab residents in Kuwait. In Lebanon, a similar situation had embroiled the country in regional feuds, turned it into a pawn in inter-Arab politics, and led to growing foreign interference. A repeat of that scenario was conceivable in Kuwait. Many commentators feared that, as in Lebanon, segments of the domestic opposition might be encouraged by foreign countries to disrupt the existing political order.

Increasing connections between the Kuwaiti left and regional opposition groups in Bahrain and Oman were also harming the al-Sabah's relations with the regimes of those and other countries in the Gulf. Saudi Arabia, in particular, was growing impatient with the apparent inability or unwillingness of the Kuwaiti government to curb the rhetoric, in parliament and elsewhere, of some of Kuwait's most militant political groups (Crystal 1992: 97). Members of Kuwait's parliament had always been too vocal for the comfort of the Saudis. In 1975–1976, increasing criticisms of Riyadh in the Kuwaiti parliament convinced the Saudis to step up pressures on the al-Sabah to crack down on dissent.

Finally, the NA was also complicating Kuwait's relation with Syria. Shortly before its dissolution, parliament had passed a resolution condemning Syria's military intervention in Lebanon and calling for a cutoff of aid to Damascus. The ruling family was especially disturbed by this highly publicized resolution, for it felt vulnerable to retaliation by Hafiz al-Asad, whom it feared might seek to destabilize the emirate.

In short, the National Assembly was dissolved because of its direct criticisms of the al-Sabah and because of its attempt to extend its authority to include issues considered by the ruling family to be its reserved domain: foreign policy, inter-Arab politics, and national security. In this context, the emir had two choices. The first would have been to accept a reduced role for the ruling family in running the affairs of the country. The second was to disband the legislature. That he chose the latter option underlines the seriousness of the threat that the assertion of parliamentary authority had come to pose to the ruling family.

A Second Try (1981–1986)

By 1980, it had become clear to the ruling family that the vital political functions that parliament had performed until 1976—creating bridges between state and society, providing avenues for political participation, providing for popular input into decisionmaking, allowing the opposition to let off steam—had not been fully taken over by any other institution since the National Assembly's disbanding. This was all the more worrisome considering that the Iranian revolution and Khomeini's attempt to export it were creating a major new regional threat. Kuwait, with its Shiite minority (a quarter of the population) and geographical proximity to Iran, seemed particularly vulnerable. Significantly, Shiite as well as Sunni fundamentalists in the emirate were becoming more active. It was vital, therefore, that the ruling family be able to point to strong domestic support for the regime, but the absence of representative institutions actually caused the government to appear isolated.

This situation, as much as the numerous petitions he received requesting the reconvening of the NA, prompted the emir to reactivate parliament. During 1979 and in early 1980, he held consultations with politicians, members of the press, and representatives of civil society. He even set up an advisory committee, entrusting it with making recommendations on how to improve the country's increasingly tense political situation. Throughout this process, he heard the same basic message: The country had to return to parliamentary life. Ultimately, he decided to oblige. In December 1980, he announced that elections would be held in early 1981 (Crystal 1992: 97–98).

To ensure an outcome favorable to the regime, the government passed a new electoral law that involved substantial gerrymandering. Until then, the country had been divided into 10 districts, each sending 5 members to the legislature. There were now to be 25 districts, each electing 2 MPs. Most of the new districts had been created in predominantly tribal areas, a stronghold of the regime. Altogether, "tribal districts" now accounted for 31 seats in parliament. By contrast, the seats allotted to predominantly Shiite districts had decreased from 10 to 4. Most important, the liberal and leftist opposition remained competitive in only 15 districts; even there, it faced strong rivals (Gavrielides 1987: 165).

The election results were devastating to the liberal-leftist alliance: Only 3 of its candidates were elected.[7] By contrast, the number of deputies from tribal areas rose from 22 in 1975 to 27 in 1981. But with its efforts to undercut pan-Arab, leftist tendencies, the government had unwisely encouraged an Islamic revival. Shiite and Sunni Islamist candidates had fared well, with the latter becoming the leading opposition bloc in the NA. Soon, members drawn from this fundamentalist following would introduce bills calling for the *sharia* to become the exclusive source of legislation, for a ban on public Christmas celebrations, and for new restrictions on women's behavior in public places.

In the elections held in 1985, as a result of several factors, the liberal-leftist opposition engineered an impressive comeback. First, the opposition had endeavored to present only one candidate in those districts where it stood a chance to win. Second, it had run tribal candidates with liberal-leftist leaning in predominantly tribal districts. Third, it had been able to capitalize on mounting discontent with governmental corruption. Finally, it had benefited from the public outcry generated by the 1982 crash of an informal stock market known as the Suq al-Manakh. Eventually, candidates with strong reformist, pan-Arab, or leftist views captured 13 seats and Sunni fundamentalists 6. The progovernment bloc, for its part, consisted mostly of 21 "tribal" MPs.

From the beginning, the 1985 parliament proved very assertive. To the surprise of many observers, the Islamic fundamentalist and pan-Arab, leftist MPs often found common ground in blocking government bills and in sponsoring legislation or resolutions against the cabinet. They immediately raised the highly sensitive issue of corruption in high places. At the initiative of Islamist MPs, the liberal-minded education minister came under pressure to resign. Simultaneously, some MPs began to interfere in the work of the Education Ministry. Without the permission of the education minister, they went to Kuwait University and questioned its president and admissions officers about tenure decisions and admission practices. This particular incident was followed by several other such instances of MPs' encroaching on the work and the prerogatives of the executive branch.

Most important, opposition MPs took a strong stand against a state bailout of investors who had been involved in the collapse of Suq al-Manakh. In particular, they publicized evidence of wrongdoings by the Fund for the Relief of Small Investors (FRSI), set up to compensate small investors who had incurred losses in the 1982 crash. Evidence had soon surfaced that the fund was actually being used to write off, at taxpayers' expense, the debts of extremely wealthy and well-connected individuals who could easily have paid what they owed. The matter was all the more sensitive in that prominent members of the ruling family were known to have benefited from the fund's largesse. This, however, did not prevent the parliamentary opposition from aggressively questioning ministers on the issue. In fact, the NA was soon able to force the resignation of the minister of justice, a member of the ruling family whose son had won compensation after he had been classified as a "small investor."[8] By then, the Council of Ministers was accusing MPs of using the oral questions merely to embarrass the government and to achieve short-term political gains.

Such criticisms, however, failed to deter the NA. It soon demanded the publication of the list of all debtors who had been compensated by the fund. It then began interpellating several ministers, asking for the resignation of the oil minister and the interior minister, both of whom belonged to the ruling family. The two ministers were blamed by the NA for inadequate security at the oil fields, after bomb attacks on oil installations had almost resulted in the closing down of the country's oil industry.[9]

On July 1, 1986, the prime minister (the crown prince) finally submitted to the emir the resignation of his cabinet, citing the NA's relentless attacks on ministers, which he argued made it impossible for the executive branch to operate. The emir responded by disbanding parliament two days later. In justifying his decision, he pointed out that the NA's tactics had paralyzed government and therefore undermined stability at a time when the country was faced by difficult regional circumstances (the Iran-Iraq war was raging and was being felt in the emirate in the form of bombings and assassination attempts carried out by members of pro-Iranian groups). Even then, the ruler was careful not to cut off all bridges to parliamentarians. In the new cabinet he appointed, four members were former deputies (Zahlan 1989: 44).

The factors that led to the disbanding of the NA in 1986 bear a striking resemblance to those that had prompted the emir to suspend it ten years earlier. In both instances, the decision came about as a result of a combination of internal and external causes. Internally, the parliamentary opposition had once again gone too far. It had directly and repeatedly attacked members of the al-Sabah family and sought to use parliament to embarrass them. It had failed to exercise restraint at a time when the emirate was already hard hit by a growing economic crisis triggered by the collapse of oil prices in 1986. Furthermore, as in 1976, security concerns generated by a tense regional situation also contributed to the assembly's demise. Particularly important in this regard was the wave of political violence that rocked Kuwait in 1985–1986, including an attempt on the life of the emir himself. The unstable regional environment, fueled by the Iran-Iraq war and replete with domestic repercussions, convinced the ruler that the country could no longer afford the divisiveness that the NA seemed to exacerbate.

In any event, the tense situation in the Gulf was pushing Kuwait to move closer to Saudi Arabia; this, in turn, was forcing the emir to become more receptive to long-standing pressures by Riyadh to shut down the NA (Crystal 1992: 99). Saudi rulers had long held negative views toward Kuwait's parliamentary experience. They regarded the existence of an elected, outspoken National Assembly as a bad influence on their own people and as a potential source of instability in a country adjacent to theirs. Moreover, Kuwait's parliament had taken a leading role in opposing some of the prerogatives (particularly in the area of collective security) that Saudi Arabia had attempted to give to the Gulf Cooperation Council when the latter was established in 1981 (Khalaf 1984: 250–251). Officials in Riyadh therefore expected that the disbanding of Kuwait's legislature would eliminate an important source of resistance to Saudi influence over the smaller Gulf states.

The Call for the Restoration of Parliament (1986–1990)

When the emir disbanded parliament in 1986, he also clamped down on the press, suspended parts of the constitution, and outlawed public meetings of more than five people. Thus, the closing of the National Assembly was part of a much broader governmental crackdown. The emir ruled by decree, and the al-Sabah were given a greater share of cabinet positions than ever before.

Meanwhile, evidence mounted of mismanagement, corruption, and incompetence in government and within the ruling family.

This authoritarian turn, however, encountered strong resistance from several segments of Kuwaiti society. The merchants, in particular, reasserted themselves. As discussed earlier, they had once been the most important source of opposition to the ruling family, but since the 1950s they had assumed a lower political profile. In the mid-1980s, however, the deal that they had struck with the ruling family came apart as a result of several factors. First, the collapse of oil prices led to a reduction in government contracts and benefits. Second, the merchants were disturbed by the increasing presence of members of the ruling family in the commercial sector. After all, the implicit bargain between the al-Sabah and the merchants had been that the former would leave business to the latter, in exchange for which the merchants would accept the ruling family's political dominance. By the 1980s, however, some of the younger members of the ruling family were becoming more and more involved in business activities, thus encroaching on the merchants' turf. These al-Sabah, furthermore, were taking unfair advantage of their privileged access to government in order to cut out some of their private-sector competitors. This generated a great deal of resentment from the merchants, who were eager to enhance governmental accountability and enforce constitutional checks on the ruling family's ability to engage in illicit practices. More generally, merchants—just like other segments of Kuwait's well-educated urban middle class—were becoming less willing to simply be bought off by the regime.

In the months that followed the August 1988 cease-fire that ended the Iran-Iraq war, prominent merchants joined with professionals, intellectuals, former parliamentarians, and even government officials in beginning to agitate for reforms. The demands of this prodemocracy movement soon focused on the restoration of parliament, the full implementation of the 1962 constitution, and the lifting of restrictions on free speech and on the right to peaceful assembly. Leading figures in this coalition found a way to circumvent the official ban on political gatherings. To spread their views and exchange ideas with each other, they began to use the traditional Kuwaiti institution known as *diwaniyyat*.[10] Former members of parliament as well as other political activists began to use *diwaniyyat* held in their homes to mobilize support for change and coordinate action. Petitions were circulated and signed by scores of prominent Kuwaitis (Crystal 1992: 117).

By 1989, the prodemocracy movement was engaged in a protracted political battle with the ruling family. In January 1990, the streets of Kuwait witnessed an unusual event: a demonstration involving several thousand people calling for the reopening of the National Assembly. Even more unusual in this city-state, which had long been known for its peaceful character and relative tolerance of political dissent, was the government's violent response to this event, which was broken up by riot police. Images of baton-wielding policemen dispersing a crowd that had merely been requesting that the government abide by the constitution created dismay in the emirate. It compounded the anger that had already been created by previous use of force by the authorities, who on several earlier occasions had used tear gas and police dogs to disperse prodemocracy meetings.

As it became evident that repression could not contain the prodemocracy movement, the emir adopted a more conciliatory tone. On January 20, 1990, he went on national television to invite the opposition to participate in a national dialogue and to inform the country that he had entrusted the crown prince—the prime minister—with the task of opening negotiations with advocates of political reform. Even though the emir let it be known that he opposed the restoration of the National Assembly—on the ground that the emirate could not afford to return to the climate of confrontation that had led to the 1976 and 1986 dissolutions—he acknowledged the need for some other mechanisms to ensure greater public participation in decisionmaking.

On April 23, 1990, the emir finally announced the establishment of an advisory National Council (Majlis al-Watani). He presented this institution as a compromise between the status quo and the reconvening of the National Assembly. The council was to have a four-year term and consist of 75 members: 50 elected and 25 appointed by the emir. Its role would be purely consultative: It would not pass legislation, and its opinions would not be binding on the emir or the cabinet. The council's most important task would be to study the advisability and feasibility of a restoration of parliament. In the event the council were to conclude in favor of reconvening the NA, it would have to suggest how this might be done without resulting in a new crisis pitting the executive branch against the legislature. The council was even empowered to propose constitutional changes. In the emir's words, it was expected "to undertake an evaluation of our parliamentary experience and propose steps for the future march of democracy." Elections to the council were to be held on June 10.

Leaders of the prodemocracy movement immediately denounced the proposed council on several grounds. First, they argued that it would delay by another four years at least the long-awaited return to the 1962 constitution. This was unacceptable to the opposition, which called instead for the immediate reconvening of parliament. Second, since the council proposed by the emir was to have a purely consultative role, it would be unable to act as a check on executive power. This seemed even more inevitable considering that progovernment politicians would make up a substantial share of the council's 50 elected members and an even larger proportion of the 25 chosen by the emir. Most worrisome was the possibility that the council would suggest a fundamental revision of the 1962 constitution. In light of the proregime bias that the opposition expected would characterize the council, such a constitutional revision would no doubt seek to institutionalize a weakening of the legislature and further concentrate power in the hands of the cabinet.

Accordingly, the opposition called for a boycott of the elections to the Majlis al-Watani. In response, the government began arresting leaders of the prodemocracy movement. In June, amid growing political tensions, elections were finally held. Turnout was unusually low. Since only progovernment tribal leaders had been willing to compete for the elected seats, the council ended up being dominated by forces sympathetic to the regime. Less than two months later, Iraq invaded a country that had become so caught up in its internal battles that it had failed to appreciate the magnitude of the threat posed by its powerful neighbor.

The 1992 Elections

When Iraqi tanks rolled into Kuwait in the early hours of August 2, 1990, the emirate was engaged in a protracted battle over its political future. The Iraqi occupation had the effect of temporarily pushing internal disagreements aside, to permit creation of the national unity needed to free the country from the grip of Saddam Hussein. But far from slowing down the forces of democratization, the Iraqi occupation would speed them up.

The Jiddah Compact

By the fall of 1990, the ruling family was under great pressure to promise that the liberation of Kuwait would be accompanied by a significant political opening. Those Kuwaitis who (unlike most of the al-Sabah) had stayed in Kuwait to organize the resistance to Iraqi forces had to be convinced that their sacrifices would not be in vain. The emir had to persuade them that the ousting of Iraqi troops would not be followed by a return to "politics as usual." Furthermore, from exile, the opposition was now petitioning the emir to formally declare his commitment to a democratization of political life in a postoccupation Kuwait. Finally, the ruling family was aware of the need to defuse criticisms in the United States of President Bush's apparent willingness to risk an armed confrontation with Iraq for the sake of freeing Kuwait. Many Americans felt uneasy about the prospect of becoming involved in an armed conflict in the Gulf merely to bring an emir back to power. They felt, in the words of *New York Times* reporter Thomas Friedman, that the United States should not go to war "to make the world safe for feudalism." By indicating a willingness to engage in real political reforms after Kuwait's liberation, the emir could facilitate the task of a U.S. administration that held the future of his country and regime in its hands. Just as important, the promise of democratization seemed necessary to unify the country behind the emir at this time of national emergency.

It is in this context that the emir sponsored a highly publicized three-day conference in Jiddah, Saudi Arabia, in October 1990. It brought together some twelve hundred representatives of all major Kuwaiti political groupings, including key opposition figures that had long been at odds with the al-Sabah. The conference concluded with a deal being made between the ruling family and the opposition. The latter agreed to stand by the emir, reaffirm its loyalty toward him, and acknowledge him as the legitimate ruler of the country. In exchange, the emir promised that liberation would be followed by far-reaching political reforms that would include the restoration of parliament—a concession that, as we saw, the emir had staunchly resisted until the Iraqi invasion.

The Setting for the Elections

The legislative elections of October 5, 1992, were thus a fulfillment of a promise that had been made two years earlier. In the meantime, the trauma of the invasion had greatly politicized Kuwaiti society. Debates were now raging on subjects such as the regime's responsibility for the Iraqi occupation; the ineptitude displayed by prominent members of the al-Sabah in the days leading up to August 2, 1990, and the mismanagement of Kuwait's overseas investments. With the exception of the ruling family and its most ardent supporters, everyone seemed to agree on the need for far-reaching political reforms. The consensus was that since the al-Sabah had failed to defend the country in 1990, they could no longer claim exclusive control over matters of national security, from defense and foreign affairs to the management of the country's financial assets. The government, it was clear, would find it difficult to return to its earlier practice of buying political loyalty through the distribution of material rewards; consequently, the ruling family had to prepare itself to share power, even in politically sensitive areas.

Campaigning for the 1992 elections was lively and vigorous. Numerous public meetings were held every day, and candidates discussed vital issues free of governmental interference. Even though only about 81,400 were allowed to vote, a very large number of those not eligible (including women and naturalized citizens) made their voices heard throughout the campaign. The intensity and quality of the public debate underscored the fact that the demand for political liberalization had such momentum that the regime could not stop it. And even though political parties remained forbidden, the various candidates were affiliated with loosely organized factions that had clear political platforms. These factions fell into three main categories: former Arab nationalists, reformists, and Islamists.[11]

Former Arab nationalists were mostly affiliated with the Kuwait Democratic Forum (Al-minbar al-dimuqrati al-kuwaiti), or KDF. The KDF was formed in March 1991, immediately following the liberation of Kuwait, as an alliance of two main Arab nationalist groups with roots in the 1960s. It included well-known and experienced figures such as Ahmad al-Khatib, Abdullah al-Nibari, and Jassim al-Qottammi, who had led the opposition in previous parliaments. The KDF's main challenge was to develop new ideas, in the wake of the diminishing appeal of pan-Arabism and leftist ideologies and the fact that many of its leaders were still tainted by their earlier embrace of the Palestinian cause.

Reformists were themselves divided into three main factions: the Constitutional Bloc (al-tajammu' al-dusturi), the Independents (al-mustaqillun), and the Parliamentarian Group (takattul al-nuwwab). The Constitutional Bloc was the main political vehicle for the wealthiest merchant families in Kuwait. Significantly, it was chaired by the president of the Kuwaiti Chamber of Commerce, Abdul Aziz al-Saqr. Among its members were the heads of Kuwait's major corporations, banks, and insurance companies. The faction known as the Independents recruited mostly among professionals and the intelligentsia, particularly lawyers and academics. Few of its members had previously held public office. By contrast, the Parliamentarian Group brought together former MPs. Formed in 1986, in the wake of the disbanding of the National Assembly, the Parliamentarian Group was headed by Ahmad al-Sa'adun, a well-known, respected, and credible opposition figure who had been speaker of parliament when the latter was suspended. The Parliamentarian Group was a particularly heterogeneous coalition whose members ranged from militantly secular to religious. However, since 1986, they had all been united in their demand that parliament be reconvened and that the emir abide by the 1962 constitution.

Islamists formed a third important political category. They, too, were divided into three main factions: the Islamic Constitutional Movement (ICM—al-haraka al-dusturiyya al-islamiyya), the Islamic Popular Alliance (IPA—al-tajammu' al-islami al-sha'bi), and the National Islamic Coalition (NIC). The Islamic Constitutional Movement was created in March 1991. It developed out of a moderate Sunni group, the Association for Social Reform (al-jami'a li'l-islah al-ijtima'i), which had gained prestige and credibility through its prominent role in the resistance to the Iraqi occupation. The ICM represented the Muslim Brotherhood in Kuwait. A highly organized group, it maintained generally good relations with the government and sought to reform the system from within. Many of its leaders held important positions in the bureaucracy and the public sector. The Islamic Popular Alliance was far more hostile to the government and lacked ties to the political establishment in general. An older organization, which had run in the 1981 and 1985 elections, it served as an umbrella for several small Sunni fundamentalist groups united in their call for the implementation of the *sharia* and an Islamization of Kuwaiti society and politics. During the Iraqi occupation, these groups had been very active in distributing food and other vital supplies to the population. Unlike the ICM, the IPA favored the creation of an Islamic state. The National Islamic Coalition was the only predominantly Shiite group and included both fundamentalist and liberal secular elements. It tended to be quite progressive on social issues, with several of its members advocating granting women the right to vote.

Candidates affiliated with the NIC campaigned on a platform centered on promoting civic equality and creating more opportunities for the Shiites, who by 1992 represented close to 30 percent of the population.

The Results

The result of the elections was a major political upset. Opposition and independent candidates captured thirty-five of the fifty seats in parliament. Several progovernment candidates believed to be "shoo-ins" were defeated, whereas most of the prominent personalities in the prodemocracy and Islamic opposition camps were elected. This outcome came as a real shock to the ruling family and as a pleasant surprise to even the most optimistic members of the opposition. For the first time since independence, the government would be unable to rely on a majority in the National Assembly.

The elections had proven that the regime would find it increasingly difficult to buy off political demands with financial rewards. Prior to the vote, the government had engaged in a massive effort to curry the favor of the electorate through such measures as writing off billions of dollars in mortgage and consumer loans; giving $2,000 grants to every individual who had been in Kuwait during the occupation; boosting monthly child allowances by 75 percent (to $175); raising by 50 percent state assistance to widows, orphans, and the poor; and implementing a 25 percent across-the-board salary increase for all public employees (nine out of ten Kuwaitis were employed by the state at the time). Despite these attempts to appease the electorate through the distribution of material benefits, the election had delivered a major blow to the government. Clearly, Kuwaiti society had become far more politicized, hence less susceptible to being co-opted by the state.

In Kuwait City and its surrounding areas, opposition and independent candidates had made a clean sweep. This showed that the various segments of the urban middle class—businessmen, professionals, intellectuals—were united in their desire for greater governmental accountability. Progovernment candidates did well only in the emirate's primarily tribal, outlying areas. Even there, however, the erosion of support for the al-Sabah was marked. Nine candidates identified with the opposition, or leaning toward it, were elected in bedouin-dominated districts, which one observer saw as "an indication that the opposition, after . . . winning all of the urban areas, is now integrating tribal areas into its machine" (Ghabra 1994: 113). The Islamist tendency, too, had made significant inroads into tribal constituencies that had long been regarded as government strongholds.

Revealing as well was the poor performance of the so-called service-candidates—old-style politicians who used their ties to the ruling family to distribute favors and benefits in exchange for votes. These political bosses, who had dominated past elections, were soundly defeated in almost every district in which they ran. That, too, highlighted the new limits on co-optation and depoliticization. It demonstrated that, in the new Kuwait, patronage from the government was no longer as important as the ability to address issues and articulate a program. In the words of a Kuwaiti politician who ran in 1992 in one of the country's remote tribal districts, "people are more enlightened than before. Their questions are different. In past elections, they were interested only in services. Now they ask questions about our investments abroad and our defense and security."[12]

The elections had also demonstrated the appeal of political Islam in the emirate. The IC Movement (moderate Sunnis affiliated with the Muslim Brotherhood) and the IPA (Sunni fundamentalists calling for an Islamic state) had won 3 seats each. In addition, at least 8 independents had been elected with the support of one or several of the religious groups. Meanwhile, the NIC (Shiites generally progressive on social issues, not all of whom are necessarily religious) had captured 3 seats. In short, parliament would now feature a group of approximately 15 deputies for whom religious issues were important. Although their positions on these issues varied a great deal, they could be expected to push cultural themes inside the new parliament. By the same token, although many if not most Islamist MPs were expected to join forces with secular independents, liberals, and leftists on issues related to governmental accountability and corruption in high places, they were seen as closer to the government on cultural and social matters.

Finally, the elections had consecrated the decline of the older, Arab nationalist tendencies to the benefit of a more accommodationist and reformist opposition. Thus, the KDF captured only 2 seats. This poor showing was mitigated by the fact that the KDF's two elected members were Ahmad al-Khatib and Abdullah al-Nibari—two political heavyweights and critics of the government who had much legislative experience and could be expected to exercise influence in the new parliament. Still, far more influential than the KDF would be the Independents, with 13 seats, and the Parliamentarian Group, with 10 seats (including one for Ahmad al-Sa'adun, the former speaker).[13] Although these two groups were quite heterogeneous, their members did not share the pan-Arab and confrontational approach of the KDF and were expected to be more flexible in dealing with the cabinet.

The Reassertion of Parliament (1992–1996)

Prior to parliament's second suspension in 1986, the emir had usually chosen only two or three ministers from among MPs. During the 1992 campaign, the opposition had repeatedly demanded that more NA members be selected for cabinet positions. Some had even called for half of all ministries—including sensitive ones such as the interior, defense, or foreign affairs—to go to deputies. Several opposition candidates had gone so far as to argue that the prime minister should no longer be the crown prince but an elected member of the NA.

In the wake of the October 1992 elections, the emir responded to these demands by giving six ministries—oil, justice, commerce and industry, education, Islamic affairs, labor and social affairs—to new MPs. Five of these MPs belonged to the opposition.[14] The emir's decision showed the ruling family's willingness to reach out to the opposition. Equally interesting was the latter's reaction. It could easily have dismissed the emir's concessions as insignificant; indeed, that is probably what it would have done in earlier times. Instead, although stressing that it had hoped for more, the opposition refrained from contesting the cabinet's composition, and it dropped the issue of separating the office of prime minister from that of the crown prince. This was an early indication that, in the new parliament, the opposition would refrain from the confrontational tactics of the past.

Still, parliament quickly showed that it would not be a rubber-stamp legislature. It elected as its speaker the outspoken Ahmad al-Sa'adun, who had held the position in the assembly that had been suspended in 1986. Soon afterward, repeated clashes took place between al-Sa'adun and the prime minister, Crown Prince Shaikh Saad al-Abdullah al-Salem al-Sabah. On several occasions, the crown prince—who made no mystery of his disdain for the legislature—tried to circumvent the NA, but his efforts were thwarted by al-Sa'adun. Parliament also kept alive the questions that had been raised by the government's response to the 1982 Suq al-Manakh crash. In a move designed to embarrass the ruling family, the NA's Finance and Economic Committee advocated the publication of the names of those who had benefited from the government bailout.

The NA asserted its prerogatives most forcefully in matters related to the use of public funds and the management of the country's overseas investments. These were areas that until then had been considered to be a prerogative of the ruling family, even though the constitution clearly gave parliament a right of oversight over them. The al-Sabah, now on the defensive, could no longer prevent the NA from adopting a more aggressive stance toward these issues. Significantly, as soon as it was reconvened, the NA launched an investigation into what came to be known as the Kuwait Investment Office (KIO) scandal.

The KIO is a London-based, Kuwaiti government agency in charge of investing the country's oil revenues. Since Kuwait's financial future depends to a large extent on how wisely the country uses proceeds from oil sales, the KIO is a vital institution. How effectively and honestly it is managed became all the more critical when, as a result of the need to finance the war with Iraq and the reconstruction effort, Kuwait's overseas assets declined from about $100 billion in 1989 to a mere $35 billion by 1993. Shortly after the liberation, however, it was disclosed that the KIO had lost an estimated $7 billion as a result of its investments in Group Torras, a Spanish holding company. Other cases pointed to the KIO's tendency to choose dubious partners and buy stocks at inflated prices. MPs as well as newspapers and magazines immediately seized upon the story. Why was the KIO pouring millions of dollars into loss-making Spanish industries? Was it as a result of a series of monumental errors? Or did it suggest, as critics of the government claimed, that officials at the KIO, most of whom were tied to the ruling family, had diverted millions of dollars to private overseas accounts? After all, no one in the KIO could account for where several billions of dollars had gone. The rapidly developing KIO scandal became all the more sensitive when the parliamentary investigation into it pointed to the involvement of Shaikh Fahd Mohammed al-Sabah, the KIO's chairman for more than twenty years and a cousin of the emir. The widening probe into the matter soon involved another cousin of the emir, the former oil minister, Shaikh Ali Khalifa al-Sabah (who had been finance minister between 1982 and 1985 and from June 1990 until April 1991).

The NA's leading role in investigating and publicizing the KIO scandal was highly significant. Prior to the Iraqi invasion, such an action would have been regarded as an unacceptable parliamentary intrusion into matters that were the prerogative of the al-Sabah and the cabinet. It might even have led to the NA's dissolution. Instead, the NA this time was allowed to perform its constitutional role as a watchdog over public investments—even though many of those in charge of managing these investments were members of the al-Sabah. This important development signaled the NA's determination to closely monitor the ruling family's use of public assets for personal enrichment or to buy political support. As such, it represented a direct questioning of what the ruling family had long considered to be "discretionary spending." The very foundations of power and authority in the emirate were thereby being challenged by parliament. Revealing as well was the financial information that, in the context of the parliamentary investigation into the KIO scandal, was provided to members of the NA and then published in newspapers. Until recently, such information would have been considered far too sensitive to be discussed in public. In this as in other respects, therefore, parliament's increasing visibility and influence contributed to an opening of political life that was felt far beyond assembly premises.

Another scandal investigated by the NA involved the Kuwait Oil Tanker Company (KOTC). In late 1992, it was revealed that former executives of the KOTC had embezzled an estimated $100 million. Ultimately, former oil minister Shaikh Ali Khalifa al-Sabah was implicated in the scandal. Shaikh Khalifa was already under fire for his catastrophic handling of the oil dispute that had erupted between Kuwait and Baghdad just prior to the Iraqi invasion in the summer of 1990. Together with the crown prince and the former ministers of defense and foreign affairs, Shaikh Khalifa was blamed for complacency in his response to Iraqi threats. The KOTC scandal made his position even more difficult in the face of repeated and aggressive questioning by NA members.

Yet, for all the publicity that surrounded them, the KIO and KOTC scandals were only two relatively minor manifestations of a much broader phenomenon: parliament's assertion of control over financial and budgetary matters, including its relentless and ultimately successful effort to win access to the accounts of public-sector companies (Aarts 1995). In 1993 and 1994, the NA passed several laws that enabled Parliament to review all expenditures by state-owned companies. One such law now requires all corporations in which the government holds 25 percent or more of the shares to report any changes in investment policies or investment portfolios to official auditors. Delays in reporting can lead to prosecution. Under the same law, officials of state-owned companies who are convicted of misusing public funds can now receive stiff sentences, including life in jail. Furthermore, financial transactions by companies in which the state owns at least 25 percent of the shares must now be ratified by the NA.

Considering that the top decisionmakers of public companies have usually been from the al-Sabah, the law creates yet new constraints on the ruling family's freedom of maneuver. Not surprisingly, it was staunchly opposed by the crown prince and the finance minister. In the end, however, neither could prevent the passing of legislation that forced the government and the ruling family to become more transparent in the management of the emirate's assets. Side by side with parliament's successful effort to pass legislation enabling it to scrutinize expenditures by public companies, it also made headway toward forcing government to fully disclose all revenues and expenditures in the state budget. Although some of these are still not made public, the government has been compelled to become far more forthcoming about details of the budget since 1993.[15]

Beyond budgetary and financial matters, parliamentarians have drawn attention to the structural weaknesses of the country's economy, including the absence of a tax base, the lack of productivity in the public sector, a bloated bureaucracy, the widening gap between state revenues and expenditures, and, more generally, the long-term problems inherent in a country that lives beyond its means, thus mortgaging the economic future of the next generations. In addition to publicizing these issues, parliamentarians have made concrete proposals to address them. Some have advocated privatizing state-owned companies. Others have insisted on the need to introduce some form of taxation. Several have had the political courage to argue in favor of rolling back Kuwait's welfare state (Aarts 1995: 17).

Finally, cultural issues played a prominent role in the debates of the 1992–1996 National Assembly. In 1993, thirty-five MPs signed a petition requesting that the second article of the constitution be changed from "The religion of the state is Islam, and the Islamic sharia shall be *a* main source of legislation" [emphasis added] to "the Islamic sharia shall be *the* main source of legislation" [emphasis added]. Subsequently, some Islamist MPs went so far as to suggest that a new state institution be created, the purpose of which would be "to direct the public to do good and refrain from evil." In both instances, the proposed legislation was defeated. Discussion of the bills did not even go beyond the appropriate committee, since there was not enough support for a debate in the plenary (Ghabra 1994: 116–117). Nevertheless, these and other examples illustrate the determination of Islamist MPs to push for legislation that would Islamize Kuwaiti society (particularly in the areas of the family and education) and inevitably curtail personal freedoms.

In July 1996, Islamist MPs scored an important victory when parliament voted to segregate Kuwait University within five years. Interestingly, the law passed because several independents, liberals, and reformers generally described as secular or part of the prodemocracy bloc in parliament voted in favor of it, in an attempt to secure the support of Islamist voters in the forthcoming parliamentary elections. Ever since parliament had been reconvened in 1992, the Islamic bloc had sought to mandate the separation of men and women in institutions of higher learning. Certainly, the July 1996 law came short of the Islamists' demand that separate educational facilities be created immediately. It gave secularist MPs hope that the next parliament would not look favorably on the prohibition of coeducational institutions and that it would repeal the July 1996 law. Still, this and other such battles in the "gender war" that often dominated the agenda of the 1992–1996 legislature showed that the fault lines in Kuwaiti politics could certainly not be reduced to government versus opposition, prodemocracy forces versus defenders of the status quo, or secularists versus Islamists. The July 1996 law demonstrated not only the importance of cultural and social matters but also the possibility that unexpected alliances might be formed on such issues.

The October 1996 Elections and Their Aftermath

New elections took place on October 7, 1996. A tense regional situation prevailed at the time, because six weeks earlier the regime of Iraqi president Saddam Hussein had deployed troops into the Kurdish "safe haven" in northern Iraq, and the United States had retaliated with missile attacks on military installations in southern Iraq. Despite this background, the campaign was remarkably free of government interference, and the election was fair. This shows the extent to which parliamentary elections have become an institutionalized and vital means for regulating political competition in Kuwait. As in Jordan's case, it would have been inconceivable two decades earlier that the emirate would hold a free and fair election in as volatile a regional environment as the one that existed in October 1996. By contrast, in 1996 the ruling family would have found it extremely difficult to justify and get away with postponing a parliamentary election—let alone canceling it—on the ground that regional politics were unstable.

In a clear indication of the interest generated by the elections, more than 80 percent of the 107,000 men eligible to vote showed up at the polls. Even though women were still not allowed to vote, they took advantage of the campaign to agitate for women's rights and against the July 1996 gender segregation bill. By doing so, they demonstrated that even in countries where restrictions are placed on parliament's mode of election and prerogatives, a legislature's contribution to political life and to prospects for democratization goes well beyond its constitutional powers.

Candidates debated vigorously, both during public meetings and through the media. The 1992 parliament came under strong criticism, and several politicians ran against what they denounced as its poor performance. They argued that the assembly elected in 1992 had failed to live up to expectations and that it had wasted precious time and energy on peripheral issues while ignoring the more serious ones facing the country. They denounced what they saw as the grandstanding and inappropriate behavior of MPs elected in 1992. Many incumbents, especially leading members of the opposition, were haunted by their failure to deliver on their promises and by the fact that their votes in parliament had often contradicted their 1992 campaign platform. In short, although the 1992 election had been accurately described as an attempt to force the government to account, the 1996 election showed the maturity of an electorate that also wanted its elected representatives to justify their record in office.

The results suggested that many voters agreed with the criticisms leveled at the 1992–1996 parliament and that there had been a tendency to "throw the bums out" (Tétreault 1997). Turnover was high, as half of the newly elected members were newcomers. Several well-known parliamentary figures—particularly among liberals, reformists, Arab nationalists, and supporters of speaker al-Sa'adun—lost their seats. The country's most prominent opposition group, the KDF, won only 2 seats. By contrast, the Islamist bloc increased its overall strength from 15 to 20 MPs (but within this bloc, turnover was high as well). Overall, the secular opposition emerged significantly weaker.

Although close to half of the assembly was made up of representatives from tribal areas, who were generally supportive of the regime, the new legislature was not expected to be docile. Independents, liberal reformers, and the Islamist opposition were bound to question and criticize the government and force it to account for its policies. Significantly, Ahmad al-Sa'adun was reelected speaker. Even MPs described as "proregime" were expected to distance themselves from the government on critical issues. As a representative institution broadly reflective of the diversity of Kuwaiti society, the 1996 National Assembly seemed as likely to assert itself as its predecessors had. That was quickly shown when during the first half of 1997 parliament confronted the government on several critical issues.[16] One was the legislation on foreign workers in Kuwait (with MPs calling for a complete overhaul of the labor code and the government arguing that only certain articles should be rewritten). Another source of friction was Kuwait's economic and military development plan. The government insisted that parliament vote on the plan as a whole. By contrast, MPs claimed the right to examine the plan item by item. Eventually, the issue was referred to the constitutional court, which decided in the government's favor.

Conclusion

Since Kuwait's first legislative elections in January 1963, parliament has been the central arena in which the battle for governmental accountability and political participation has been waged. When in session, the National Assembly has been active and influential. It has provided for a measure of control over the actions of the cabinet and individual ministers and has made vital contributions to the debate over national issues. It is revealing that, in both instances when the NA was dissolved, its absence created a political vacuum that no other institution was able to fill. It is also significant that even when closed, parliament served as a powerful political symbol, and its reopening soon emerged as the key demand of advocates of political reform. This was shown by the growing call for the reconvening of the NA in 1980–1981, by the prodemocracy movement of 1989–1990, and by the period immediately following Kuwait's liberation from Iraq on February 28, 1991.

Several of the factors that have complicated executive-legislative relations in the emirate present a striking similarity to those that, until recently, had also led to repeated dissolutions of parliament elsewhere in the region, as in Morocco and Jordan. To begin with, Kuwait's ruling family has been reluctant to see parliament encroach on what it considers to be its reserved domain: national security and foreign affairs. Similarly, as shown in Chapter 7, King Hussein's attempt to retain control over foreign policy and national security issues has profoundly affected the nature of his relationship with the Jordanian legislature. Another cause of executive-legislative tensions has been the vulnerability of the country and the turbulent regional environment in which it operates. Kuwait is a very small country surrounded by powerful neighbors that resent its wealth and harbor designs over it. Predictably—and again not unlike the situation in Jordan—on those occasions when the regime has felt under serious external threat, it has hardened its attitude toward parliament. This has been particularly true when the Assembly has acted in ways that could be construed as undermining national unity. Whenever developments in the Arab world have heightened tensions within Kuwait, the ruling family and/or the cabinet has tried to curb the NA's power. By contrast, when the al-Sabah and the government have felt more secure, they have usually been willing to broaden the space within which parliament operates. Ironically, however, when regional tensions prompted the ruling family to disband parliament (in 1976 and 1986), the absence of a legislature left the al-Sabah more isolated and vulnerable than ever, leading the emir to subsequently reconvene the National Assembly, but this time with additional power for the opposition.

Until 1990 at least, the tendency of the parliamentary opposition to look to other Arab countries for support and inspiration also fueled the government's distrust of the NA. The same can be said of the opposition's attempt to mobilize the support of the large Palestinian expatriate community and of its embrace of pan-Arab ideologies and causes, such as Nasserism or the Palestinian struggle. Such behavior intensified the fears of a regime that already felt vulnerable to destabilizing forces coming from the outside and made it easier for the more conservative members of the al-Sabah to perceive or portray the opposition as a "fifth column" and to cast suspicion on its patriotism and ultimate motives.[17]

Even worse was the tendency of some of the most outspoken members of the parliamentary opposition to question the very legitimacy of the regime or to deliberately focus their attacks on members of the ruling family. In their inflammatory speeches, these deputies often seemed to be driven primarily by a desire to embarrass the government. This type of behavior, as much as the opposition's connections to foreign movements, countries, or ideologies, was bound to fuel the regime's perception that a large segment of the opposition was "disloyal." As many examples in this book demonstrate, such a situation usually leads to political stalemate, which frequently results in the legislature's disbanding.

More generally, the two suspensions of parliament and the unwillingness of the ruling family to reopen it between 1986 and the Iraqi invasion were largely due to the inability of the al-Sabah and the opposition to agree on the parameters within which the NA should be allowed to operate. The opposition often insisted on stretching to the limits the prerogatives that parliament could legitimately invoke under the 1962 constitution. It also refused to abide by the unwritten norm that criticism of the ruling family was not acceptable. For its part, the ruling family was unwilling to live with all the constraints that the 1962 constitution had placed on its power. This lack of agreement on the rules of the game explains the constant bickering and the mistrust that came to plague executive-legislative relations.

Since October 1992, parliament has become more forceful and effective—even taking into account what Kuwaitis themselves saw as the inappropriate behavior of many members of the 1992–1996 legislature and the latter's unsatisfactory record. Moroever, the NA's assertion of its constitutional prerogatives has not led to a replay of previous executive-legislative impasses and governmental crackdowns. This has come about mostly for three interrelated reasons. First, Kuwaitis are very much aware that debilitating internal bickering contributed to the disaster that befell their country in August 1990. They are determined not to repeat a mistake that would once again turn their country into an easy prey for ambitious neighbors. Also critical to parliament's enhanced role in the "new Kuwait" has been the ruling family's realization that it can no longer resist genuine reforms. The Iraqi invasion radically changed the balance of power in the emirate. The emir and the ruling family understand that they must learn how to share power with parliament. Indeed, their ability to do so has become a condition of their long-term survival. Finally, changes in the composition, outlook, and behavior of the opposition have diminished the potential for violent confrontations between the ruling family and the cabinet on the one hand, and parliament on the other. The opposition is no longer identified with pan-Arab issues and movements. That, in turn, has limited the extent to which it is seen as dangerous or disloyal by the regime.[18] The opposition has become far less ideological as well. As a rule, its members are less prone to posturing and rhetorical excesses than their predecessors. They are more likely to cooperate with the regime in finding concrete solutions to the country's problems. In general, they are content with an incremental approach to political reform and seem genuinely interested in putting into practice the program on which they ran, both in 1992 and 1996. This new pragmatism and spirit of cooperation have allowed for productive bargaining and negotiations between the regime and the opposition.

Notes

1. For instance, the state deliberately stayed out of certain sectors, such as construction and trade. In addition, the government also made a tacit promise that members of the ruling family would not engage in commercial activities that would encroach on the merchants' turf.

2. For instance, a law was passed in 1960 that required that Kuwaitis have 51 percent (the majority) of control of all companies operating in the country. Other laws were adopted that gave Kuwaiti firms preferential treatment in the bidding for state contracts and that required that foreign firms take Kuwaiti partners.

3. The tradition whereby the emir usually appoints the crown prince as prime minister presents several advantages. For one, it gives the crown prince the opportunity to act publicly and therefore to gain political experience and maturity before he becomes the ruler. It enables him in particular to develop a close relationship with the National Assembly. As a result, by the time he becomes emir, the crown prince typically has familiarized himself with the executive and the legislative branches of government and has developed intimate working relationships with both.

4. Laws passed by the NA are referred to the emir for promulgation. The emir is bound by the constitution to promulgate these laws within thirty days from the time he receives them, unless the NA, by a simple majority, has classified a law as urgent, in which case the emir has to promulgate it within seven days. The constitution specifies

that laws not promulgated within the legal period and not returned to the NA for reconsideration are considered de facto laws, even though the emir did not officially promulgate them. If the emir decides not to promulgate a law, he can return it to the NA within the legal period, requesting reconsideration and providing reasons for his decision. If the assembly reaffirms its position by a two-thirds majority, the emir must promulgate the law within thirty days. However, if the NA fails to muster a two-thirds majority, the law dies and cannot be discussed in the same legislative session. If during the following legislative session the NA upholds the same law by a simple majority, the emir must promulgate it within thirty days.

5. Under Article 114, the NA is empowered to establish investigative committees.

6. Interpellation sessions are to be scheduled seven days after the request has been made, in order to give the cabinet minister the opportunity to prepare his defense and to allow time for the possible reconciliation and compromises that would render the interpellation session unnecessary.

7. The opposition's electoral humiliation was due to more than gerrymandering. In each district where it might have had a chance, the opposition was represented by too many candidates. Ahmad al-Khatib was among those who failed to win a seat.

8. The motion of no-confidence in the minister of justice was approved by 44 of parliament's 50 members.

9. Previously, several MPs had accused the oil minister of having used his office for private gain.

10. *Diwaniyyat* are informal gatherings of men who are relatives, friends, or close associates. These meetings typically take place once a week, in the home of one of the members of the group. They provide opportunities for individuals to socialize, exchange views, and find ways of helping each other. *Diwaniyyat* discussions frequently turn to business or politics.

11. For information on these groups, see Alshayeji 1992: 41–46; Aarts 1994: 21–22; Ghabra 1994: 106–107; and Dabaghy and Melki, 1995: 17.

12. Quoted in "Who's Responsible?" *The Middle East*, November 1992, p. 6.

13. The only member of the Constitutional Bloc who was elected was its leader, Jassem al-Saqr. This outcome, however, did not represent the true strength of the Constitutional Bloc, which had contributed to the victory of several candidates running as independents.

14. The Oil Ministry went to Ali Ahmed al-Baghli, a Shiite who ran as an independent and won both Sunni and Shia votes. Meshari Jassem al-Anjari and Ahmed al-Rubai, both members of the Parliamentarian Group, received, respectively, the justice and the education portfolios. Three Islamist MPs also entered the cabinet. Two of them belonged to the ICM (Jamaan Fa'ih al-Azmi, who became minister of Islamic affairs, and Abdullah Rashid al-Hajiri, who was appointed minister of commerce and industry). The third one was affiliated with the IPA (Jassem Mohammed al-Aoun, who was given the labor and social affairs ministry).

15. See David Gardner, "The World Is a Tougher Place," *Financial Times*, May 23, 1995, p. 1.

16. See Kathy Evans, "Kuwait: The Progress of Democracy," *The Middle East*, May 1997, pp. 11–12.

17. The opposition's behavior may also have caused it to lose potential supporters frightened by its foreign connections.

18. This particular change in the opposition is largely due to the fact that the very forces that Kuwait's pan-Arab leftist opposition had long supported showed little sympathy for the emirate following Saddam Hussein's invasion; indeed, they often sided with Iraq, as was the case of the PLO.

9

Yemen

The Republic of Yemen (ROY) was born in May 1990 when the Yemen Arab Republic (YAR—North Yemen) merged with the People's Democratic Republic of Yemen (PDRY—South Yemen). Since then, the ROY has ridden a political roller coaster. In 1992 and 1993, despite the negative repercussions of the 1991 Gulf War on its economy, Yemen appeared to be demonstrating that a country located on the edge of the Arabian Peninsula could experience a rapid and dramatic breakthrough to democracy. This new form of government, it seemed, would also serve to legitimate and cement the union, in addition to providing the basis upon which the new country could tackle pressing economic and other problems. The proliferation at that time of political parties and voluntary associations was met with regional and international acclaim, as were the April 1993 parliamentary elections. Discussions among observers of Yemen of the possibility that its traditions of tribal egalitarianism and consultation might serve as foundations for an immediate transition to a full-fledged democracy were reminiscent of nineteenth-century debates among Marxists over whether Russia's village-based communities might provide the basis for a leap from feudalism to socialism.

Alas, the bright and often unrealistic hopes of 1992 and 1993 were dashed by the civil war that broke out between the north and the south in April 1994. By July, the war had been won by the north, but with this victory came growing uncertainty regarding Yemen's prospects for democracy. Parliament, which had been the institutional embodiment of hopes for democracy, was now seen by many as a rubber stamp for an executive branch dominated by a president strengthened by the war and its aftermath.

Yet, this new pessimism was perhaps as excessive as the often naive optimism that had prevailed in 1992 and 1993, when enthusiasm for Yemen's experiment had ignored underlying tensions and unresolved problems. The war's impact on democracy was in fact complex. Certainly, in the short to medium term, the hostilities were followed by a constriction of political freedoms and numerous attempts by the regime to intimidate its opponents.

Nonetheless, the war also highlighted the resiliency of some democratic institutions, including parliament. Developments since 1995 suggest that despite
President Ali Abdullah Salih's attempt to impose his views, the Yemeni political system remains pluralistic. It features several political parties, a relatively
free press, vigorous debates, and political demonstrations. Parliament certainly has not been weakened to the extent suggested by many analysts. Its
speaker, Shaikh Abdullah al-Ahmar, remains one of the key power holders in
the country. On many critical issues, his views conflict sharply with those of
President Salih, who cannot afford to ignore him.

It is also significant that fixing the date and the modalities of the 1997
parliamentary election assumed great importance in political debates in
Yemen during 1996. If the legislature were not seen as an influential institution, capable of providing political actors with an opportunity to publicize
their ideas and affect policymaking, the issue of when elections should take
place and under what format would not have been as contested as it was.
Moreover, when these elections were finally held on April 27, 1997, they
were deemed by international observers to have been free and fair. Women
participated, both as voters and as candidates. Even though there were no
women among the candidates presented by the largest and most influential
party, the General People's Congress (GPC), women's registration prior to the
elections had grown by a much larger percentage than that of men. In addition, an Islamist party was allowed to compete, in contrast to countries such
as Egypt and Tunisia that, despite their much longer history with constitutional government, ban parties based on religion.

The 1997 legislative elections were the second such ballot since unification
and the onset of democratization. That they took place on schedule and were
democratic and generally peaceful (despite isolated incidents of violence) reveals the extent to which multiparty parliamentary elections are becoming an
institutionalized means of regulating political competition. In short, considering
the short life of Yemen's experiment with democracy and parliamentary politics, the balance sheet of the 1990s—despite the civil war of 1994, continued
domestic tensions, and the regime's heavy-handed tactics since 1995—remains
a positive one thus far. As of mid-1998, there are certainly many reasons to
worry about the future of democracy in Yemen. These concerns, however,
should not be allowed to obscure the political achievements of the country,
which become clearer when they are examined in a broad historical perspective.

Historical Roots of Yemen's Parliamentary Experiment

The present role of parliament in the ROY has been shaped far more by the
legacy of the YAR in the north than by that of the PDRY in the south. The

PDRY's much smaller size and population, the ultimate defeat of forces loyal to its ruling party in the 1994 civil war, and the fact that its political institutions were inspired by the discredited Soviet version of Marxism-Leninism all contributed to rendering the PDRY's political and electoral experience less relevant to developments in the ROY. It is thus to the politics of the YAR that one must look for an understanding of the roots of Yemen's experiment with parliamentary politics.

The YAR was created in 1962, when a military coup overthrew the ruling dynasty. The new regime, led by Brig.-Gen. Abdullah al-Sallal, was a republic in name only. Dominated by the military and faced with a royalist uprising in the northeastern part of the country, the regime did not initially provide for a legislature that might restrict the powers of the executive. In 1969, however, Sallal's successor, Abd al-Rahman al-Iryani, appointed a National Council of forty-five members drawn principally from the tribes. The end of the civil war and the reconciliation between royalists and republicans in 1970 resulted in a relaxation of authoritarian rule and the reintegration of tribal leaders into the formal power structure. One manifestation of this phenomenon was the expansion of the National Council to sixty-three members. Although the Council had only token powers and was subordinate to the executive branch and the army, it was chosen by the ruling elite to serve as the conduit for the promulgation and legitimization of a new constitution in December 1970. This decision points to the regime's awareness that, despite its very limited authority, the Council was seen by the population as reflecting popular will and Yemeni sovereignty more accurately than did the executive branch.

The main objective of the 1970 constitution was to institutionalize political relationships in the wake of the return to Yemen of exiled royalists. The constitution retained the principle of collective executive leadership in the form of a three-person Presidential Council, a prime minister, and a cabinet. In addition, however, it created a Consultative Council (Majlis al-Shura) of 179 members. Twenty of this new body's members were to be appointed by the president, the other 159 being chosen through a combination of direct elections (in the main towns) and indirect elections (in villages and rural areas).

Although this first Consultative Council could not initiate legislation, and thus was not a true legislature, it came to play an important political role. Many of its members were tribal leaders and other notables who actively sought to oversee the executive. They felt that, in the name of "modernization," the government was seeking to gather all power into its hands. On numerous occasions, the Consultative Council blocked legislation and the annual budget proposed by the executive. In many other ways, too, it asserted its independence from the Presidential Council and the cabinet. Individual members were often successful in identifying executive abuses and demanding their rectification. Led by its speaker, Shaikh Abdullah al-Ahmar, the Consultative Council reflected the continuing power of tribes (especially those of the Hashid tribal confederation) while also embodying the political hopes of a much wider range of Yemenis, including modernists and democrats. (More than twenty years later, al-Ahmar would become speaker of the ROY's elected legislature.)

On June 13, 1974, a bloodless coup led to the ascent to power of Lt.-Col. Muhammad al-Hamdi. Al-Hamdi's first official act was to prorogue the Consultative Council. Executive and legislative powers were vested in an enlarged Command Council of ten members, which replaced the three-member Presidential Council. Within a matter of months, however, the new government recognized that a ten-member executive council could neither mask the rule of al-Hamdi and the military, nor adequately legitimate it. Accordingly, the 1970 constitution and the Consultative Council were reinstated, and the Command Council was reduced to seven members. Less than a year later (in October 1975), the Consultative Council's term came to an end. Although the government issued a decree later that year for the preparation of an election according to the constitution, that election had not been held when al-Hamdi was assassinated on October 11, 1977. The military, acting through the Command Council, nominated Col. Ahmad al-Ghashmi as al-Hamdi's successor.

Politically weaker than his predecessor, al-Ghashmi sought to legitimize his ascent to power by appointing a ninety-nine-member People's Constituent Assembly, which then formally authorized the Command Council to select al-Ghashmi as president. By establishing a legislature intended to provide at least symbolic legitimation of a presidential succession that had been engineered elsewhere, al-Ghashmi began the process of restoring a semblance of constitutional rule. In addition, the Assembly was granted the right to review and approve the legislation and budgets formulated by the executive, even though the prime minister and cabinet were made responsible not to the Assembly but to the president.

When al-Ghashmi was assassinated in June 1978, the Assembly met immediately to choose a new provisional Presidential Council of four members, headed by the speaker of the Assembly. The next month, the Assembly elected Ali Abdullah Salih as president. The new president appointed sixty additional Assembly members, most of whom were tribal leaders. Salih was from a minor tribe of the Hashid tribal confederation, and his strategy was to mobilize tribal elements behind his presidency. Al-Ghashmi had departed from Yemeni tradition in appointing as members of the Assembly primarily urban, educated people. Salih, instead, was bent on shifting the political balance back toward tribes. Apparently, he also understood the political benefits to be derived from institutionalizing political participation, as suggested by his creation in 1982 of the top-down mobilizational GPC, over which he presided as secretary general until the mid-1990s.

The term of the People's Constituent Assembly was extended for four more years in 1983. Thereafter, the Assembly debated and approved a number of important laws that laid the basis for criminal and civil legal codes, court structures and processes, and authorities and jurisdictions of other state institutions. Politically, the very existence of the Assembly and its relative vigor helped legitimize the government while demonstrating to it that political participation carried significant benefits and might safely be expanded. Accordingly, the People's Constituent Assembly passed legislation to hold the long-promised but repeatedly postponed elections for a new Consultative Assembly. The new body, which was intended to be a much stronger legislature, would be elected and endowed with the legal capacity to amend or reject (but not initiate) legislation and to debate motions of no confidence in the executive.

Elections were held on July 5, 1988, in 128 single-member electoral districts. The remaining 31 members of this 159-member assembly were appointed by the president. About 1.1 million voters chose from among 1,293 candidates, with the majority of winners being tribal leaders or their sons. The electoral law passed by the People's Constituent Assembly had permitted candidates to hold political rallies and put up posters but not to campaign on "divisive issues" or use partisan labels, for political parties remained illegal. Informally, however, partisan identifications were made known, and the election was seen in part as a competition between candidates backed by the GPC, individuals identified with the secular opposition (particularly Baathists and Nasserites), and Islamists. The Islamists were represented primarily by members of the Muslim Brotherhood, who won about one-quarter of the seats, including all six in the capital, Sana'a. A week after the election, the Consultative Assembly held its first session, during which it elected the vice president, Abd al Karim al-Arashi, as speaker. The following week, it overwhelmingly reelected Salih to a third five-year term by a vote of 152 for, 2 abstentions, and 5 absentees.

The parliament elected in 1988 immediately challenged the president by seeking the transfer from the executive to the legislative branch of control over the Central Organization for Control and Accounts (COCA), the governmental accounting agency. Although ultimately unsuccessful, those efforts served notice on the executive that parliament would attempt to gain meaningful control over the purse strings and to enforce accountability.

The election of a parliament endowed with significant prerogatives had taken about a quarter of a century since the 1962 coup that had established the republic. During that period, legislative powers had been vested in an executive council. All of Yemen's rulers, however, ultimately came to the conclusion that their legitimacy depended in part on convening a consultative council broadly representative of the population. Over time, these councils assumed greater importance, and elections to them became a political demand that the regime found increasingly difficult to resist.

The Unification and Its Aftermath
(1990–1992)

Legitimation of the union between the YAR and the PDRY was provided through separate meetings of their respective legislatures on May 21, 1990, one day before the ROY officially came into being. The Consultative Assembly (Majlis al-Shura) of the north and the Supreme People's Council (Majlis al-Sha'ab al-'Aliy) of the south approved the new country's draft constitution, which was embodied in a document known as the Aden Declaration. That document also specified the modalities of a thirty-month transition period leading up to general elections. Relevant provisions included the creation of a 301-member Chamber of Deputies (Majlis al Nuwwab), consisting of the 159 members of the former northern Consultative Assembly, the 111 members of the now-defunct southern Supreme People's Council, and 31 new members appointed by the president. With a mere 20 percent of the population of the new country, the south was therefore clearly overrepresented in the transition parliament. The Chamber of Deputies was to be a full-fledged lawmaking institution, and its term was set for two and one-half years. Dr. Yassin Said Nu'man, a southerner, was chosen as its speaker.

The executive branch was divided between a five-member presidential council and a thirty-nine-member cabinet headed by a prime minister. The presidential council, to be elected by the Chamber of Deputies, was to select a president and vice president from among its members. Former president of the YAR Ali Abdullah Salih became president, and the vice presidency was given to Ali Salim al-Bidh, the former president of the PDRY. The prime minister was to nominate his cabinet for approval by the president. Before the cabinet could be installed, however, it had to receive a vote of confidence from the Chamber of Deputies. A southerner, Haidar Abu Bakr al-Attas, was chosen as prime minister.

Finally, unification involved a tacit understanding that, during the transition period at least, all key posts in the executive branch would be distributed roughly 60:40 between north and south, whereas positions within the bureaucracy would be divided evenly. However, whereas northerners generally assumed that this quota system was temporary and would ultimately give way to majority rule, southerners believed that power would continue to be divided more or less equally between north and south. This fundamental misunderstanding was never resolved, and as will be seen, it eventually led to the civil war that broke out in April 1994.

Parliament Under the 1991 Constitution

The constitution adopted at unification was an amended version of the 1970 constitution of the YAR. It remains in place today, although constitutional amendments and legal changes were effected in the wake of the 1994 civil war. As will be discussed subsequently, the intents and consequences of these amendments were to further advantage the executive branch at the expense of the legislature and the north at the expense of the south. In addition, the 1994 amendments replaced the presidential council with a president. By and large, however, the prerogatives of parliament today remain those defined in the 1991 constitution, and so we review them here.

Under the 1991 constitution, the Chamber of Deputies was assigned powers to grant or withhold its vote of confidence in the council of ministers (Article 72), approve the budget (Article 49) and other laws (Article 50), question ministers (Article 75), override presidential council vetoes (Article 79), and initiate subjects for debate (Article 69). The constitution empowered parliament to debate and approve the program of the cabinet, which must be submitted to the legislature prior to a vote of confidence in the cabinet. Members of parliament (MPs) were provided immunity from arrest and/or trial, unless they were caught in a situation of flagrante delicto or unless parliament voted to take that immunity away from them. The constitution assigned to the Chamber the right to elect its leaders and create permanent, ad hoc, and special investigatory committees as it deems necessary. This right, however, must be exercised through the promulgation of laws, which means that the presidential council (the president since November 1994) may veto the proposed law, although the Chamber can override this veto by an absolute majority of voting members.

Constitutional constraints on parliament include a provision for its dissolution by the president, an act that requires approval by referendum. In addition, the president has thirty days to prevent a bill passed by parliament from becoming law. (If the president fails to act within thirty days, the bill automatically becomes law.) If rejected by the president, the bill is returned to parliament. In that case, however, only an absolute majority is required to override the presidential veto—not a two-thirds majority as is the case in the United States and many other countries. This indicates a desire on the part of the framers of the Yemeni constitution to elevate the legislature relative to the presidency. Finally, although parliament cannot alter provisions of the budget without the cabinet's approval, it can reject the budget in its entirety.

Although the constitution empowered the presidential council (the president since 1994) to decree laws when parliament is not in session, laws passed by decree must be submitted for review by parliament within thirty days of it reconvening. This latter provision, however, was systematically abused by the executive in the period between unification and the April 1993 elections. During Ramadan in 1991, thirty-one key laws were decreed by the presidential council, and more than forty laws were decreed in the following Ramadan. Included in legislation enacted in this fashion was Law 1 of 1991, which established the administrative structures, jurisdictions, and procedures of the judicial branch. Parliament did not challenge the executive over these violations of the spirit, if not the letter, of the constitution.

Yemen's political and constitutional framework resembles that of Jordan, where, as was shown in Chapter 7, the cabinet is assigned the role of political shock absorber between parliament and the monarch. In both Yemen and Jordan, the chief executive (the president in Yemen, the king in Jordan) is in charge of all major policies and decisions, and the cabinet is responsible for presenting and selling these decisions to the legislature and then implementing them. Criticisms of these policies or their implementation by parliament are addressed to the cabinet, not to the king or president. This three-actor political game enables the head of state to act as a national symbol as well as an umpire in conflicts between political groups or between parliament and the cabinet. The performance of these roles has been perfected by King Hussein, but President Ali Abdullah Salih, too, has demonstrated considerable skill in rising above the fray, leaving cabinet members to deal with challenges from parliament.

Immediately after the constitution was adopted, the new Chamber assumed its responsibilities and began to formulate a program to strengthen its internal capacity. It passed important laws on the press, political parties, and elections, thus setting the parameters within which political activity was to take place in the ROY. Still, the Chamber did not assert itself vis-à-vis the executive in the period leading up to the April 1993 elections, primarily because of the absence of a viable opposition, the imbalance of resources between parliament and the executive branch, and the serious economic crisis that the ROY faced in the wake of the Gulf War.

From Elections to Civil War (April 1993–June 1994)

The April 1993 multiparty elections, the first ones ever to be held in Yemen, were reasonably free and fair and were heralded as signaling the onset of real democracy. However, they also undermined the informal agreement upon which unification had been achieved. Southern leaders saw themselves as equal partners to their northern counterparts, even though southerners made up only one-fifth of Yemen's population. They believed that power should be divided more or less evenly between north and south, even after the general elections. The leadership of the Yemeni Socialist Party (YSP), which had ruled over South Yemen, had assumed all along that it would capture in northern constituencies enough seats to enable it to achieve rough parity with the north's former ruling party, the GPC. These expectations, however, were dashed by the apparent lack of appeal of the YSP in the north and by the entry into the election of the northern tribal-Islamist Yemeni Party for Reform, popularly known as the Islah. In the April 1993 elections, the YSP won only 57 of the 301 seats, behind not only the GPC, with its 123 seats, but also the Islah, which captured 62 seats.

Intensely suspicious of a perceived tactical alliance between the GPC and the Islah, the leader of the YSP, Vice President Ali Salim al-Bidh, concluded that his and his party's future within the new union was bleak, and he now claimed to have been tricked by President Ali Abdullah Salih into joining that union. YSP apprehension was further heightened by the election of Islah leader Shaikh Abdullah al-Ahmar as speaker of the Chamber. Al-Ahmar was the paramount shaikh of the Hashid tribal confederation, to which President Ali Abdullah Salih's Sanhan tribe belonged. Also disturbing to al-Bidh and his associates was the appointment of a member of Islah to the five-person presidential council. Southern leaders were indeed being marginalized—but not, as they claimed, as a result of a "conspiracy" of religious and tribal elements in the north. Their loss of influence instead was due to their electoral defeat and, more generally, to the poor skills they displayed at the game of coalition building with which northern elites were so comfortable.

In this context, al-Bidh repaired to the former southern capital of Aden and began to prepare the ground for either secession or a renegotiation of the unity agreement. He now wanted the union to provide for much greater decentralization, thereby diluting the power of the central government within which he and the YSP had been marginalized. These developments were accompanied by threatening military moves on both sides. In this already volatile environment, Saudi Arabia played a critical destabilizing role. Yemen's northern neighbor had never welcomed the prospect of a unified, democratic Yemen that could challenge Saudi dominance of the peninsula and might inspire Saudi reformers to question dynastic rule. In addition, the Saudi regime had not forgotten Yemen's attempt at neutrality during the 1990–1991 Gulf crisis. Riyadh therefore went out of its way to fuel the antagonism between north and south, and to thwart attempts at mediation (including that by King Hussein in February 1994). Some independent sources in Yemen go so far as to suggest that the Saudi regime paid al-Bidh up to a quarter billion dollars to encourage him to break away. Be that as it may, the south did formally secede in April 1994, and a civil war immediately broke out.

Between the April 1993 elections and the outbreak of hostilities a year later, the functioning of the Chamber of Deputies, like that of other governmental institutions, was severely impeded by the brewing political conflict. Nevertheless, throughout that period parliament provided virtually the only arena within which the leaders of the three main political parties could interact. During the war, the Chamber continued to meet and ratified all of President Salih's decisions. The president thus acted within the bounds of the constitution and with the backing of parliament, whereas the YSP leadership behaved in an unconstitutional fashion. Significantly, many YSP deputies parted company with their party's leadership. They chose to remain in parliament and to respect constitutional provisions. That they stayed in Sana'a and continued to attend the sessions of the Chamber was evidence of their hopes to use that body to mediate the conflict and to play a major role in the process of political reconstruction after the war. In these and other respects, the conflict strengthened parliament's importance in the political system.

The Civil War's Significance

Political developments in Yemen between 1990 and 1994 validated the model of negotiated transitions to democracy presented in this book. They demonstrated that dramatic breakthroughs to democracy are unlikely and that attempts to bring such breakthroughs about are risky. They showed that elections can actually threaten democratization if their results are inconsistent with the understandings reached between competing elites at the onset of the democratization process.

Analysts have usually described the 1994 civil war as a major defeat for democracy in Yemen. At the very least, this view should be qualified. In reality, the conflict was a major test for the country's new democratic institutions. That these institutions survived the challenge suggests that the war was less a case of democratic breakdown than a proof of the resiliency of the democratic framework established between 1991 and 1993. In addition, the northern-based political coalition that won the civil war is more likely to provide a long-term basis for the consolidation of democratic practices and institutions than would have been a victory by a YSP intent upon perpetuating a Leninist style of politics. As its behavior in the wake of the 1993 elections demonstrated, the YSP leadership was not ready to accept the logic of democratic politics. It continued to believe that political power and offices should be divided evenly between north and south irrespective of electoral results. The defeat of this outlook and agenda can hardly be described as a blow to democracy.

By contrast, for all its flaws, the northern leadership was not only willing to play the game of democratic politics but effective in doing so. This is primarily because the north has long had a political system based on coalition formation and the seeking of compromise. Primarily a tribal, therefore pluralistic society, the north has never had a central government strong enough to dictate political terms to tribal constituencies. Instead, government in the north has to a large extent been the product of interactions between traditional sociopolitical units that perform the functions normally associated with more modern institutional and organizational forms. This is why the political leaders of the north had all along assumed that unification was bringing into the polity yet another political actor, the YSP, who would be a potential coalition partner or an opponent, depending on circumstances at any given time.

Parliament in the Wake of the Civil War
(July 1994–April 1997)

Shortly after the civil war ended, constitutional amendments were adopted that altered the structure of government in order to consolidate more power in the presidency. The five-member Presidential Council, which had previously exercised the executive function, including the appointment of ministers, was abolished. Its powers were transferred to the president. According to a new constitutional provision, in the future the president was to be elected not by parliament but by universal suffrage; the president was to be limited to two five-year terms. It was decided, however, that this limit would not apply retrospectively. As a result, President Salih was provided the constitutional option of remaining in power for up to ten more years. On October 1, 1994, Salih was reelected president by parliament, the last time that the legislature was to exercise this power. Following his reelection, Salih transferred the National Security Organization (the secret police) from the Ministry of Interior to the presidency and renamed it the Political Security Organization.

The enhancement of presidential power after the civil war does not mean that parliament was marginalized. It is true that the legislature was stripped of its power to elect the president. It is also the case that the abrogation of the presidential council eliminated an institution that acted as a counterbalance to the president. However, the establishment of a presidential system had been anticipated before the civil war broke out. Most of the key players during the 1990–1993 period saw the presidential council as a temporary institution that would ultimately give way to a strengthened presidency. In addition, it is significant that all constitutional amendments effected after the civil war were referred to parliament and that the government also sought (and received) the legislature's approval of personnel changes during and after the hostilities. This respect for constitutionalism reflects the government's awareness of the public's desire to see a legislature check the decisions of the executive. Furthermore, when parliament resumed its activities in the fall of 1994, it did so with considerably greater vigor than in the year following the 1993 elections, when the crisis between the YSP and the GPC had largely immobilized Yemeni politics. As soon as the war ended, the speaker of parliament also emerged as a major counterweight to the president. As head of a powerful tribal federation and political party, and possessing excellent linkages to the Saudi Arabian political elite, Shaikh Abdullah al-Ahmar showed himself capable of forestalling several presidential initiatives that he opposed.

In short, the balance of power between president and parliament was not profoundly affected by the creation of a truly presidential system. This was evidenced in 1995 and 1996 when the Chamber asserted its constitutional prerogatives. In particular, conflicts with the executive over the issues of parliamentary immunity and approval of the budget demonstrated that legislators were intent on preserving and indeed expanding constitutionalism.

With regard to the question of immunity, more than seventy deputies walked out of parliament in July 1995 to protest the detention of a YSP member and alleged murderer, Muhammad Nagi Said. The Chamber then decided to summon Interior Minister Hussein Muhammad Arab to explain why Said had been arrested in apparent violation of his parliamentary immunity. Arab refused to attend the session to which he had been summoned, claiming that he had received a "message" from parliament sanctioning Said's detention—this "message" being assumed to be a communication from the speaker, Shaikh Abdullah al-Ahmar. Arab did, however, release the accused. The issue was ultimately resolved, and the constitutionally enshrined principle of immunity preserved in typical Yemeni, traditional fashion. Shaikh Abdullah al-Ahmar, possibly seeking to avoid further embarrassment, mediated between the two tribes involved. Meanwhile, President Salih authorized the payment of $21,500 in blood money to the victim's relatives.

The struggle over the 1996 draft budget also reflected the widespread desire of parliamentarians to force the executive to adhere to constitutional provisions. The constitution stipulated that the proposed budget should be presented to parliament two months prior to the commencement of the fiscal year on the first of January. However, conflict between the GPC and the Islah over the magnitude of budgetary cutbacks had caused the government to miss the budget deadline. In response, parliament voted in mid-January 1996 to give the government another four days in which to produce the budget, failing which the legislature would demand that all government expenditures cease. The cabinet complied with the request, and the Chamber commenced its deliberations of the budget. Like the cabinet, parliament was deeply divided over the issue of adopting stringent economic stabilization and structural adjustment measures. As a result, its debate of the budget dragged on until mid-March. Finally, on March 19, the legislature voted with the narrowest possible majority to approve the budget, with 150 deputies supporting it, 53 opposing, 11 abstaining, and 13 walking out during the voting in protest. The legal requirement for the proposed budget to be passed is one-half of the deputies. The speaker ruled that since four seats of the 301-member parliament were then vacant, 150 votes in favor met the legal requirement. Although parliament had not rejected the government's budget, it had succeeded in forcing the cabinet to produce one and had then subjected that budget to careful scrutiny and extensive debate.

Paradoxically, parliament's political importance was heightened by the narrowing of other channels through which to express political dissent. Following the war, the government attempted to intimidate its critics by tightening censorship over the media and by invoking restrictive provisions in the laws regulating political parties. The YSP was specifically targeted. Most of its regional offices were closed, and many of its supporters were removed from public employment. The regime also engaged in a variety of human rights abuses, including physical coercion and imprisonment. In addition, the government repeatedly seized issues of newspapers containing information damaging to its image. Several newspapers were temporarily suspended.

In this environment, parliament became the principal "political lung" through which the YSP and other, smaller opposition parties could continue to "breathe." Despite their embattled, minority status within the Chamber, opposition parties came to rely on the legislature as the forum from which they could continue to make their views known. It is significant that, despite the government's harassment of their party, most YSP deputies resumed their parliamentary activities after the war ended. Having realized that it could not eliminate its rivals or establish joint dictatorial rule with the GPC, the YSP had to compromise. It engaged in issue-specific coalition building, forming alliances with the Bathists, Nasserites, the GPC, and even the Islah, depending on the particular political matter in question. From the perspective of this book, two points therefore deserve emphasis. First, the war forced the YSP to change its behavior and outlook in a way that is far more conducive to democratic consolidation in Yemen. Second, parliament played a key role in making this transformation possible, providing the YSP with avenues through which that party could experiment with the politics of conciliation and deal making.

Between 1995 and 1997, the legislature became the main venue within which the opposition was able to formulate common positions and undertake joint actions. In addition, the lack of unity within the parliamentary wings of the GPC and the Islah, as well as the increasingly bitter competition between them, presented many opportunities for YSP members to cooperate with dissidents from these two parties in pressing demands on the government. Some YSP deputies even came to contemplate a more substantial alliance with the Islah.

Parliament also provided a platform from which members of the Islah attacked the president on what they saw as his lack of commitment to an Islamization of Yemeni society. At the very end of 1995, Islah deputies used the floor of the Chamber to criticize Salih for his November announcement that Aden would be made a free port to attract foreign investment and tourism. They saw this as leading to the revival of tourist areas and the possible reopening of the brewery, both of which had been badly damaged by radical Islamists when they entered the city at the end of the civil war. But the Islamists scored their biggest victory in the struggle over Islamic banking, when they succeeded in passing legislation mandating Islamic practices for the banking sector. President Salih, who opposed the legislation, was thus forced to return the draft law to parliament, where he applied pressure on GPC deputies to ensure that his nominal veto was not overridden.

Yet another indication of parliament's role was its performance of a wide variety of ceremonial duties that reflected its status as the institutional embodiment of Yemeni sovereignty. For example, between 1995 and 1997, parliament received numerous foreign officials, including three Arab members of the Israeli Knesset in March 1996. Remarkably, the legislature also demonstrated a willingness to question the executive over its conduct of foreign and defense policy. Islah deputies objected, although without apparent effect, to Yemen's participation in the November 1995 Amman economic summit, a step that they saw as giving the country's blessings to normalization of relations with Israel. Similarly, in the wake of a successful attempt in late 1995 by Eritrean forces to land on and consolidate control over Hanish Island in the Red Sea, parliament demanded from the government an explanation of how the military disaster had occurred. The legislature also passed a resolution urging the government to retake Hanish by force if Eritrea refused to withdraw its forces. The removal of several top military officers with responsibility for the bungled defense of the island may have resulted from pressure from parliament and been an attempt to placate its members.

Parliament's Internal Capacity

On the eve of the 1997 elections, Yemen's parliament was seriously lacking in internal capacity. Like Tunisia's legislature, it was housed in a former royal palace. Although architecturally stunning, the building is singularly unsuited for its contemporary purpose. It is difficult to access because it has virtually no parking on site and is entered through a narrow side street. It has fewer committee rooms than committees and no personal rooms for members, including committee chairpersons. It does not even have adequate spaces in which deputies can congregate informally. In 1997, the building had but one lavatory to serve the 301 members when they were in plenary session. Although a neighboring building has been acquired by parliament that does provide some committee rooms and additional facilities, the Yemeni legislature remains inadequately housed.

Other facilities are similarly primitive. Security is provided principally by the private bodyguards of the members, so the forecourt in front of the ornate building teems with armed men during sessions. The only telephones are to be found in the offices of the speaker, his three deputies, and the chief administrators. The parliament owns very little office equipment, and much of what it has is not in working order. The few desktop computers available are not in use. The parliamentary library is minuscule, even by the not very demanding standards of the region. Members are not provided any support staff. Each of the seventeen permanent committees is assigned three staff members, but those staffers are not required to possess specialized knowledge of the committee's subject area. Fewer than 10 percent of the total staff of some 250 have a university degree. In sum, with regard to both physical and human resources, the Yemeni parliament is less well endowed than any other in the region. Compounding the problems associated with inadequate resources are difficulties arising from poor relations between members and staff, inappropriate rules of procedure, and an institutional culture of suspicion and distrust, all of which in turn are manifestations of a parliament in the process of transition away from single-party dominance.

During interviews conducted in 1995, members of all parties expressed the view that even the personnel assigned to them were unresponsive to their needs. Significantly, members had little control over their own staffs, who were permanent civil servants accountable primarily to the director general, the top-ranking governmental official within parliament. It seemed clear in 1995 that members and staff had antagonistic, competitive relationships, possibly caused by the widespread belief among senior staffs that the parliament was really their institution and that the members were an unfortunate annoyance. During interviews, several staff members expressed the view that the vast majority of deputies were poorly educated and unable to perform their tasks properly. They preferred previous parliaments, such as that of 1988, in which many members were appointed, for in the opinion of senior staffs those deputies were better educated and more competent. This attitude is at least partially a self-serving one, for staff compete with members for benefits provided by foreign donors, including overseas trips, and therefore have an interest in conveying the impression that it is they, rather than members, who really run the institution. It is also true that assistance provided to the Yemeni parliament has disproportionately concentrated on staff and failed to address the issue of facilitating the development of professional, apolitical relationships between staff and members.

Parliament's bylaws, as well as breaches of them, are also a testament to the legacy of one-party rule. Those bylaws prevent bills reported out of committee from being amended on the floor of the Chamber. They also require the reading of bills line by line, a procedure that consumes vast amounts of time and reduces the role of members to that of editors rather than conceptualizers of basic issues underlying legislation. Probably the most serious deficiency of the bylaws is that they do not include provisions for enforcement. So, for example, signatures of twenty members are in theory sufficient for an interpellation of a minister or government official. The government, however, ignores this legal provision with impunity when it so chooses. On such occasions, the speaker's loyalty has appeared to lie with the government rather than with parliament, for he has not pressed the issue. Similarly, the requirement that parliament consider all decrees issued by the president when it is out of session has never been adhered to in form or content, despite the fact that over one hundred such decrees have been issued since unification.

As typically is the case with parliaments that have recently become multiparty bodies, the Yemeni parliament is characterized by relations of distrust between members of opposing parties. Opposition members of parliament (MPs) are particularly suspicious of the speaker and his close allies. One manifestation of that suspicion in 1995 was the widespread belief among opposition deputies that the speaker had the newly installed voting machine damaged. That machine's sudden breakdown was attributed by opposition deputies to the speaker's desire to have less formal ways of recording votes so that he could manipulate the vote count. Assurances by representatives of the agency that had provided the voting system that it was damaged as a result of electrical malfunctions did nothing to convince these deputies.

In short, the Yemeni parliament is plagued by inadequate resources and the difficulties normally associated with transition from being a single- to a multiparty institution. Fortunately, deputies are keenly aware of both problems and willing to express themselves privately and publicly about them. Members have also demonstrated that they are willing to work on solutions to these problems. Such actions have included demands articulated on the floor of the Assembly for allocation of further resources as well as joint undertakings by opposition MPs to enforce the bylaws by engaging in walkouts and boycotts. In other words, the Yemeni parliament has begun the processes of building its institutional capacity and adjusting to its new status of being a multiparty institution. Those processes will take considerable time, but their relative progress since 1990 suggests that an optimistic, rather than pessimistic, assessment is the more appropriate one.

The April 1997 Elections and Their Significance

On April 27, 1997, less than three years after the north had defeated the south's military bid to break away from the union, the ROY held its second multiparty, universal suffrage parliamentary election. The election indicated that, to say the least, all was not well with Yemen's democratization experiment. To draw attention to their claim that the elections would be rigged to favor President Salih's ruling GPC and to protest the government's failure to return all YSP offices, property, and funds confiscated during and after the war, the YSP (as well as two other smaller, southern-based opposition parties) decided to boycott the elections. Largely as a result of this boycott, voter turnout in Yemen's southern governorates was much lower (49 percent of registered voters) than in the north (62 percent). The elections thus confirmed that in the south—where approximately 19 percent of Yemen's population lives—a significant segment of the electorate feels alienated from national politics. This discontent must be reduced if Yemen's democratic experiment is to succeed.

More generally, at 57 percent of registered voters (as compared to 81 percent in 1993), overall turnout was a disappointment. Any explanation of this decrease of 24 percentage points in turnout must take into account the widespread perception that, despite the competition that characterized the electoral campaign, Salih and the GPC controlled most of the cards and were rather heavy-handed in taking advantage of this situation. This turned off a lot of potential voters and explains why the euphoria of 1993 gave way to a great deal of cynicism.

Still, the elections were a success in several respects. First, they generated a great deal of interest, as approximately two thousand candidates (three-quarters of them running as independents) competed for the Chamber's 301 seats. Second, despite fears that they would be canceled at the last minute or that they would be marred by violence and/or widespread irregularities, the elections were deemed by international observers to have been free and fair on the whole, and their results were accepted by all key players. Third, most political parties—eleven out of the fourteen operating in Yemen at the time—took part in the electoral process. Several YSP members of the outgoing parliament even defied their party's boycott and ran as independents.

The elections resulted in an overwhelming victory for the ruling GPC, which won 187 seats out of 301 (it had 123 members in the outgoing Chamber). The Islah's seats decreased from 62 to 53. Independents, whose political orientations varied greatly, received 54 seats. The Nasserite Unionist People's Party and the Arab Socialist Baath party captured 3 and 2 seats respectively. As in 1993, two women were elected. The impressive performance of the GPC was due mostly to the YSP boycott. Faced with a choice between the GPC and the Islah, many voters (especially women) who were not necessarily well disposed toward the ruling party nevertheless voted for it because of their fear of Islamism (Katz 1997: 49; Hawthorne and Wolfe 1997).

Conclusion: Yemen's Parliament in Historical Perspective

By both regional and global standards, the evolution of parliamentary politics in Yemen has been remarkably rapid. Until 1962, North Yemen had one of the most absolutist governments in the world, with no formal, institutional mechanisms even for consultation, let alone representation. South Yemen, for its part, was ruled by a Marxist-Leninist regime until unification in 1990. By 1970, however, North Yemen had already enshrined into law the principle of representation through an elected legislature with some power to contribute to public policy and oversee the executive. Thereafter, successive governments in the north found it necessary to convene assemblies that, whether appointed or partially elected, were designed to accommodate popular desires for participation and accountability and give executive decisions the necessary stamp of approval. By the late 1980s, even communist South Yemen felt compelled to seek legitimacy through elections.

It is also significant that the political leaders of both north and south concurred in 1990 that for their proposed unification to be perceived as legitimate, it had to be accompanied with a democratization that included free and fair elections to a legislature. Such an election took place in 1993. In short, within three years, Yemen was able to establish the constitutional framework and the electoral, press, and party laws within which an elected legislature could function. That is a considerable accomplishment. This new legislature, furthermore, became the sole arena within which members of the northern and southern political elites continued to interact throughout the crisis leading up to the brief civil war, and then during the fighting itself.

Despite the additional powers given to the presidency after the civil war, the legislature has remained feisty. This status is due in considerable measure to the fact that the war resulted in the YSP's leaving government and forming the opposition. It is also the result of growing confidence and capacity on the part of parliamentarians, who are becoming more resolute and skillful in their effort to ensure that the executive respects constitutionalism. Furthermore, the strength of the legislature should not be interpreted only in terms of its adversarial relationship with the executive. Parliament and the executive share certain interests, the pursuit of which serves to strengthen the legislative branch. The most important of these interests is the provision of an arena within which agreements can be reached over issues of public policy, the rules of the political game, or even the allocation of power and resources among political actors.

Although Yemeni politics remain highly informal, negotiations over key issues have been conducted in parliament. Even agreements reached through negotiations conducted outside the parliamentary arena have subsequently been ratified in the legislature. In the wake of the civil war, parliament's function of providing an arena for negotiations has remained significant, for the president has sought to use the Chamber as a channel through which he can maintain contact with the opposition and use that opposition as a counterbalance to the Islah, if the need should arise. The executive has, therefore, developed a stake in ensuring that the YSP be able to utilize parliament to retain its political visibility and to defend its interests as well as contribute to debates on important issues of public policy. During interviews conducted in 1995, YSP deputies confirmed that although their party was subject to harassment at the branch level, their treatment in parliament was no different than that of members of any other party and that they were provided equal opportunity to fully participate in parliament's activities.

Yemen's legislature is also becoming a power base for at least some of its members. Many MPs have realized that the institution does provide significant political resources, and they therefore have developed a stake in further enhancing the Chamber's influence. This attitude prevails not only with regard to the provision of constituency services, but also concerning high-level political issues, including, as was shown, the areas of foreign affairs and national security. Because parliament is the YSP's and other, smaller opposition parties' principal means of access to decisionmaking and even to the public, these parties have a significant stake in the expansion of the institution's power.

Paradoxically, this is also the case of Shaikh Abdullah al-Ahmar, the speaker of parliament and leader of Islah. As the head of the main tribal confederation in a country where tribal alliances still underlie the power of the state, al-Ahmar has other bases of power besides parliament. Still, his parliamentary role both complements and legitimates his exercise of that power and provides him with further resources with which to serve the interests of the tribal constituencies he represents. During the debate over the budget in 1996, for example, Shaikh al-Ahmar, who was opposed to several of the stabilization measures proposed in it, used his position as speaker to influence that debate and to embarrass the government. As speaker he also is engaged in the conduct of foreign affairs and to some extent held personally accountable for the performance of the Chamber, a matter over which he is frequently interviewed in the press.

Finally, the daily television broadcasts of parliamentary sessions for approximately one-and-a-half hours (from 2 P.M. to 3:30 P.M.) provide an important window on Yemen's political process. For all the authoritarian leanings of Salih and the GPC, important issues are debated during these sessions, which are followed with great interest by Yemenis from all walks of life. The educational function of legislatures, discussed throughout this book, is therefore evident in Yemen and may help that country overcome the numerous obstacles that still stand in the way of its ability to consolidate its nascent democratic institutions.

10

Egypt

The Egyptian parliament has an impressive capacity. Among Arab legislatures, it has the longest history, dating back to 1866. It occupies the largest premises, which include an Italianate, domed building with appropriate baroque trimmings as well as a neighboring high-rise housing ample committee rooms and a comparatively large library. It employs some one thousand staff, several hundred of whom have university degrees, thereby giving it an administrative and research capacity that is the envy of the Arab world. Total membership in the upper and lower houses (Maglis al-Shura and Maglis al-Sha'b) approaches seven hundred, the greatest number of legislators in any Middle Eastern or north African country.

This capacity is presently underutilized, and full utilization would require political centrality, which for the most part has eluded the Egyptian parliament during its 130-year history. Evidence of this is the fact that only three of Egypt's elected parliaments since 1923 have completed their constitutional terms. At critical historical moments, and especially when executive power has temporarily weakened, the legislature has asserted itself. But when those crises have passed and executive power has reconsolidated, the legislative branch has been marginalized, as is presently the case.

Because the political centrality of the Egyptian parliament has ebbed and flowed but never persisted long enough to be consolidated, it is tempting to argue that such consolidation is precluded by the bureaucratic-authoritarian nature of politics and government in Egypt. And yet, even when parliament has been overshadowed by the executive branch, it has performed important political functions, as it does today. The very fact that the opposition has consistently sought to use parliament when challenging the established order suggests that the legislature's potential power is widely recognized, even when it seems to be politically dormant. Whether that potential can ever be realized in the form of institutionalizing a constitutional, democratic order with an ap-

propriate balance of power among the three branches of government remains
to be seen. The historical evidence is not encouraging, but democratic transitions have occurred in other bureaucratic-authoritarian polities, and such a
change is possible in Egypt as well.

Although Egypt embarked upon political liberalization in the mid-
1970s—years earlier than any other Arab country—it has now fallen behind
the polities examined in previous chapters. The costs of unfulfilled hopes are
apathy, cynicism, despair, and, on the other side of that coin, radicalism and
political violence. Egypt's stalled transition has eroded interest in parliament
and even debased that institution's reputation. Still, parliament remains *a*, if
not *the*, major arena for which government and opposition contest, and the intensity of that competition has increased in recent years. So, although the
stalled liberalization has undermined the status of parliament, that institution
remains central to the political calculations and behavior of government and
opposition alike. When and if the stalled liberalization is to regain forward
momentum, it will be the legislature that both benefits from it and provides
much of the impetus for it.

History of Parliament

The first assemblies in modern Egypt were the council established by
Napoleon during his short-lived occupation of the country (1798–1801) and
the Advisory Council (Maglis al-Mashwara) created in 1829 by Muhammad
Ali (the founder of the dynasty that ruled Egypt from 1805 until 1952). Both of
these were purely consultative bodies that had no legislative powers or executive oversight functions. In 1866 Khedive Isma'il—Egypt's hereditary ruler,
who nominally was a governor accountable to the Ottoman sultan but was in
practice independent—convened a Consultative Assembly of Delegates
(Maglis Shura al-Nuwwab). That Assembly consisted of seventy-five members
elected for a three-year term through a system of indirect elections. Isma'il had
intended it to be a docile gathering of rural notables who would approve his actions, thus helping him reduce domestic criticism of his profligate expenditures while enhancing his standing with Western creditors. Instead, the Assembly grew increasingly vociferous in its criticism of the khedive, becoming in
the late 1870s a focal point for mobilization against him and against Western
interference in Egypt's internal affairs (Brown and Amit 1994: 184).

For the first time in Egyptian history, the Assembly provided members of
the country's indigenous elite with a forum in which to examine and criticize
the policies of the ruler. It enabled them to express publicly their concerns
over issues such as taxation and government expenditures. Inspired by both
nationalism and economic considerations, the Assembly steadily imposed
more constitutional constraints on the executive branch. It agitated for greater

popular representation and governmental accountability and for mobilization against foreign penetration. In 1882, during the military revolt led by Colonel Ahmad 'Urabi, it even promulgated a draft parliamentary constitution. However, the draft was abrogated and the Assembly was disbanded after the rebellion was put down by British intervention (Lewis 1994: 50).

Great Britain's occupation of Egypt in 1882 slowed down—but did not eliminate—this trend toward constitutionalism and the restriction of monarchical absolutism. An organic law promulgated in May 1883 provided for two partially elected bodies: a legislative council of 30 members, 14 of whom were nominated and permanent and 16 of whom were indirectly elected for six years; and a General Assembly made up of the khedive's ministers, the members of the legislative council, and 46 others elected for six years. These bodies functioned regularly from 1883 to 1912, "asserting their views and rights against the khedive and sometimes against the occupying power" (Lewis 1994: 51).

In 1919, a nationalist uprising compelled the British to proclaim Egypt's formal independence, with important restrictions that actually left Britain as a key player in the country's political life. Four years later, King Fu'ad promulgated Egypt's first constitution, which was a product of negotiations among the three dominant forces in the country at the time: the monarch, the British, and the nationalist movement represented principally by the Wafd Party. Fearful of the nationalist movement, the British stood by the king in his demands for extensive constitutional powers. Accordingly, the 1923 constitution gave the king the right to appoint the prime minister, dismiss the cabinet, delay legislative sessions, and disband the legislature. (The constitution provided for a bicameral legislature, which consisted of a Senate and a Chamber of Deputies.) In addition, all bills had to be approved by the king, who was also responsible for appointing the president of the senate and one-fifth of its members.

Even though the 1923 constitution gave overwhelming power to the king, the latter repeatedly violated its provisions or suspended it (with the tacit or active support of the British) whenever he felt constrained by it. As a result, the Wafd, which originally had condemned this constitution as antidemocratic, came to be its major defender. Still, because of preponderant executive power and continued political manipulation by the British, the Wafd held government for only seven years between 1923 and 1952, even though it was far and away the country's most popular political party.

Executive-legislative relations established during that period are mirrored in today's practices. To subordinate parliament to his will, the king not only utilized the constitutional and even unconstitutional methods described above but also rigged elections and created several small, palace-dependent parties to do his bidding in parliament or in the cabinet. He relied on executive patronage to ensure his electoral control over the countryside and on gerrymandering of electoral districts to perpetuate the subordination of the more radical urban centers to conservative rural areas. These abuses of power undermined the credibility of the legislature and gave democracy and parliamentary politics a bad name in Egypt. They also eroded support for the political system, which was overthrown by a group of army officers on July 26, 1952. That coup created the regime that still rules Egypt today. From 1954 until 1970, that regime was dominated by Gamal Abdel Nasser.

Parliament During the Nasser Era (1952–1970)

What is remarkable about parliament under Nasser is that it was able to play any meaningful political role at all. It had been discredited during the previous era as a result of its manipulation by the executive. When Nasser and other Arab nationalists made parliament, along with democracy more generally, a scapegoat for all that ailed Egypt, parliament was further curtailed by Nasserist constitutions. The 1956 constitution substituted a presidential for a parliamentary system of government. It made the president responsible for appointing and dismissing ministers. It also established a single political party and empowered that party to approve all candidates for parliament, which was a unicameral National Assembly of 350 members. When these constitutional constraints on parliamentary independence failed to prevent members of parliament (MPs) from criticizing executive performance, they were further tightened in the 1964 constitution, which was decreed by the government two weeks before the new parliamentary session was to commence. The 1964 constitution required that half of the members of the National Assembly be workers or peasants. This provision guaranteed executive control over those seats, since "workers" were drawn from the civil service and public sector and thus were more or less nominated by the executive branch, whereas "peasant" MPs were typically enmeshed in the government rural patronage network and hence beholden to it. In addition, the 1964 constitution stipulated that the president would not be directly elected but would be nominated by the National Assembly and then confirmed in a popular referendum.

These lopsided constitutional arrangements were supplemented by executive practices intended to further subordinate the legislature. Principal among these was the selection of candidates by the ruling party, itself a creature of the executive. The high turnover of deputies was also critical. For example, only 76 of the 360 deputies elected to the 1964 Assembly had previously sat in parliament. High turnover resulted from the executive's strategy of rotating political patronage within the ruling party. This practice enabled the executive to derive maximum political control from patronage and to prevent the emergence of a cadre of skilled, experienced parliamentarians. This strategy is still used today.

Still, the legislature proved intermittently feisty in the face of executive power. On occasion, it even was able to force the cabinet to retreat. The 1964

Assembly, for example, attacked the government for implementing its new higher education policy through a presidential decree rather than through a bill proposed to parliament. (The government had acted under the guise of an alleged condition of "urgency" or "emergency," a tactic of dubious constitutionality used repeatedly by all of Egypt's rulers since King Fu'ad.) Parliamentary criticisms resulted in the postponement of the proposed reforms for a full year (Dekmejian 1971: 155–158).

In this instance as in most other similar cases, the Assembly's partial success stemmed primarily from the president's political calculations. By permitting certain constituencies to use parliament to voice their opposition to specific policies, Nasser was hoping to gain a measure of legitimacy and support for himself and his regime while providing a relatively safe outlet for the expression of grievances. For instance, academics and university administrators (professions that were more politically prominent then than they are now) were dismayed by some of the changes envisioned by the 1964 higher education policy that the cabinet was trying to implement. By allowing these professions to voice their opposition through parliamentary channels, Nasser gained a measure of support from them. In addition, parliamentary criticism of cabinet members created a check on those ministers' political ambitions and a means of stimulating and monitoring their performance. Finally, attacks on ministers or their programs in parliament gave Nasser justification for jettisoning those individuals or their policies whenever he needed to do so.

Intra-elite rivalries also contributed to parliament's occasional ability to stand up to executive power. During the Nasser era, leftists congregated in the only party, the Arab Socialist Union (ASU). Meanwhile, their opponents often relied on the National Assembly to mobilize support for their views. Thus the ASU and the Assembly were competitors and came to be seen as representing left and right, respectively. Significantly, the speaker of the Assembly from 1961 to 1969 was Anwar al-Sadat, who was strongly antagonistic to the left and its leadership. Sadat recruited Sayed Marei, a veteran politician and member of parliament during the ancien régime, as his deputy speaker. The two skillfully drew upon the material and political resources provided by the Assembly in their ongoing intra-elite struggle with the left. It was in Sadat's and Marei's interests to defend the constitutional role of the Assembly and to seek to bolster its status in the political system. By doing so, they illustrated a common feature of so-called bureaucratic-authoritarian systems—namely, that they are politically more heterogenous than is implied by that label. Factionalism within the elite provides opportunities for the assertion of authority by legislatures, as was the case of the Assembly during the Nasser era.

In the wake of the 1967 Arab-Israeli war, which significantly weakened the regime, the Assembly managed to circumvent the provision that the ASU screen all candidates to parliamentary seats. As a result, opponents of the left became ensconced in the Assembly, and their interests were served by strengthening the power of the legislature. That the Assembly played a role in the succession struggle that pitted Anwar al-Sadat against leftists is testament to the fact that it managed not only to survive but in some respects to prosper in the Nasser era.

The Legislature Under Sadat (1970–1981)

Nasser died in September 1970. His successor, Sadat, relied on parliament—the institution within which he had the greatest support—to legitimate and to some extent even to orchestrate his so-called Corrective Revolution of May 1971, which amounted to a purge of his political enemies. Within months a new constitution was adopted. That constitution remains in force today, although with several amendments. Like the document it replaced, the 1971 constitution concentrates power in the presidency. It gives the president the right to rule by decree and to disband the legislature, which was renamed the People's Assembly. In addition, it grants the president extensive powers over legislation and makes him responsible for appointing and dismissing ministers and the vice president.

Subsequent events illustrate a pattern noted earlier: Parliament asserts itself in times of executive weakness only to be subdued after the executive consolidates power. Caught in a "no war, no peace" situation with Israel and having yet to establish fully his personal legitimacy and control of the state apparatus, Sadat remained in a precarious position until the October 1973 Yom Kippur war broke out. In the meantime, the People's Assembly was invigorated by new elections held in November 1971 and by the president's announced intention of creating "a state of institutions." As John Waterbury noted, following the November 1971 elections "new MPs emphasized the fact that they were directly and 'popularly' elected to their seats, while noting that ASU representatives at all levels were often indirectly elected or appointed. The parliament therefore became the symbol of the return to a more democratic and liberal style" (Waterbury 1983: 365). The legislature immediately showed new dedication in carrying out its constitutionally mandated roles. In its first session (1971–1972), it considered and passed three times as many bills as it had in the previous session (1970–1971). In addition, it rejected more than a quarter of the legislation introduced by the government. Executive oversight, in the form of questions, requests for information, and creation of special and fact-finding committees, doubled. The ratio of bills introduced by MPs increased from 1 in 10 to 5 in 10—although of all bills that passed, those introduced by members rose only from 7 to 18 percent (Cooper 1982: 162–168). These data suggest that in the immediate wake of the Corrective Revolution, the Assembly was becoming a significant counterbalance to executive authority and was even moving, albeit tentatively, into the domain of lawmaking. In sum, it was leading a political liberalization over which the president had only partial control.

Following the October 1973 war, however, the Assembly's influence plummeted as the president brought the process of liberalization under his control and thereafter regulated its direction and progress. After 1973, the number of MP-initiated bills dropped dramatically, as did oversight activities. Still, the decline of parliament did not follow a straight downward path. Confident that he had accumulated sufficient power to contain serious challenges, Sadat in 1976 embarked on a controlled liberalization that included new parliamentary elections. Candidates did not have to be approved by the ASU and were allowed to run under the pseudoparty labels of left, center, or right or as independents. From this last category, 48 candidates were elected, making them a principal opposition force and inaugurating the conflict between independents and government that has continued through the Mubarak era. The center, which inherited the structure and executive support of the ASU and which within three years evolved into the National Democratic Party (NDP), won four-fifths of the seats. The right won 10 seats and the left 3.

The struggle to create a multiparty political system occurred primarily in parliament, which was charged by the executive with the task of drafting a law to govern the creation and operations of parties. The debate over that law revealed both the strengths and weaknesses of the legislature in the condition of controlled liberalization. Parliament's strength was reflected in the fact that the president felt compelled to legitimate the regulation of political parties by having the legislature pass the appropriate legislation; by the fact that not only the government, but also independents and members of the left introduced bills; and by the protracted and intense nature of parliamentary maneuver and debate that resulted in the passage of Law 40 of 1977. This law is still in effect, even though many of its provisions have subsequently been modified by judicial decisions.

By contrast, the weakness of parliament was indicated by both the content of Law 40 and the method by which it was passed. With respect to the former, the law created various obstacles to the founding of parties, including support by twenty MPs and certification by a committee composed of members of the executive, the ruling party, and the judiciary. As for the way in which the law was passed, it violated normal procedures. Parliament's bylaws indeed required that the legislative "traffic cop," the Committee for Legislative Affairs (CLA), issue reports on all bills that pertained to the same subject upon referring those bills to the floor. In this particular case, however (and in many subsequent cases, for that matter), the CLA made no mention of the bills introduced by independents and the left when it reported on the government's draft legislation (El-Mikawy 1991: 113–119).

Having first reined in the relatively spontaneous liberalization, Sadat was then forced to abort the more controlled one. His trip to Jerusalem in November 1977, followed by negotiations that resulted in a peace treaty in March 1979, stimulated domestic criticism that he was not prepared to tolerate. Be-

ginning in early spring 1978, he steadily tightened the screws on political activity, with parliament being the principal arena in which executive pressure
was brought to bear. For criticizing Sadat's policies, several MPs were
stripped first of their parliamentary immunity and then of their membership.
Furthermore, a newly created party called the New Wafd provoked Sadat's
ire, prompting him to push through parliament Law 33 of 1978, which pro-
hibited political parties "that did not espouse the principles of the July [1952]
Revolution." In this fashion, Sadat forced the New Wafd to dissolve one hundred days after it had come into existence. A few months later, he similarly
rammed through parliament Law 36 of 1979, which banned all parties that
opposed the peace with Israel.

Shortly thereafter, Sadat dissolved the People's Assembly and held new
elections. They were contested by four parties: the progovernment NDP, the
left-wing National Progressive Unionist Party (NPUP, or al-tagammu'), the
Liberal Party (the successor to the right wing of the former ASU), and the Labor Party, which Sadat had brought into existence with the intention of creating a credible "loyal opposition." Also taking part in the elections were some
1,192 independents. The NDP won an overwhelming 347 seats, 200 of which
were occupied by newcomers. Since no NPUP candidate was elected, the Labor Party, with 29 seats, became the official opposition. Independents, who
had been particularly outspoken in their criticism of Sadat, managed to win
only 10 seats (in 1976, by comparison, 48 of 897 independent candidates had
been elected).

Although Sadat must have believed that such an Assembly would be little
more than a rubber stamp for his policies, that did not turn out to be the case.
The first task of the new parliament was to ratify various laws that Sadat had
decreed prior to the commencement of the session. Article 147 of the constitution states that the president can issue decrees in the absence of the Assembly under "conditions which cannot suffer delay." However, such decrees
must then be approved by parliament when it reconvenes. The speaker provided MPs with copies of Sadat's decrees, now embodied in draft legislation,
only minutes before they were called upon to vote on them. Several independent and Labor MPs objected, demonstrating thereby that even rigged elections do not guarantee the absolute quiescence of parliament. Sadat refused to
brook even this limited criticism. He induced almost half of the Labor MPs to
defect to the NDP, thereby reducing parliamentary opposition to a mere handful of deputies.

Because of his own experience as speaker during the 1960s, Sadat knew
that even a weak parliament can be used by opposition forces to further their
agenda. This may explain why much of the energy he devoted to domestic
politics in the last three years of his life focused on subordinating the People's
Assembly to his will. Ultimately, he more or less succeeded in that effort.
This strategy, however, caused him to become increasingly isolated, leaving

him with little other than repression or the threat of it as a means to rule. By undermining the political autonomy of parliament, Sadat had eroded his own legitimacy. This contributed to the tense political atmosphere that prevailed until his assassination on October 6, 1981.

Parliament Under Mubarak (1981–)

Three characteristics of the relationship between the executive branch and parliament that became apparent during the Sadat era have become yet more pronounced under his successor, Husni Mubarak. The first is that access to parliament is the principal point of contention between government and opposition. The second is that the centrality of parliament varies inversely with the degree to which the executive has consolidated power. The final characteristic is that presidential legitimacy is largely a function of the representation of the opposition within the legislature: the fewer opposition MPs in parliament, the lower the level of presidential legitimacy.

These three characteristics are closely related. During the 1980s, Mubarak sought to exchange a limited increase in the access to, and centrality of, parliament for recognition of his right to rule. The parliament that presided over his succession to the presidency in 1981 was the one produced by Sadat's vengeful 1979 elections, in which he had sought to purge the legislature of all meaningful opposition. That parliament was thus too weak to provide real legitimacy for the new president. Accordingly, although wary of the consequences of free and fair elections, Mubarak sought through the election of a slightly more representative legislature in 1984 to provide some substance to his claim to be a democrat, a claim by which he hoped to bolster his popularity.

Mubarak prepared the ground carefully for the 1984 elections, as he has done for subsequent ones in 1987, 1990, and 1995. In the lead-up to the 1984 elections, opposition spokespersons (including those for the Wafd Party, which had been brought back to political life by a 1983 decision of the Supreme Constitutional Court) demanded that Egypt's long-standing constituency-based, multimember, simple majority, winner-take-all electoral system be changed to a proportional representation system. With this demand the opposition unwittingly played into the hands of the executive and the leadership of the NDP. A proportional representation, party-list system was bound to give the NDP's leadership much greater control over candidate selection. It also would prevent independents from even contesting the elections.

Not surprisingly, the government accepted the demand and then incorporated into the electoral law additional provisions designed to screen out opposition candidates. One such stipulation was that a party could enter parliament only if it captured a minimum of 8 percent of the vote nationwide. In addition, a complex formula for distributing votes was adopted that favored the dominant party. The electoral importance of candidates' local support bases was also reduced by increasing the number of seats from 350 to 448 while simultaneously enlarging the districts and bringing their number down from 175 to 48. Finally, each party was required to field two lists of candidates in every district. The official rationale for this decision was to deal with the contingency of some candidates' withdrawing from a party's original list. In reality, the new measure was designed to work against opposition parties, which find it much harder than the ruling NDP to present two lists of candidates. Ignored were opposition demands that judges rather than local officials of the Ministry of Interior supervise elections and that an improved voter identification system be adopted.

The 73 percent of the vote won by the NDP translated into 391 seats, or 87 percent of the total. Meanwhile, the combined vote of opposition parties, which was 27 percent, resulted in those parties' receiving only 13 percent of parliamentary seats. No independents were elected. The Socialist Labor Party fell one percentage point short of that required for representation in parliament, so its votes, as well as those of NPUP and the Liberals (which in total amounted to 11.9 percent of all votes cast), were allocated to the NDP. Ultimately the courts ruled that the complex and largely unfair formula for distribution of votes had been fraudulently applied in several districts and that those NDP deputies elected as a result should be unseated. Parliament, however, refused to comply: Its speaker, supported by more than four-fifths of the NDP contingent, contested the courts' jurisdiction over the legislative branch. The opposition electoral coalition of the Muslim Brotherhood (MB) and the Wafd, which had won 58 seats, became the principal parliamentary opposition and proceeded to use its limited presence to good effect. In the 1984–1985 session, for example, MPs associated with the Wafd-MB alliance submitted 22 percent of all bills (El-Mikawy 1991: 364).

In December 1986 the Supreme Constitutional Court ruled that the electoral law was unconstitutional because it prevented independent candidates from contesting elections. Accordingly, new elections were held the following year. The revised election law passed by the People's Assembly stipulated that independents could compete for one seat in each of the forty-eight districts. That this concession to independents was so limited reflected governmental apprehension about their potential role in parliament. Three years later the Supreme Constitutional Court ruled that this revised electoral law was also unconstitutional, thereby precipitating the 1990 elections, for which the party-list system was abolished.

Despite the constraints of the electoral law, the opposition managed to capture 22 percent of the seats in the 1987 Assembly. Eight independents— not including those more or less aligned with the NDP—also won. The legislature elected in 1987 thus revealed the underlying weakness of the NDP's appeal to voters. The ruling party's percentage of the vote had fallen to 68.8, the poorest showing for the incumbent party since 1950. Even if the votes of

NDP-aligned independent candidates are added to the total, the NDP obtained no more than 77 percent of the votes, that is, 5 percent less than the ruling party's performance in the relatively free 1976 elections. The 1987 election, in short, signaled to government and opposition alike that their competition was becoming a more equal one. In particular, the election of 56 deputies from the new MB, Labor, and Liberal Party alliance, of which 36 were from the MB, reflected the MB's electoral appeal (which, largely as a result of restrictions on its activities, was only partially translated into votes and parliamentary seats). With the Wafd's 36 MPs, the combined opposition controlled 92 of the 448 Assembly seats.

The weakness of the NDP, then as now, is in fact much greater than the aggregate vote or even distribution of seats suggests. That weakness is due to the party's relative lack of appeal in urban and industrialized areas. Only through gerrymandering and the overrepresentation of rural areas does the NDP actually manage to win its lopsided parliamentary majorities. In 1987, for example, the NDP won a mere 51 percent of the votes in Cairo, only 42 percent of those in Port Said, and 39 percent of those in Suez. To secure its overwhelming parliamentary majorities the government thus has to inflate the value of those rural votes it can more easily control. Significantly, border provinces, where the governmental bureaucracy dominates and where the NDP typically captures overwhelming majorities, are vastly overrepresented in parliament. With a population of just over half a million in 1987, those provinces elected 20 MPs, whereas Egypt's largest cities, with a combined population of almost 10 million—twenty times as much—elected only 90 MPs (El-Mikawy 1991: 334). Partly to facilitate this gerrymandering, the government discourages voter registration, especially in urban areas. In rural areas, voter registration is done en bloc by families and clans, who receive encouragement from officials. In cities, by contrast, social solidarities are less compelling, and governmental involvement is of a negative, rather than positive, nature. Until 1994, when the voter registration law was amended to extend the registration period from November to February, that law permitted new voters to register only during the month of December and through a relatively cumbersome procedure at that.

Turnout rates reflect the government's desire to encourage rural and discourage urban voters. In 1987, for example, fewer than 2 million of the almost 10 million inhabitants of Egypt's largest cities were registered voters, compared to over 200,000 registered voters out of just over 500,000 residents in the border governorates. Of just over 20 million residents of the Delta, 7 million were registered voters. Thus border governorate residents were more than twice as likely, and Delta residents 50 percent more likely, to be registered voters than were inhabitants of the large cities. As Mark Cooper noted, the ruling party has, through patronage networks, "gained control over the traditional political structures of the agricultural areas and in the fringe," but it is unable to "dominate the politics of the cities and the industrial areas," which constitute "the real constituency for a policy of political liberalization" (Cooper 1982: 233–234).

Despite these obstacles the opposition fared comparatively well in the 1987 elections. Its strong position in parliament resulted in a series of confrontations with the government. Islamist MPs utilized the power of interpellation to harry the minister of interior over allegations of torture of detainees. When in March 1988 the government rammed through legislation to extend the state of emergency, not only did all opposition MPs vote against it, but they were joined by three NDP deputies.

In the event, however, the opposition was unable to capitalize on its comparatively strong position in the 1987 legislature. Its failure to do so resulted in part from it own miscalculation. When new elections were declared as a result of the Supreme Constitutional Court's decision invalidating the election law under which that parliament had been elected, opposition parties, with the exception of the NPUP, announced that they would boycott those elections unless supervision was to be conducted directly by the judiciary, as opposed to the Ministry of Interior. Hoping to exploit the government's need to demonstrate its popularity in the lead-up to the Gulf War, and assuming that the government would also feel pressure to legitimate the Assembly prior to the upcoming presidential election, the opposition overplayed its hand. As it transpired, the government was less concerned about its democratic legitimacy than it was worried by the prospect of yet stronger opposition in the legislature. It therefore refused to give ground. Consequently, of the significant opposition parties, only the NPUP contested the elections, and it won a mere 6 seats. The NDP, including independents aligned with it, captured 385 seats, or 86 percent of the total. Able to marshal at most twenty-five votes on important bills (most of which after 1991 were intended to further constrict political participation), the opposition lost the capacity it previously had enjoyed to utilize parliamentary procedures to embarrass the government and occasionally induce it to change its approach.

The opposition realized its mistake almost immediately after the 1990 elections and determined forthwith to prepare thoroughly for the scheduled 1995 elections. However, the Islamist insurgency that broke out in 1992 raised political tensions to a level with which Egypt's fragile institutions for representation and protection of the rule of law could not cope. The government, apparently worried equally by the legal, aboveground opposition and the militant Islamist insurgency, embarked in 1993 on a series of steps that led in the fall of 1995 to a situation reminiscent of that just before Sadat's assassination in October 1981.

The thrust of governmental measures was to make no distinction between the formal, legal opposition and the insurgents. From February 1993 until the November-December 1995 elections, the severity of these measures increased steadily. In February 1993, alarmed by the growing influence of the Islamist movement within professional syndicates, the government rammed through parliament the so-called Law to Guarantee Democracy Within Professional Syndicates, the impact of which was to place most syndicate elections directly under government control. In October of that year the government tightened pressure on journalists, amending the Journalists Syndicate law to place all promotions under governmental supervision. In March 1994, parliament passed legislation to terminate the century-old practice of electing village mayors and deputy mayors, a step the government apparently deemed necessary because the opposition, especially the MB, had performed comparatively well in the 1992 local government elections. Less than a month later, parliament extended the Emergency Law for a further three years, with only twelve dissenting votes being cast (as compared to some five times that number in the 1987 parliament). In May 1995, the government forced the legislature to pass in a matter of hours Law 93, which drastically increased penalties on journalists accused of libeling government officials. In the summer of 1995 the government moved to close down human rights organizations active in Egypt.

Coupled with these measures was a security crackdown that was progressively extended until it ultimately included scores of candidates in the 1995 parliamentary elections. Several journalists were arrested on spurious charges or simply beaten up by government thugs. The new antiterrorism law legalized the practice of sending civilians to trial in military courts. That practice steadily gained momentum until, two months before the election, virtually the entirety of the Muslim Brotherhood leadership, including many candidates for parliament, was sent to military courts for offenses of considerably lesser magnitude than those on which alleged Islamist terrorists were being tried. Fifty-four members of the MB were sentenced to jail terms immediately prior to the elections, at which time the government also announced that the MB was "inextricably linked to terrorist organizations." The Ministry of Interior closed and sealed MB headquarters on the grounds that its members had been holding secret meetings there. The former leader of the MB parliamentary delegation was sentenced to five years' hard labor.

To ensure the overwhelming defeat of the opposition, the government manipulated the election law. The National Dialogue conference of July 1994 had discussed whether the country should revert to a proportional representation system, but no definitive conclusion had been reached. The government had promised to take the matter under advisement. Then it delayed its decision for more than a year, thereby severely limiting the time opposition parties would have to prepare their slates of candidates, which was no simple task given the expansion of the number of districts from 48 to 222. By reducing the lead time before the election, the government created uncertainty and confusion within opposition parties.

Although since 1992 the government has relied primarily on the stick in its approach to the opposition, it also has brandished the carrot intermittently, hoping that some elements of the opposition would choose to receive benefits rather than be harassed. The most noteworthy example of this was the National Dialogue. President Mubarak had announced during his presidential acceptance speech before parliament in October 1993 that he wanted to conduct a dialogue with the opposition. In reality the National Dialogue was intended, as have been virtually all subsequent "carrots," as a device to split the secular from the Islamist (i.e., Muslim Brotherhood) opposition. That effort failed, largely because the government was unwilling to make sufficient concessions to the secular opposition in the form of guarantees of political freedoms. Consequently, the National Dialogue became a stage-managed event that produced no tangible results. In the final days of the 1995 election campaign, and even as the votes were being counted, the government made overtures to several prominent secular and semisecular opposition political figures, including the NPUP leader Khaled Muhyi al-Din and Labor Party activist Adil Hussein. When those politicians and others rejected these overtures, the government ensured their electoral defeats. In the case of Khaled Muhyi al-Din, it did so after it had first tentatively declared his victory.

The irregularities of the 1995 elections were reminiscent of those of 1979, and they produced remarkably similar results. The NDP took 417 of 444 seats, with opposition parties winning but 14. Only one candidate representing Islamism, a member of the MB running as an independent, succeeded in winning a seat. The Wafd Party became the leader of the opposition, with a mere 6 seats (the exact number as those held by the NPUP when it constituted the opposition's leadership in the 1979 Assembly). All opposition MP stalwarts were removed from parliament. Ibrahim Shukry, for example, leader of the Labor Party, was defeated in Daqhaliya, where he had won in every election since 1950 (with the exception of the 1990 election, which he boycotted). Fikri al-Gazzar, a popular, veteran independent MP with a reputation as the most outspoken critic of the government in the 1990–1995 parliament, was also defeated.

The political uproar produced by governmental transgressions during the campaign and by the conduct and the results of the election may have been greater than the president had anticipated. The U.S. government issued a statement emphasizing its concern about reports of irregularities and expressed the hope that the Egyptian government would investigate them. Such veiled criticism from the United States, combined with domestic dissatisfaction, probably contributed to the decision on January 3, 1996, to replace Prime Minister Atif Sidqi, the longest-serving prime minister in Egypt's history, with former deputy prime minister Kamal al-Ganzuri. Because a month earlier President Mubarak had flatly declared that there would be no change of government after the elections, this step was widely seen as an attempt to provide at least the image of change, since the elections had failed to provide the reality of it.

Still, although neither free nor fair, the 1995 elections paradoxically demonstrated that substantial potential exists for a negotiated transition to democracy in Egypt. All legal parties participated actively in the campaign. The MB defied governmental intimidation and its leaders risked lengthy prison sentences in order for some of its members to contest seats as independents or to run in alliance with the Labor and Liberal parties. The poor showing of the opposition reflected in part the sharp divisions in its ranks. Rivalry between secularists and Islamists was intense in districts where both fielded candidates. Fierce as well was the competition between candidates who subscribed to opposing economic philosophies, with the Wafd and Liberals endorsing neoliberalism and the Nasserists and NPUP adhering to various versions of Arab socialism. Such competition suggests the maturation of the political system into one in which parties provide voters with choices between reasonably coherent political-economic philosophies.

The Islamic insurgency was certainly not the only cause of the government's heavy-handed tactics in the mid-1990s. After all, by the fall of 1995 that insurgency had been at least temporarily contained. Instead, the government's increasing intolerance of political autonomy was driven primarily by the ruling elite's concern about the legal opposition, which seeks access to power through the ballot box. As discussed above, the electoral base of the ruling party is fragile and in decline. The strongest organized political tendency in the country is Islamism. Were free and fair elections to be held, the MB would very likely win more votes than any other party. The regime, therefore, has felt that it has no choice but to turn its back on democracy and impose its will by the threat or use of physical coercion and by electoral fraud and interference. The resulting popular discontent, however, has contributed to growing public support for political change, which in turn has brought increased political pressure to bear on the ruling party.

The consequences of that pressure manifested themselves during and after the 1995 election. The large number of former NDP stalwarts who contested seats as independents was due in part to their awareness of the unpopularity of the ruling party. Indeed, some 140 candidates running as independents won, with the overwhelming majority of them then joining the NDP bloc in parliament. However, because of its lack of popularity, the NDP has only a limited capacity to enforce discipline among its members in the People's Assembly. This explains why the NDP parliamentary majority has been so critical of the government in areas of "low policy," especially those connected to service delivery. Far from being a monolithic organization, the NDP is so fragmented that its various factions compete actively against one another, especially in the parliamentary arena.

Manifestations of intraparty contestation within the People's Assembly have occurred with increasingly regularity since the 1995 election. When the new parliamentary session commenced in November 1997, for example, the speaker, backed up by Kamal al-Shazli (who is the minister of state for parliamentary affairs and thus the key "enforcer" in the body), sought to railroad through the government's choice for the deputy speakership for Upper Egypt. Amal Osman, who had been the long-serving minister of social affairs, had just been elected to the Assembly from a constituency in Upper Egypt that was the site of her ancestral home but where she had few remaining connections. NDP deputies representing Upper Egypt revolted; they refused to support her candidacy and voted instead for a senior member with much closer associations with that region. Al-Shazli immediately intervened, inducing that member to withdraw his candidacy, thereby enabling Osman, who had the next highest number of votes, to assume the deputy speakership. For weeks thereafter, NDP deputies from Upper Egypt took every opportunity to complain to the press about this incident and about the lack of proper representation of their region.

Possibly at least partially in retaliation for this incident, MPs in the following month upbraided the Assembly's leadership (i.e., Fathi Surour and al-Shazli) for having allowed a U.S. Agency for International Development (USAID) project designed to strengthen both the lower and upper houses to proceed without formal approval by either house. When some senior deputies, including onetime presidential adviser Mustafa al-Fiqi, joined the chorus of criticism, Surour and al-Shazli gave way, suspending the project and agreeing to renegotiate it before presenting it for approval.

In short, electoral irregularities in the 1995 elections reflected the relative weakness of the ruling party. They also detracted from the government's legitimacy, thus further weakening it vis-à-vis the opposition. Because the People's Assembly produced by the elections does not accurately reflect public opinion, it cannot legitimize the government. In this context, factionalism within the NDP encourages sniping at governmental policies and performance, thereby further weakening both that party and the government. Egypt in the late 1990s therefore suggests that elections and parliaments—even when thoroughly subordinate to the executive branch—can create pressure for a transition toward more democratic forms of government.

Determinants of Parliament's Role in the Political System

Having highlighted the main themes and patterns in Egypt's parliamentary history, we now turn to an analysis of the political, economic, and constitutional context in which parliament operates.

The Political Economy

The Egyptian government's extensive control of the economy puts a vast array of political tools at its disposal. Among them is the political exploitation of the approximately six million persons who are on the state's payroll. This constituency is constantly reminded of its dependence on government. It is deployed for election rallies in support of government-backed candidates. It is used to fill the "worker" contingent of the People's Assembly, and since the Sadat era it has typically provided about one-third of the membership of the lower house. In sum, public-sector workers and civil service employees make up the government's principal political foot soldiers.

Other divisions of "political infantry" are provided by rural inhabitants, whose livelihoods remain heavily influenced by governmental regulation of agriculture. For rural producers, to earn the antipathy of government is an invitation to economic disaster. This economic dependence gives the government enormous political leverage. Consequently, although Egypt's cities are the sail of the political system, rural Egypt is its anchor. That anchor, however, is of illusory steadfastness, in part because of the gradual retraction of state intervention in the rural economy and in part because of the gap between formal and informal political processes. The paradox of Upper Egypt's being the region along the Nile that provides the ruling party with its greatest electoral margins while also being the location of the most protracted insurgency in Egypt's modern history points to the shallowness of formal political structures and processes in rural areas.

"Officers" in the government's political army are recruited from the thousands of high-ranking civil servants, managers and board members of public companies, and party apparatchiks. In their roles as "political officers" they fill a host of appointed political positions, although those in parliament are nominally elected ones. The Maglis al-Shura, for example, which Sadat created in 1980 to counterbalance the People's Assembly, is elected through a party list system that awards all seats to the party that wins a majority of votes. The opposition, which wants this upper house adjourned *sine die*, has never contested Maglis al-Shura elections, which are held every three years for half the full membership. Virtually all members who have served in the Maglis al-Shura have been pensioned off from the universities, the civil service, the public sector, or (in the case of former ministers) the political system. All have been from the NDP.

The lower house (People's Assembly) is also used to reward the government's political foot soldiers and officers. Membership brings prestige and legal immunity; the latter has been exploited by numerous con men. Membership also provides access to government, which in turn opens the door to favors that can be either directly consumed or passed on to constituents for political or material rewards. As corruption has spread, parliamentary seats have become increasingly attractive investments, and competition for them consequently has increased. Significantly, 4,277 candidates contested the 1995 elections, the highest number in history. Of those candidates, 1,350 had formerly been of the NDP, but when they failed to receive nominations from that party, they contested seats as independents. Of this group, 90 had sat in the preceding Assembly. The government manipulates NDP endorsement, hence governmental patronage, to maintain the allegiance of its political army.

The government also parachutes cabinet ministers into the lower house to bolster their status and further ensure governmental control over that body. Almost three-quarters of sitting ministers were elected to the People's Assembly in the 1995 elections, a record absolute number and proportion of cabinet ministers. The minister of state for parliamentary affairs, Kamal al-Shazli, won 100 percent of the votes in his district (that constituency's other seat was won by his brother Shahin). Of the seven ministers elected in the first round of voting, two (al-Shazli and People's Assembly speaker Fathi Surour) are the government's "political officers" for parliament. The longest-serving cabinet member in Mubarak's Egypt, Amal Osman, in 1995 confronted her toughest election campaign. As minister of social affairs, Osman had enforced the onerous provisions of Law 32 of 1964, by which private voluntary associations are brought under strict governmental control. Running against a popular Islamist candidate (the son of a former supreme guide of the MB), Osman was widely predicted to lose were the elections even to approach being free and fair. The government, fearing the embarrassment that her defeat would cause, rounded up the opposition candidate's poll watchers before voting began, clearing the way for Osman's landslide victory.

The overwhelming role of the government in Egypt's political economy provides it with almost limitless means to influence election outcomes and formal political behavior more generally. The ruling elite sees parliament more as yet another component of the vast state spoils system than as a representative body that is to oversee the executive, legislate, or perform other tasks normally associated with legislatures. Since the great majority of MPs owe their seats to this spoils system and sit in parliament primarily for the purpose of exploiting it, development of the institution is a difficult task indeed.

The Legal/Constitutional Framework

The constitutional framework establishes a bicameral legislature. The lower house is elected every five years unless dissolved by the president. Half of the members of the consultative upper house are elected every three years. The two houses meet on alternate weeks from October until July. The very existence of the consultative upper house, the membership of which is essentially appointed by the president, tilts the balance of legislative-executive relations further toward the latter.

Constitutional arrangements in Egypt have tended to reflect rather than to create power relationships. The basic law adopted by the Assembly in 1882 was the only constitution put forward by the legislature rather than by the executive. Egypt's two most recent constitutions, those of 1964 and 1971, were both decreed by the president a matter of weeks prior to the commencement of parliamentary sessions. The latter constitution, which remains in effect as amended, is built around an extremely strong presidency. Elected for six years, the president is head of state and commander of the armed forces. He appoints the prime minister and cabinet and can both convene and dissolve the People's Assembly at any time. He can call and chair cabinet meetings and even serve as prime minister. Article 147 permits him to rule by decree in cases of emergency, and Article 108 provides him the power to unilaterally declare laws during a period stipulated by the Assembly. Articles 74 and 152 provide him the power to hold referenda by which the Assembly can be bypassed. Although the Assembly can vote no-confidence in the Council of Ministers, the president can then ask the Assembly to reconsider. If it refuses, the president can then hold a referendum that, if in favor of the president, causes the Assembly to be dissolved. The president may appoint up to ten additional members to the People's Assembly.

Typical powers of a legislature that are assigned to the Egyptian parliament by the 1971 constitution include the right to initiate legislation and to reject laws proposed by the government or decreed by the president. The legislature is also empowered to participate in the budgetary process and to oversee the executive through fact-finding investigations, questions, or interpellations of ministers. In 1976 Sadat placed the Central Audit Organization under the People's Assembly, a move that endowed that body with the potential capacity to investigate executive abuses. Virtually unique is the constitutional requirement that half of MPs be workers or peasants. This provision favors the government because "opposition parties have difficulty cobbling together tickets that meet the stipulation" and because it "reduces the representation in the Assembly of members of the liberal professions, such as lawyers, who are apt to be active in debate and legislation" (Lesch 1996: 621).

Constitutional imbalance is tilted yet further in favor of the executive by the state of emergency under which Egypt has lived for almost half a century. First decreed in the 1950s and then renewed for a decade in the wake of the 1967 war, the current state of emergency was reimposed in the wake of Sadat's assassination in 1981. Since then "it has become a general pattern [for the Assembly] to approve the extension of the Emergency Law within one day, without any room for debate or opposition" (Rabie 1995: 422). On April 11, 1994, amid howls of protest by opposition deputies, it was renewed for a further three years. Under the state of emergency the president may order arrests, forbid meetings, and prevent citizens from moving and have them searched for contraband material. MPs are not immune from these provisions; under Mubarak, they repeatedly have been prevented by the police from attending meetings and election rallies. In the 1995 parliamentary election campaign, the president utilized the state of emergency to enable the Ministry of Interior to arrest scores of actual and potential candidates. That ministry even violated the provision of the Emergency Law that specifies that suspects who have not been convicted of a crime can be detained for "only" six months. In reality, the ministry detained for seven months potential candidates to parliament who had been arrested in January 1995. Then, in July 1995, it simply referred these candidates to military courts for trial, taking advantage of the fact that there is no time limit for detention under the military legal system.

Interaction Among the Three Branches of Government

The nominal powers of the legislature are further constricted in practice by an executive that engages in dirty tricks and extralegal behavior. Mention has already been made of manipulation of the party and election laws and of actual violations of the latter by the government. Other means utilized to prevent opposition candidates from winning parliamentary seats include limiting these candidates' access to the electronic media and intimidating the opposition press. The leadership of the New Civic Forum, a think tank with informal links to the Wafd Party, complained at the end of the 1995 election campaign that in the past thirty years the Wafd had been provided exactly eighty minutes of television time to present its program and candidates. Press Law 93 of 1995 imposes draconian penalties on journalists who "libel" members of the executive branch. During the 1995 parliamentary campaign the government interrogated the editor of *al-Wafd* under the provisions of that law. It also threatened to try Magdi Hussein, editor of *al-Sha'b*, the mouthpiece of the Socialist Party–Muslim Brotherhood alliance, on the basis that his paper had violated provisions of the law.

Despite these restrictions, the press remains active and outspoken. During the 1995 campaign and the election itself, opposition newspapers highlighted governmental abuses. Press Law 93 stirred up a hornet's nest of enraged journalists, including prestigious editors and writers from the government's own newspapers. Acting through their syndicate, journalists were able to force the government to concede to the creation of a special committee to propose an amended press law. In the event, the lack of inclusion of representatives of the opposition press on that committee created yet another furor that was reported in detail in opposition newspapers. Throughout 1997, *al-Sha'b* relentlessly attacked the minister of interior, Hassan al-Alfi, alleging that he had benefited improperly from real estate dealings and claiming that his ministry was shot through with corruption. (Al-Alfi was relieved of his post in the wake of the November 17, 1997, attack on tourists in Luxor and ended up in court defending himself against *al-Sha'b*'s charges.) In short, Egypt's fourth estate is too well developed and has enjoyed substantial freedom of expression for too long for the government to muzzle it without expending huge sums of political capital.

Parliamentary immunity is utilized in carrot-and-stick fashion by the executive to force MPs to toe its line. In 1977, for example, Ahmad Yunis, a prominent deputy who had a powerful base of support in the agricultural cooperatives, let it be known that he was contemplating leaving the ruling party to join the newly formed Wafd Party. The government responded by announcing that he was under investigation for corruption and that his parliamentary immunity was to be lifted. In numerous other cases since that time the NDP has refused to lift the immunity of those of its MPs who have been caught up in corruption scandals. In 1997 some deputies revolted temporarily against the speaker when he sought to strip former minister of economy Mustafa al-Said of his immunity because of allegations of improper and illegal business dealings. Whether those members did not want to set a precedent, or whether they truly believed insufficient evidence had been presented, is not clear. In any case the relevant committee initially refused to endorse the request. However, after more revelations about al-Said's business dealings were revealed in the press, the speaker reintroduced the motion. This time, he secured its passage, although not without continued grumbling by many members who remained opposed to the lifting of immunity and believed that the government was seeking to punish the former minister out of other considerations.

In sum, even though the executive enjoys constitutional-legal powers considerably superior to those of the legislative branch, it does not even feel compelled to abide by the constitutional framework. Moreover, parliament has been unable to force the executive to respect the constitution. Still, by highlighting the ruling elite's various excesses, such as the abuse of immunity, the opposition has intermittently embarrassed the government.

The legislature—precisely because it poses a greater potential threat to the executive than does the judiciary—is more strictly controlled by that executive. Enjoying considerably more autonomy, courts have provided a measure of protection for the individual rights of Egyptians. However, they have been unable to force the executive to adhere to the constitutional-legal framework that nominally governs its relations with the legislature.

Under Sadat the relative autonomy of the court system was considerably expanded, largely because he sought to utilize that system to contain his opponents within the political elite and to provide additional means to monitor and supervise the sprawling bureaucracy (Rosberg 1994). The 1971 constitution provides for the independence of administrative courts and endows them with the power to review decisions taken by governmental agencies. In 1972 legislation was passed that increased the autonomy of the Council of State, under which the administrative courts operate. The Supreme Administrative Court was also removed from the Ministry of Justice and placed under a general assembly of judges. Further legislation in 1984 enabled the Council of State to take more control over the appointment and postings of senior judges.

As a result of these legal-constitutional changes, the administrative courts have become a principal venue for Egyptians who seek redress of grievances that arise from their dealings with government. Increasingly this has included cases involving abridgements of personal political freedoms. Because the political opposition has enjoyed much greater success in pursuing its claims through the legal system than it has in parliament, it has sought to subordinate some aspects of parliamentary activity to the judicial branch. Most important in this regard is the supervision of parliamentary elections, which the opposition would rather be in the hands of judges than in those of parliament, where the ruling party ensures that key decisions are made to the detriment of the opposition.

The constitution states that the People's Assembly has the power to determine the legality of elections. Nevertheless, the Supreme Administrative Court has ruled that since the agencies that review the eligibility of candidates for elections and that supervise them are administrative, their acts and decisions can be appealed to the Council of State. As a result, opposition candidates have increasingly appealed to the courts to intervene in parliamentary elections. In 1989 the Supreme Administrative Court ruled that thirty-nine members of the NDP had been fraudulently elected, and it awarded their seats to members of opposition parties. The leadership of the People's Assembly refused to obey this decision. The constitutional crisis that ensued was resolved when the Supreme Constitutional Court ruled that the electoral law was unconstitutional, to which President Mubarak responded by dissolving the Assembly.

Following the 1990 elections, sixty-nine deputies were ruled to have been elected fraudulently, but the Assembly again rejected the court's claim for jurisdiction, this time with impunity. In 1995 opposition parties appealed to the courts immediately following the first stage of elections and obtained rulings in numerous cases to freeze results pending investigations into allegations of fraud. The Ministry of Interior ignored the decisions, and the Assembly subsequently seated those NDP candidates whose election had successfully been contested in court.

The courts' responsiveness to the opposition has led to numerous conflicts between the judicial and legislative branches, largely over the issue of jurisdiction over elections and parliamentary immunity. In these conflicts NDP deputies argue the case for the autonomy of the legislative branch, which is a tactical response, for they certainly do not contend that the principle should be extended to legislative-executive relations. The opposition's infatuation with the judicial branch is similarly tactical. For both sides, the strategic prize is the legislature.

Exercise of Power Within Parliament

During the 1990s, NDP members of the lower house have repeatedly exercised power in ways that have violated the spirit and, in some cases, the actual content of the Assembly's bylaws. NDP domination of key positions and resources makes such behavior possible. The speaker and his two deputies are elected at the outset of each parliamentary term, as are the eighteen committee chairpersons. No supporter of the political opposition has yet been elected to any of these positions in Republican Egypt.

The role of speaker is particularly important, for he or she controls the Assembly's agenda and the progress of business generally by deciding who can speak, for how long, and on what issues. The flow of debate on the floor is guided by Article 297 of the Internal Operating Procedures, which permits the Speaker to close discussion on any topic upon the request of twenty MPs or to ignore such a request. He or she also decides how long the Assembly will remain in session and when and if ministers requested to answer questions and interpellations actually appear before the Assembly. In the 1980s speakers permitted some three-quarters of requests for interpellations to be ignored by the cabinet (El-Mikawy 1991: 407). In the 1994 session the speaker promoted a decision by the Assembly to restrict interpellations to two per month, a clear violation of Article 125 of the Constitution, which grants freedom to all deputies to request clarification from the government on any issue (Rabie 1995: 429). The speaker appoints all committee members.

Speakers use their powers to support the government, although in differing degrees. Under Sadat, Speaker Sayed Marei sought to play a middleman role, serving as a broker between the president and opposition elements within the Assembly. Marei did not hesitate, however, to utilize his powers to structure the Assembly's agenda to favor the government's case, as in its deliberation of the political party law in 1977, when he ensured that alternative draft legislation was not reported out to the floor (El-Mikawy 1991: 347). Marei's mediating style ultimately foundered as a result of political polarization caused by Sadat's determination to make peace with Israel.

Subsequently, the role of speaker became more authoritarian. Sufi Abu Talib, for example, stated that parliament should question the executive only with regard to service delivery and not with regard to policies concerning "sovereignty, [because] that should be in the hands of the symbol of the nation, the president." Accordingly, he refused to implement certain requests for ministers to respond to questions and interpellations (El-Mikawy 1991: 347).

Speaker Rifat Mahgub, who was assassinated in 1991, became particularly high-handed, regularly speaking on behalf of governmental legislation from the podium rather than descending to the floor of the Assembly.

Although the current speaker, Fathi Surour, does at least observe that provision of the bylaws, his general demeanor toward MPs, especially those from opposition parties, is to treat them as children who require instruction and tutelage. Moreover, Surour has presided over the Assembly as violations of the bylaws have intensified. In November 1994, for example, he hailed decrees that Mubarak had issued the previous month abolishing Sadat's 1978 Law on the Protection of the Internal Front and the infamous 1980 Law of Shame. In fact, both laws were dead letters in any case because they had previously been struck down by court decisions. Praising from the floor Mubarak's decisions as manifestations of "the restoration of freedom," Surour then dismissed from the podium complaints that the president's actions were unconstitutional (since there was no state of emergency, Mubarak should have introduced the legislation in parliament rather than decreeing it).

Surour has also allowed the government not to introduce its annual program at the outset of the parliamentary session, which legally it is required to do. By not providing that program until as late as the forty-sixth day after the session commenced, the government has avoided having to respond to questions and has essentially frozen all oversight procedures. On May 27, 1995, Surour railroaded Law 93 for the press through the Assembly in a matter of hours and with virtually no debate.

Vagueness in the Assembly's internal operating procedures is exploited by the leadership of that institution. For instance, the size of committees is not specified in the bylaws, so committees tend to be expanded or contracted to advantage the NDP. Similarly, the Committee on Suggestions and Complaints (CSC), to which all bills are sent for review before they are forwarded to the CLA, has frequently abused its powers. In theory, the task of the CSC is merely to make sure that bills do not violate the constitution and are technically sound before they can be considered by the CLA. In practice, however, the CSC has determined on numerous occasions that bills proposed by independents or members of opposition parties are unconstitutional or deficient in some technical regard. In this fashion, the CSC has been able to kill such bills before they can even reach the CLA. This method has been used to prevent the Assembly from debating sensitive political issues, such as the electoral system, or even more mundane questions, such as the Port Said Free Zone law or the allocation of public-sector shares to workers (El-Mikawy 1991: 395).

In the 1994 session, the CSC did not even make the case that the relevant bills contained technical defects; it simply rejected them on substantive grounds, decisions that are in clear violation of the Assembly's bylaws (Rabie 1995: 427). And when the CSC has failed to prevent independents' and opposition members' bills from reaching the CLA, the latter has usually succeeded in making sure that these bills will not be debated by the Assembly as a whole.

In short, parliamentary life has been seriously eroded as a result of the domination of the legislature by the NDP and through the manipulation of parliamentary business by those acting on behalf of the executive branch. The opposition has too few seats in the Assembly to take its own initiatives or adequately oversee the executive, which appears to have become accustomed to only muffled criticism from parliament. The limited pluralism that remains within parliament results primarily from intraparty competition between prominent deputies from the NDP. Committee chairpersons, for example, vie with one another and with other leading party members for the political limelight. Demonstrating independence from the NDP's executive leadership is one way of boosting personal popularity. Committee chairpersons frequently utilize that strategy in policy areas that are not deemed by the leadership to be of vital political significance. In service delivery areas, freedom of debate remains largely unaffected by the growing restrictions on political pluralism and participation. It in fact has flourished as NDP deputies seek popularity with their constituents and as contending elites within the ruling party jostle for position.

Consequences of the Stalled Transition

Parliament's failure to become more central to the political system has had several negative consequences. The decay of political parties, for example, is due in large measure to the fact that the legislature does not serve as an arena within which they can contribute to the making of public policy, control the executive, or perform any other vital functions that would engender popular support for them. The rebirth of a multiparty system in 1977 led to a short period of growth and vigor for political parties. Since the 1980s, however, parties have atrophied—with the exception of the MB, which remains illegal. The NPUP's membership, for example, declined from a claimed 160,000 in 1976 to 30,000 in 1987 and is probably much less now (El-Mikawy 1991: 170). Significantly, that party, like the others, no longer releases membership figures.

Parliament's weakness in the face of the executive might also contribute to voter apathy. Reliable data on turnout rates are unavailable, but evidence suggests that in urban districts participation did not exceed 15 percent in either the 1990 or the 1995 election. Moreover, the inverse relationship between urbanity and voter turnout appears to be increasing, which suggests that although support for the formal political system may be stagnant in rural Egypt, it is decaying in the large cities. Among city dwellers, the level of commitment to the political system may have reached dangerously low levels. Certainly, the proposition that voting rates would increase were the legislature to become more politically central remains untested. Still, the relative enthusiasm that surrounded the comparatively free and fair 1976 elections and the first two elections held under Mubarak (1984 and 1987) suggests that Egyptians would probably turn out to vote in significantly greater numbers if they felt their vote was counted fairly and really meant something. The 1995 elections demonstrated that even local issues and personal competition between candidates engender considerable voter interest. Were it to become apparent that political liberalization had recommenced and that there was a real possibility of ultimate democratization, apathy would in all likelihood be very quickly supplanted by a surge of participation.

Another product of parliament's marginalization is the resurgence, especially in rural areas, of familism and traditionalism, replete with the vendettas and violence usually associated with such politics. At least forty persons were killed during the 1995 parliamentary elections, the greatest number in Egypt's Republican history. The rise in religious sectarianism and violence as well as the exacerbation of primordial loyalties have no doubt been fed by the decline of parliament and of other institutionalized means for resolving political disputes. Indeed, the stalled political liberalization, including the erosion of parliament, probably contributed to the low-level insurgency that broke out in Egypt in 1992 and that took almost four years and massive use of force to contain. As most channels of legal political participation have been progressively restricted or entirely closed, many of those seeking to effect policy and personnel changes have turned to extralegal means. Parliament has become too marginalized to serve as an effective political shock absorber. Nor is the legislature now capable of legitimizing the government.

Nevertheless, even in its current, politically impoverished state, parliament remains a focal point of contestation between government and opposition. As a result, the government could seek to enhance the legitimacy of the political system that it dominates by granting greater access to the legislature. If this step were taken, it would immediately reinvigorate the stalled liberalization. Indeed, no other initiative that the regime could take would demonstrate its commitment to democratization more clearly than would the easing of the opposition's access to the People's Assembly.

PART THREE
Conclusion

11

Legislatures and Democratic Transitions: Lessons for the Twenty-First Century

The recent fascination with sweeping democratic changes in Eastern and Central Europe, the former Soviet Union, and some Latin American countries has diverted attention from what is historically the most common form of democratization—namely, piecemeal, gradual reforms implemented by incumbents seeking to enhance their legitimacy by accommodating pressures from below. This book focused on that particular process of incremental change. As a research strategy, this approach allowed us to capture the significant transformations that are reshaping the political systems analyzed in this book. We found that, over the long haul, reforms implemented in this gradual fashion are more durable because they have been accepted and negotiated with those segments of society that have more to lose from democratization (i.e., those forces that are represented in the executive branch and the military). Although these forces are reluctant to approve the more thorough transformations that prodemocracy advocates would like to see taking place, the changes they do accept are less likely to be reversed.

This book focused more specifically on the contribution that legislatures are making to this process of transition through negotiation. During the 1990s, Arab parliaments have provided vital mechanisms and arenas through which pressures for democratization have been worked into the political system in nondestabilizing ways. In exchange for playing that role, these legislatures have seen their freedom of maneuver increase. Certainly, this process is not unilinear and can be temporarily reversed—as has been demonstrated since 1994 by the examples of Jordan and, especially, Yemen. Nevertheless, we believe that the overall trend is positive and will continue to be so.

Continued Constraints on Centrality

Our cautious optimism regarding prospects for parliamentary development in the Arab world must be balanced against the recognition that even the legislatures we analyzed continue to operate under powerful political constraints. Sometimes, even though the constitution empowers these legislatures to act in certain areas, they in fact may not venture there because of the existence of implicit "red lines." And when they fail to respect these informal political boundaries, they are likely to pay a price for their transgression.

The Lebanese Chamber of Deputies best illustrates this phenomenon. Constitutionally, it can claim all the prerogatives of a legislature under a strong parliamentary system. In practice, however, it operates under strenuous political restrictions. The presence of Syrian troops, the Israeli occupation in the south, and the existence of a national resistance movement against that occupation all limit the legislature's ability to deal openly with certain sensitive topics relevant to these security issues. It is not that political debates about these issues are absent from the media and informal discussions. In fact, the Lebanese media (whether based in Lebanon or elsewhere) deal with these subjects on a regular basis. However, all of Lebanon's political institutions, including the legislature, have refrained from engaging in open and frank discussions of these questions for fear of the political costs involved in doing so, including the possibility that it might lead to renewed domestic violence and unnecessary divisions.

In Morocco as well, the lines that the legislature may not cross are clear. They include criticism of the dominant position of the monarchy and any questioning of the king's religious authority. The legislature must also use extreme caution when dealing with security and foreign policy concerns, especially with regard to the Western Sahara dispute. The military and its role in politics are equally sensitive topics that are discussed neither in the press nor in other public forums such as the legislature. Significantly, the defense component of the budget is never contested or even debated by parliament. In Jordan, too, the legislature must tread carefully when the institution of the monarchy and the Arab-Israeli peace process are concerned. Even though since 1994 parliament has shown surprising audacity in expressing criticism of the peace treaty with Israel, the king has been successful in defending his prerogatives in security and foreign affairs matters. He has successfully fended off the many attempts by the legislature to seize the initiative in those areas.

In Kuwait, the legislature remains similarly constrained in its ability to influence defense and foreign policies. Kuwait's relationships with Saudi Arabia, the United States, and Iraq are particularly sensitive topics. In Yemen, meanwhile, the governing party's comfortable majority in the Chamber of Deputies has allowed the regime to scuttle discussions it wants to avoid. The situation is somewhat similar in Egypt, where the ruling party's dominance of the legislature has made that institution stay clear of the Middle East "peace process," security matters, and ways and means of dealing with the challenges of political Islam and terrorism.

One common feature of all six countries on which this book focused— and indeed of all polities in the region—is the existence of serious domestic or external threats to the survival of the regime and in several cases to the country's very sovereignty and territorial integrity. That characteristic represents the single most significant constraint on all Arab legislatures. Whenever domestic or regional tensions have increased to the point of posing a national security challenge, the executive branch in all the countries we studied has tended to react by restricting political debates on security-related matters. A fundamental question facing policymakers, intellectuals, and reformers in those countries is whether such political restrictions are effective ways of dealing with these threats or whether they tend to be counterproductive.

Still, the fact that the legislatures we discussed operate under severe constraints does not mean that they are powerless or politically insignificant. All parliaments, including those in mature democracies, face constitutional and political limitations. Students of legislatures in nascent democracies or semi-authoritarian regimes too often assume that a "true legislature" must have a range of prerogatives that in reality very few parliaments have. Some analysts also make the mistaken assumption that a legislature's political significance depends exclusively on its influence on policymaking. In fact, as previous case studies illustrated, a parliament may have little impact on policymaking and still make vital contributions to political development in areas such as national integration; the facilitation of constituents' access to the bureaucracy; the management of political, cultural, and socioeconomic conflicts; the striking of societal bargains on the rules of the political game; allowing political incumbents and challengers to relate to each other in more productive ways than they would in the absence of a legislature; educating the public on important policy issues; improving executive performance and adherence to the rule of law by increasing the political costs associated with failed policies and abuses of power and authority; and providing the incentives that will progressively entice political parties that have nondemocratic leanings into playing by democratic rules.

Legislatures and the Accommodation of Political Islam

One of the main problems facing Arab countries in their quest for democracy is the rising tide of Islamist political movements. Some analysts see these movements as inherently antidemocratic and believe that Islamist parties should not be allowed to participate in the electoral process, since they are bound to seek to subvert that process. Other commentators claim instead that Islamist movements should be encouraged to take part in elections so that they can become integrated into the political system.

The evidence analyzed in previous chapters provides support for the second line of reasoning. Where Islamists have been allowed to take part in elections and gain access to parliament, they have shown themselves to be responsible and willing to abide by the rules of the democratic game. In Lebanon, Hizballah (the Party of God), which was originally intent on turning the country into an Islamic state, found itself embracing Lebanon's multisectarian political system and playing by its rules. Indeed, Hizballah's behavior in parliament has been remarkably similar to that of secular political parties. Hizballah members of parliament (MPs) have been eager not to endanger the status and influence that they have gained as a result of their presence in the Chamber of Deputies. Accordingly, they have shown themselves to be adept at the politics of conciliation and compromise and have played the role of a loyal opposition.

Jordan, Morocco, and Kuwait similarly have managed to integrate political Islam into their legislatures. In Jordan, the Islamic bloc was even the largest one in parliament from 1989 until 1997. In Kuwait, the Assembly includes outspoken and active Islamist deputies. Yemen, too, has provided Islamists with access to parliamentary power and resources. Since 1993, the Islah has been the second largest party in the Chamber of Deputies, and its leader, Shaikh al-Ahmar, has been the institution's speaker. Only in Egypt have Islamic groups been excluded from representation in the last two parliaments (those elected in 1990 and 1995). This phenomenon may well have contributed to the recurrent outbreaks of violence that have rocked that country in the 1990s. The bloodshed in Algeria, too, can be invoked to illustrate the dangers associated with denying political Islam access to the formal political process. Many of the gruesome massacres that have occurred there since 1992 have their roots in the ruling party's decision to deny the Islamists an electoral victory.

Regime Type, Party System, and Political Succession

The evidence provided in this book suggests that Arab monarchies such as Morocco and Jordan may be better equipped to accommodate the political demands stemming from party pluralism than is the case of regimes such as those in Egypt or Yemen. The fundamental reason for this phenomenon lies in the potential danger that elections pose for the chief executive. Leaders such as Husni Mubarak and Ali Abdullah Salih owe their positions to having been elected. Furthermore, under the constitutional frameworks of these countries, the head of state (who is also the de facto head of government) cannot implement his policies unless he enjoys the support of the majority of the members of parliament. In fact, in both Egypt and Yemen parliament plays a leading role in the election of the chief executive. In Egypt, the People's Assembly nominates the president, who must then be confirmed by popular referendum. (Popular referenda thus far have been a mere formality.) In Yemen, the Chamber of Deputies elects the president. In addition, in both countries the cabinet is essentially an instrument of the president. To be elected and remain in power the president thus needs a majority party to support him. A defeat of that party means a defeat for him, an outcome the president usually feels he cannot tolerate.

King Hassan and King Hussein operate under no such constraints. That is because their legitimacy does not depend on the results of an election or on the support of a majority party. Both rulers have shown that they can work with a variety of parliamentary majorities and party leaders, even those with Islamist or leftist tendencies, as long as those leaders do not challenge the legitimacy of the monarchy and its dominant role in the political system. The prime ministers and cabinet members that King Hassan and King Hussein have chosen or approved over the years have ranged very broadly in their ideological orientations. In any event, an election that does not go the way either king had wished does not mean that he has to step down; at the very most, it implies that he must take advantage of his considerable constitutional and political prerogatives to maneuver more carefully than he might have had to do under different circumstances. As discussed earlier, on February 4, 1998, King Hassan appointed a socialist prime minister, even though the Socialist Union of Popular Forces and parties aligned with it had failed to win an absolute majority in the lower house. For their part, the king of Jordan and the emir of Kuwait have shown a willingness to include in government former opponents of theirs, independents, and opposition members. One remembers in particular the entry of four members of the Muslim Brotherhood in the Jordanian cabinet in January 1991 as well as the Kuwaiti emir's decision to give a handful of portfolios to opposition and independent MPs in the wake of the October 1992 elections.

It is not so easy for elected leaders of pseudorepublican regimes such as Egypt's or Yemen's to allow a wide variety of political currents to gain access to decisionmaking circles. Significantly, no such effort has taken place in Egypt thus far. As for Yemen, the uneasy coalition government that President Ali Salih formed with the Yemeni Socialist Party in the wake of unification ended tragically with the war of secession. The outcome of that war amounted to a de facto victory by Salih over his Yemeni Socialist Party challenger, and the new parliament elected in April 1997 consecrated the dominance of Salih's party, the General People's Congress.

Ultimately, the litmus test of a regime's democratic nature resides in its ability to regulate political succession in a peaceful and widely agreed upon manner. Here again, we find that constitutional monarchical systems are more likely to manage this issue successfully than is true of military-dominated presidential regimes. In the monarchies, the process by which succession is to take place as well as the outcome of that succession are known in advance. This characteristic reduces uncertainty while still providing for adequate levels of contestation and participation, especially as kings assume the role of umpires who let political parties compete for leadership positions in the legislature and the cabinet.

In military-dominated presidential systems such as Egypt's and Yemen's, by contrast, the issue of succession is inherently more problematic. As was just shown, the leaders of these regimes cannot afford to lose an election. Therefore, they may well manipulate elections and repress political forces that threaten their dominance. In such conditions, politics tends to take on many of the attributes of a zero-sum game. This, in turn, makes peaceful and democratic political succession very difficult.

History provides few examples of chief executives who showed themselves willing and able to change their status from leader of a political party—and of the segment of society represented by that party—to head of the entire nation, not tied too closely to specific political interests and agendas. And that, indeed, will remain a central challenge for many Arab polities as they enter the twenty-first century.

Acronyms

ASU	Arab Socialist Union
CLA	Committee for Legislative Affairs
COCA	Central Organization for Control and Accounts
CSC	Committee on Suggestions and Complaints
FDIC	Front for the Defense of Constitutional Institutions
FFS	Socialist Forces Front (Algeria)
FIS	Islamic Salvation Front (Algeria)
FLN	National Liberation Front
FRSI	Fund for the Relief of Small Investors
GPC	General People's Congress
IAF	Islamic Action Front
ICM	Islamic Constitutional Movement
IMF	International Monetary Fund
IPA	Islamic Popular Alliance
KDF	Kuwait Democratic Forum
KIO	Kuwait Investment Office
KOTC	Kuwait Oil Tanker Company
LA	Legislative Assembly
LCP	Lebanese Communist Party
MB	Muslim Brotherhood
MDS	Movement of Social Democrats
MNP	Popular National Movement
MP	member of parliament
NA	National Assembly
NCC	National Consultative Council
NCP	National Constitutional Party
NDP	National Democratic Party
NGO	nongovernmental organization

NIC	National Islamic Coalition
NLP	National Liberal Party
NPUP	National Progressive Unionist Party
NSP	National Socialist Party
OADP	Organization of Democratic and Popular Action
PDRY	People's Democratic Republic of Yemen
PLO	Palestine Liberation Organization
PND	National Democratic Party
PPS	Party of Progress and Socialism
PSP	Progressive Socialist Party
RC	Representative Council
RCD	Rally for Culture and Democracy
RNI	National Rally of Independents
ROY	Republic of Yemen
SAP	Structural Adjustment Program
SSNP	Syrian Social Nationalist Party
UNFP	National Union of Popular Forces
USAID	U.S. Agency for International Development
USFP	Socialist Union of Popular Forces
YAR	Yemen Arab Republic
YSP	Yemeni Socialist Party

References

Aarts, Paul. 1993. "Les limites du 'tribalisme politique': Le Koweit d'après-guerre et le processus de démocratisation." *Maghreb-Machrek*, no. 142 (October-December): 61–79.

———. 1994. "The Limits of Political Tribalism: Post-War Kuwait and the Process of Democratization" (Part One). *Civil Society* (Cairo): 17–22.

———. 1995. "The Limits of Political Tribalism: Post-War Kuwait and the Process of Democratization" (Part Two). *Civil Society* (Cairo): 16–18.

Abu Jaber, Kamel S. 1972. "The Jordanian Parliament." In Jacob M. Landau, ed., *Man, State, and Society in the Contemporary Middle East*, 91–121. New York: Praeger.

AbuKhalil, As'ad. 1993. "The Study of Political Parties in the Arab World: The Case of Lebanon." *Journal of Asian and African Affairs* (Fall): 49–64.

Adelman, Irma, and Cynthia Taft Morris. 1973. *Economic Growth and Social Equity in Developing Countries*. Stanford: Stanford University Press.

Ágh, Attila. 1994. *The Emergence of East Central European Parliaments: The First Steps*. Budapest: Hungarian Centre for Democracy Studies.

———. 1995. "The Experience of the First Democratic Parliaments in East Central Europe." *Communist and Post-Communist Studies* 28, no. 2: 203–214.

Al-Haj, Abdullah Juma. 1996. "The Politics of Participation in the Gulf Cooperation Council States: The Omani Consultative Council." *Middle East Journal* 50, no. 4 (Autumn): 559–571.

Almond, Gabriel, and James Coleman. 1960. *The Politics of the Developing Areas*. Princeton: Princeton University Press.

Almond, Gabriel, and Sidney Verba. 1963. *The Civic Culture*. Princeton: Princeton University Press.

Alshayeji, Abdullah K. 1992. "Kuwait at the Crossroads: The Quest for Democratization." *Middle East Insight* 18, no. 5 (May-June): 41–46.

Anderson, Lisa. 1986. *The State and Social Transformation in Tunisia and Libya*. Princeton: Princeton University Press.

———. 1987. "The State in the Middle East and North Africa." *Comparative Politics* (October): 1–18.

Ansari, Hamied. 1986. *Egypt: The Stalled Society*. Albany: State University of New York Press.

Apter, David. 1965. *The Politics of Modernization*. Chicago: University of Chicago Press.

Baaklini, Abdo. 1976. *Legislative and Political Development: Lebanon, 1842–1972.* Durham: Duke University Press.

———. 1978. "The Future of Legislatures in the Middle East." *Parliamentary Affairs* 30, no. 7 (May): 396–407.

———. 1982. "Legislatures in the Gulf Area: The Experience of Kuwait, 1961–1976." *International Journal of Middle East Studies* 14 (August): 361–379.

Baaklini, Abdo, and Alia Abdul-Wahab. 1979. "The Role of the National Assembly in Kuwait's Economic Development: National Oil Policy." In Joel Smith and Lloyd D. Musolf, eds., *Legislatures in Development: Dynamics of Change in New and Old States*, 311–333. Durham: Duke University Press.

Badeau, J. 1959. "The Revolt Against Democracy," *Journal of International Affairs* 13, no. 2.

Bahout, Joseph. 1996. "Lebanese Parliamentarism: Shadow Plays and the Death of Politics." *The Lebanon Report*, no. 1 (Spring): 27–31.

Baktiari, Bahman. 1996. *Parliamentary Politics in Revolutionary Iran: The Institutionalization of Factional Politics.* Gainesville: University Press of Florida.

Bardhan, Pranab. 1989. "The New Institutional Economics and Development Theory: A Brief Critical Assessment." *World Development* 17, no. 9: 1389–1395.

Beblawi, Hazem, and Giacomo Luciani. 1987. *The Rentier State.* London: Croom Helm.

Be'eri, Eliezer. 1969. *Army Officers in Arab Politics and Society.* Jerusalem: Israel Universities Press.

Ben-Dor, Gabriel. 1983. *State and Conflict in the Middle East: Emergence of the Post-colonial State.* New York: Praeger.

Bill, James A. 1972. *The Politics of Iran: Groups, Classes, and Modernization.* Columbus: Charles E. Merrill.

Bill, James A., and Robert Springborg. 1994. *Politics in the Middle East.* New York: HarperCollins.

Binder, Leonard, ed. 1966. *Politics in Lebanon.* New York: Wiley.

———. 1978. *In a Moment of Enthusiasm: Political Power and the Second Stratum in Egypt.* Chicago: University of Chicago Press.

Boynton, G. R., and Chong Lim Kim, eds. 1975. *Legislative Systems in Developing Countries.* Durham: Duke University Press.

Brown, Nathan, and Roni Amit. 1994. "Constitutionalism in Egypt." In Daniel P. Franklin and Michael J. Braun, eds., *Political Culture and Constitutionalism: A Comparative Approach*, 184–197. London: M. E. Sharpe.

Bryce, James. 1921. *Modern Democracies.* London: Macmillan.

Butt, Ronald. 1967. *The Power of Parliament.* London: Constable.

Close, David. 1995. "Introduction: Consolidating Democracy in Latin America— What Role for Legislatures?" In David Close, ed., *Legislatures and the New Democracies in Latin America*, 1–15. Boulder: Lynne Rienner Publishers.

Close, David, ed. 1995. *Legislatures and the New Democracies in Latin America.* Boulder: Lynne Rienner Publishers.

Collings, Deirdre, and Jill Tansley. 1992. "Peace for Lebanon? Obstacles, Challenges, Prospects." Working paper 43, Canadian Institute for International Peace and Security, Ottawa.

Cooper, Mark N. 1982. *The Transformation of Egypt.* Baltimore: Johns Hopkins University Press.

Copeland, Gary W., and Samuel C. Patterson. 1994. *Parliaments in the Modern World: Changing Institutions.* Ann Arbor: University of Michigan Press.

Crow, Ralph E. 1970. "Parliament in the Lebanese Political System." In A. Kornberg and L. Musolf, eds., *Legislatures in Developmental Perspectives,* 273–302. Durham: Duke University Press.

Crystal, Jill. 1990. *Oil and Politics in the Gulf: Rulers and Merchants in Kuwait and Qatar.* Cambridge: Cambridge University Press.

———. 1992. *Kuwait: The Transformation of an Oil State.* Boulder: Westview Press.

Curtis, Gerald L. 1997. "A 'Recipe' for Democratic Development." *Journal of Democracy* 8, no. 3 (July): 139–145.

Dabaghy, Jean, and Roger Melki. 1995. "Koweït: Un pays en voie de re-naissance." *Arabies* (February): 12–19.

Damgaard, Erik, ed. 1992. *Parliamentary Change in the Nordic Countries.* Oslo: Scandinavian University Press.

Dann, Uriel. 1989. *King Hussein and the Challenge of Arab Radicalism: Jordan, 1955–1967.* New York: Oxford University Press.

———. 1992. "King Hussein's Strategy of Survival." Policy papers 29, Washington Institute for Near East Policy, Washington, DC.

Davidson, Roger H. 1992. *The Postreform Congress.* New York: St. Martin's Press.

Davison, Roderic H. 1963. *Reform in the Ottoman Empire, 1856–1876.* Princeton: Princeton University Press.

———. 1968. "The Advent of the Principle of Representation in the Government of the Ottoman Empire." In William R. Polk and Richard L. Chambers, eds., *Beginnings of Modernization in the Middle East: The Nineteenth Century,* 93–108. Chicago: University of Chicago Press.

Deeb, Marius. 1980. *The Lebanese Civil War.* New York: Praeger.

De Jouvenel, Bertrand. 1957. *Sovereignty.* Chicago: University of Chicago Press.

Dekmejian, R. Hrair. 1971. *Egypt under Nasir: A Study in Political Dynamics.* Albany: State University of New York Press.

———. 1975. *Patterns of Political Leadership: Lebanon, Israel, Egypt.* Albany: State University of New York Press.

Denoeux, Guilain, and Laurent Gateau. 1995. "L'Essor des associations au Maroc: À la recherche de la citoyenneté." *Maghreb-Machrek,* no. 150 (October-December): 19–39.

Deutsch, Karl. 1961. "Social Mobilization and Political Development," *American Political Science Review* 55 (September): 493–514.

Devereux, Robert. 1963. *The First Ottoman Constitutional Period: A Study of the Midhat Constitution and Parliament.* Baltimore: Johns Hopkins University Press.

Di Palma, Giuseppe. 1990a. *To Craft Democracies: An Essay on Democratic Transitions.* Berkeley: University of California Press.

———. 1990b. "Parliaments, Consolidation, Institutionalization: A Minimalist View." In Ulrike Liebert and Maurizio Cotta, eds., *Parliament and Democratic Consolidation in Southern Europe: Greece, Italy, Portugal, Spain, and Turkey,* 31–51. London: Pinter Publishers.

Dominguez, Jorge. 1993. "The Caribbean Question: Why Has Liberal Democracy (Surprisingly) Flourished?" In Jorge Dominguez, ed., *Democracy in the Caribbean: Political, Economic, and Social Perspectives,* 1–25. Baltimore: Johns Hopkins University Press.

Easton, David. 1957. "An Approach to the Study of Political Systems." *World Politics* 9 (April): 383–400.

Ecevit, Bülent. 1993. "Prospects and Difficulties of Democratization in the Middle East." In Ellis Goldberg et al., eds., *Rules and Rights in the Middle East: Democracy, Law, and Society,* 141–163. Seattle: University of Washington Press.

El-Mikawy, Noha M. 1991. "Transition to Liberal Democracy in Egypt: The Predicament of Consensus-Building." Ph.D. diss., University of California–Los Angeles.

Entelis, John P. 1974. *Pluralism and Party Transformation in Lebanon: Al-Kata'ib, 1936–1970.* Leiden: Brill.

Evans, C. Lawrence, and Walter J. Oleszek. 1997. *Congress Under Fire: Reform Politics and the Republican Majority.* Boston: Houghton Mifflin.

Evans, Peter B., Dietrich Rueschemeyer, and Theda Skocpol, eds. 1985. *Bringing the State Back In.* New York: Cambridge University Press.

Flinterman, Cees, Aalt Willem Heringa, and Lisa Waddington, eds. 1994. *The Evolving Role of Parliaments in Europe.* Antwerp: MAKLU Uitgevers.

Foley, Michael W., and Bob Edwards. 1996. "The Paradox of Civil Society." *Journal of Democracy* 7, no. 3: 38–52.

Franks, C.E.S. 1987. *The Parliament of Canada.* Toronto: University of Toronto Press.

Freij, Hanna Y., and Leonard C. Robinson. 1996. "Liberalization, the Islamists, and the Stability of the Arab State: Jordan as a Case Study." *The Muslim World* 86, no. 1 (January): 1–31.

Gavrielides, Nicolas. 1987. "Tribal Democracy: The Anatomy of Parliamentary Elections in Kuwait." In Linda L. Layne, ed., *Elections in the Middle East: Implications of Recent Trends,* 153–183. Boulder: Westview Press.

Gellner, Ernest, and John Waterbury, eds. 1977. *Patrons and Clients in Mediterranean Societies.* London: Duckworth.

Gerschenkron, Alexander. 1962. *Economic Backwardness in Historical Perspective.* Cambridge: Harvard University Press.

Ghabra, Shafeeq. 1991. "Voluntary Associations in Kuwait: The Foundation of a New System?" *The Middle East Journal* 45, no. 2 (Spring): 199–215.

———. 1994. "Democratization in a Middle Eastern State: Kuwait, 1993." *Middle East Policy* 3, no. 1: 102–119.

Gilmour, David. 1983. *Lebanon: The Fractured Country.* New York: St. Martin's Press.

Goldberg, Ellis, Resat Kasaba, and Joel Migdal, eds. 1993. *Rules and Rights in the Middle East: Democracy, Law, and Society.* Seattle: University of Washington Press.

Gordon, David C. 1983. *The Republic of Lebanon: Nation in Jeopardy.* Boulder: Westview Press.

Graz, Liesl. 1992. *The Turbulent Gulf: People, Politics and Power.* London: I. B. Tauris.

Grofman, Bernard, and Arend Lijphart, eds. 1986. *Electoral Laws and Their Political Consequences.* New York: Agathon.

Gubser, Peter. 1988. "Jordan: Balancing Pluralism and Authoritarianism." In Peter J. Chekowsky and Robert J. Pranger, *Ideology and Power in the Middle East: Studies in Honor of George Lenczowski,* 89–114. Durham: Duke University Press.

Hahn, Jeffrey W., ed. 1996. *Democratization in Russia: The Development of Legislative Institutions.* New York: M. E. Sharpe.

Hall, Peter. 1986. *Governing the Economy: The Politics of State Intervention in Britain and France.* New York: Oxford University Press.

Halpern, Manfred. 1963. *The Politics of Social Change in the Middle East and North Africa.* Princeton: Princeton University Press.

Harik, Iliya F. 1975. "Political Elite of Lebanon." In George Lenczowski, ed., *Political Elites in the Middle East,* 201–220. Washington, DC: The American Enterprise Institute.

———. 1980. "Voting Participation and Political Integration in Lebanon, 1943–1974." *Middle Eastern Studies* 16, no. 1 (January): 27–48.

Harrold, Deborah. 1995. "The Menace and Appeal of Algeria's Parallel Economy." *Middle East Report,* no. 192 (January-February): 18–22.

Hawthorne, Amy, and Ronald Wolfe. 1997. "IFES' Pollworker Training Project for Yemen's 1997 Parliamentary Elections: Final Report." Washington, DC: International Foundation for Election Systems (IFES).

Hermassi, Elbaki. 1972. *Leadership and National Development in North Africa.* Berkeley: University of California Press.

Hertzke, Allen D., and Ronald M. Peters, Jr., eds. 1992. *The Atomistic Congress: An Interpretation of Congressional Change.* Armonk, NY: M. E. Sharpe.

Hooglund, Eric. 1991. "Government and Politics." In Helen Chapin Metz, ed., *Jordan: A Country Study,* 181–220. Washington, DC: Library of Congress, Area Handbook Series.

Horowitz, Donald L. 1993. "Comparing Democratic Systems." In Larry Diamond and Marc F. Plattner, eds., *The Global Resurgence of Democracy,* 127–133. Baltimore and London: Johns Hopkins University Press.

Hottinger, Arnold. 1961. "Zu'ama' and Parties in the Lebanese Crisis of 1958." *The Middle East Journal* 15, no. 2 (Spring): 127–140.

———. 1966. "Zu'ama in Historical Perspective." In L. Binder, ed., *Politics in Lebanon,* 85–105. New York: Wiley.

Hourani, Albert. 1976. "Ideologies of the Mountain and the City." In Roger Owen, ed., *Essays on the Crisis in Lebanon,* 33–41. London: Ithaca Press.

Hudson, Michael. 1966. "The Electoral Process and Political Development in Lebanon." *The Middle East Journal* 20, no. 2 (Spring): 173–186.

———. 1968. *The Precarious Republic.* New York: Random House.

———. 1977. *Arab Politics: The Search for Legitimacy.* New Haven: Yale University Press.

Huntington, Samuel. 1968. *Political Order in Changing Societies.* New Haven: Yale University Press.

Hurewitz, J. C. 1969. *Middle East Politics: The Military Dimension.* New York: Praeger.

Issawi, Charles. 1956. "Economic and Social Foundations of Democracy in the Middle East." *International Affairs* 32 (January): 27–42.

Jewell, M. E. 1973. "Linkages between Legislative Parties and External Parties." In Allan Kornberg and Lloyd Musolf, ed., *Legislatures in Comparative Perspective,* 203–234. New York: David McKay.

Jogerst, Michael. 1993. *Reform in the House of Commons: The Select Committee System.* Lexington: University Press of Kentucky.

Karl, Terry Lynn. 1990. "Dilemmas of Democratization in Latin America." *Comparative Politics* 23 (October): 1–21.

Karl, Terry Lynn, and Philippe Schmitter. 1991. "Modes of Transition in Latin America, Southern and Eastern Europe." *International Social Science Journal* 43: 269–284.

Katz, Mark N. 1997. "Election Day in Aden." *Middle East Policy* 5, no. 3 (September): 40–50.

Kayali, Hasan. 1995. "Elections and the Electoral Process in the Ottoman Empire, 1876–1919." *International Journal of Middle East Studies* 27: 265–286.

Kedourie, Elie. 1992. *Democracy and Arab Political Culture.* Washington, DC: Washington Institute for Near East Policy.

Khalaf, Jassim Muhammad. 1984. "The Kuwait National Assembly: A Study of Its Structure and Function." Ph.D. diss., State University of New York at Albany, Graduate School of Public Affairs, Department of Public Administration.

Khalaf, Samir. 1987. *Lebanon's Predicament*. New York: Columbia University Press.

Khatib, Abdullah A. 1975. "The Jordanian Legislature in Political Development Perspective." Ph.D. diss., State University of New York at Albany, Graduate School of Public Affairs, Department of Public Administration.

El-Khazen, Farid. 1994. "Lebanon's First Postwar Parliamentary Elections, 1993." *Middle East Policy* 3, no. 1: 120–136.

Khoury, Nabeel A. 1981. "The National Consultative Council of Jordan: A Study in Legislative Development." *International Journal of Middle East Studies* 13: 427–439.

Khoury, Philip S. 1987. *Syria and the French Mandate: The Politics of Arab Nationalism*. Princeton: Princeton University Press.

Kliot, N. 1987. "The Collapse of the Lebanese State." *Middle Eastern Studies* 23, no. 1 (January): 54–74.

Koelble, Thomas A. 1995. "The New Institutionalism in Political Science and Sociology." *Comparative Politics* 27, no. 2 (January): 231–243.

Kornberg, Allen, ed. 1973. *Legislatures in Comparative Perspective*. New York: David McKay.

Kornberg, Allan, and Lloyd Musolf, eds. 1970. *Legislatures in Developmental Perspective*. Durham: Duke University Press.

Krasner, Stephen D. 1978. *Defending the National Interest*. Princeton: Princeton University Press.

Langlois, R. N. 1986. *Economics as a Process: Essays in the New Institutional Economics*. Cambridge: Cambridge University Press.

Layne, Linda. 1987. "Tribesmen as Citizens: 'Primordial Ties' and Democracy in Rural Jordan." In Linda L. Layne, ed., *Elections in the Middle East: Implications of Recent Trends,* 113–153. Boulder: Westview Press.

Lenczowski, George, ed. 1975. *Political Elites in the Middle East*. Washington, DC: American Enterprise Institute.

Lerner, Daniel. 1958. *The Passing of Traditional Society*. New York: Free Press.

Lesch, Ann Mosely. 1996. "Egypt." In Gabriel A. Almond and G. Bingham Powell, eds., *Comparative Politics Today*. New York: HarperCollins.

Lewis, Bernard. 1994. *The Shaping of the Modern Middle East*. New York: Oxford University Press.

Liebert, Ulrike. 1990a. "Parliament as a Central Site in Democratic Consolidation: A Preliminary Exploration." In Ulrike Liebert and Maurizio Cotta, eds., *Parliament and Democratic Consolidation in Southern Europe: Greece, Italy, Portugal, Spain, and Turkey*, 3–30. London: Pinter Publishers.

———. 1990b. "Parliaments in the Consolidation of Democracy—A Comparative Assessment of Southern European Experiences." In Ulrike Liebert and Maurizio Cotta, eds., *Parliament and Democratic Consolidation in Southern Europe: Greece, Italy, Portugal, Spain, and Turkey*, 249–272. London: Pinter Publishers.

Liebert, Ulrike, and Maurizio Cotta, eds. 1990. *Parliament and Democratic Consolidation in Southern Europe: Greece, Italy, Portugal, Spain, and Turkey*. London: Pinter Publishers.

Linz, Juan J. 1990. "The Perils of Presidentialism." *Journal of Democracy* 1 (Winter): 51–69.

Linz, Juan J., and Alfred Stepan. 1996. *Problems of Democratic Transition and Consolidation: Southern Europe, South America, and Post-Communist Europe.* Baltimore: Johns Hopkins University Press.

Linz, Juan J., and Alfred Stepan, eds. 1978. *The Breakdown of Democratic Regimes.* Baltimore: Johns Hopkins University Press.

Linz, Juan J., and Arturo Valenzuela. 1994. *The Failure of Presidential Democracy.* Baltimore: Johns Hopkins University Press.

Lipset, Seymour Martin. 1959. "Some Social Requisites of Democracy." *American Political Science Review* 53 (March): 69–105.

———. 1960. *Political Man.* Garden City: Doubleday.

———. 1993. "The Centrality of Political Culture." In Larry Diamond and Marc F. Plattner, eds., *The Global Resurgence of Democracy*, 134–137. Baltimore: Johns Hopkins University Press.

———. 1994. "The Social Requisites of Democracy Revisited." *American Sociological Review* 59 (February): 1–22.

Loewenberg, G., and S. C. Patterson. 1979. *Comparing Legislatures.* Boston: Little, Brown.

Loewenberg, Gerhard, ed. 1971. *Modern Parliaments: Change or Decline?* Chicago: Aldine-Atherton.

Mainwaring, Scott, and Donald Share. 1986. "Transitions through Transaction: Democratization in Brazil and Spain." In Wayne Selcher, ed., *Political Liberalization in Brazil*, 175–215. Boulder: Westview Press.

March, James G., and Johan P. Olsen. 1984. "The New Institutionalism: Organizational Factors in Political Life." *The American Political Science Review* 78, no. 3 (September): 734–749.

———. 1989. *Rediscovering Institutions: The Organizational Bases of Politics.* New York: Free Press.

Marongiu, Antonio. 1968. *Medieval Parliaments: A Comparative Study.* London: Eyre and Spottiswoode.

Melnik, Constantin, and Nathan Leites. 1958. *The House without Windows.* Evanston: Row, Peterson.

Mezey, Michael L. 1979. *Comparative Legislatures.* Durham: Duke University Press.

———. 1985. "The Functions of Legislatures in the Third World." In Gerhard Loewenberg, Samuel C. Patterson, and Malcolm E. Jewell, eds., *Handbook of Legislative Research,* 733–772. Cambridge, MA: Harvard University Press.

———. 1996. "Studying Legislatures: Lessons for Comparing the Russian Experience." In Jeffrey W. Hahn, ed., *Democratization in Russia: The Development of Legislative Institutions,* 221–240. New York: M. E. Sharpe.

Moe, Terry M. 1990. "Political Institutions: The Neglected Side of the Story." *Journal of Law, Economics, and Organization* 6: 213–253.

Moore, Barrington. 1966. *Social Origins of Democracy and Dictatorship: Lord and Peasant in the Making of the Modern World.* Boston: Beacon Press.

Morris-Jones, W. H. 1983. "The Politics of Political Science: The Case of Comparative Legislative Studies." *Political Studies* 31: 1–24.

Munck, Gerardo L. 1994. "Democratic Transitions in Comparative Perspective," *Comparative Politics* (April): 355–375.

Nabli, Mustapha K., and Jeffrey B. Nugent. 1989. "The New Institutional Economics and Its Applicability to Development." *World Development* 17, no. 9: 1333–1347.

Nordlinger, Eric. 1981. *On the Autonomy of the Democratic State.* Cambridge: Harvard University Press.

North, Douglas C. 1981. *Structure and Change in Economic History.* New York: W. W. Norton.

North, Douglas C., and R. Thomas. 1973. *The Rise of the Western World.* Cambridge: Cambridge University Press.

Norton, Augustus Richard. 1997. "Lebanon: With Friends Like These . . ." *Current History* (January): 6–12.

Norton, Augustus Richard, ed. 1995. *Civil Society in the Middle East.* New York: E. J. Brill.

Norton, Philip. 1990a. *Parliaments in Western Europe.* London: Frank Cass.

———. 1990b. "Parliaments: A Framework for Analysis." *West European Politics* 13, no. 3: 1–9.

———. 1991. "The Changing Face of Parliament: Lobbying and Its Consequences." In Philip Norton, ed., *New Directions in British Politics,* 53–75. Aldershot, England: Edward Eigar.

———. 1992. "The House of Commons: From Overlooked to Overworked." In Bill Jones and Lynton Robins, ed., *Two Decades in British Politics*, 139–154. Manchester: Manchester University Press.

———. 1993. *Does Parliament Matter?* New York: Harvester Wheatsheaf.

———. 1994. "Representation of Interests: The Case of the British House of Commons." In Gary W. Copeland and Samuel C. Patterson, *Parliaments in the Modern World: Changing Institutions*, 13–28. Ann Arbor: University of Michigan Press.

O'Donnell, Guillermo. 1973. *Modernization and Bureaucratic-Authoritarianism: Studies in South American Politics.* Berkeley: University of California Press.

O'Donnell, Guillermo, and Philippe Schmitter. 1986. *Transitions from Authoritarian Rule: Tentative Conclusions About Uncertain Democracies.* Baltimore: Johns Hopkins University Press.

Olson, David. 1994. *Democratic Legislative Institutions: A Comparative View.* Armonk, NY: M. E. Sharpe.

Olson, David M., and Philip Norton. 1996. "Legislatures in Democratic Transition." *The Journal of Legislative Studies* 2, no. 1 (Spring): 1–15.

Ostrom, Elinor. 1995. "New Horizons in Institutional Analysis." *American Political Science Review* 89 (March): 174–178.

Owen, Roger. 1992. *State, Power and Politics in the Making of the Modern Middle East.* London: Routledge.

———. 1993. "The Practice of Electoral Democracy in the Arab East and North Africa: Some Lessons from Nearly a Century's Experience." In Ellis Goldberg et al., eds., *Rules and Rights in the Middle East*, 17–40. Seattle: University of Washington Press.

Özbudun, Ergun. 1987. "Turkey." In Myron Weiner and Ergun Özbudun, eds., *Competitive Elections in Developing Countries*, 328–365. Durham: Duke University Press.

Packenham, Robert. 1970. "Legislatures and Political Development." In Allan Kornberg and Lloyd Musolf, eds., *Legislatures in Developmental Perspective.* Durham: Duke University Press.

Palmer, Monte, Leila Ali, and El Sayed Yassin. 1988. *The Egyptian Bureaucracy.* Syracuse: Syracuse University Press.

Patterson, Samuel C., and Gary W. Copeland, eds. 1994. "Parliaments in the Twenty-first Century." In Gary W. Copeland and Samuel C. Patterson, eds., *Parliaments in the Modern World: Changing Institutions*, 1–11. Ann Arbor: University of Michigan Press.

Piro, Timothy. 1992. "Parliament, Politics, and Pluralism in Jordan: Democratic Trend at a Difficult Time." *Middle East Insight* 8, no. 6 (July-October): 39–44.

Pollard, A. F. 1964. Reprint. *The Evolution of Parliament.* New York: Russell and Russell. Original edition, London: Longmans, Green and Co., 1920.

Polsby, Nelson W. 1975. "Legislatures." In Fred I. Greenstein and Nelson W. Polsby, eds., *Handbook of Political Science.* Vol. 5: *Governmental Institutions and Processes,* 257–319. Reading, MA.: Addison-Wesley.

Putnam, Robert D. 1993. *Making Democracy Work.* Princeton: Princeton University Press.

Rabie, Amr Hashem. 1995. "The People's Assembly." In *The Arab Strategic Report, 1994.* Cairo: Al Ahram Center for Political and Strategic Studies.

Rae, Douglas. 1967. *The Political Consequences of Electoral Laws.* New Haven: Yale University Press.

Remington, Thomas F., ed. 1994. *Parliaments in Transition: The New Legislative Politics in the Former USSR and Eastern Europe.* Boulder: Westview Press.

Remmer, Karen. 1991. "New Wine or Old Bottlenecks? The Study of Latin American Democracy." *Comparative Politics* 23 (July): 479–495.

Richards, Alan. 1993. "Political Economy Review of Jordan." Written for Chemonics International and the United States Agency for International Development (USAID), Near East Bureau. Washington, DC.

Richards, Alan, and John Waterbury. 1996. *A Political Economy of the Middle East.* 2d ed.) Boulder: Westview Press.

Robins, Philip J. 1991. "Politics and the 1986 Electoral Law in Jordan." In Rodney Wilson, ed., *Politics and the Economy in Jordan,* 184–207. London: Routledge.

Robinson, Glenn E. 1997. "Can Islamists Be Democrats? The Case of Jordan." *Middle East Journal* 51, no. 3 (Summer): 373–387.

Rosberg, James. 1994. "Causes and Consequences of Judicial Independence in Contemporary Egypt." Paper presented to the annual conference of the Middle East Studies Association, Phoenix, Arizona.

Rustow, Dankwart A. 1970. "Transitions to Democracy." *Comparative Politics* 2: 337–364.

Salamé, Ghassan, ed. 1987. *The Foundations of the Arab State.* London: Croom Helm.

———. 1994. *Democracy Without Democrats.* New York: St. Martin's Press.

Salih, Kamal Osman. 1991. "Kuwait: Political Consequences of Modernization." *Middle Eastern Studies* 27, no. 1 (January): 46–66.

Sartori, Giovanni. 1976. *Parties and Party Systems: A Framework for Analysis.* Cambridge: Cambridge University Press.

Sassine, Fares. 1996. "Is Parliament's Credibility in the Red?" *The Lebanon Report,* no. 1 (Spring): 32–36.

Schmitter, Philippe C. 1991. "The Consolidation of Democracy and the Choice of Institutions." East-South System Transformations working paper 7, University of Chicago, Department of Political Science.

Shaw, Stanford J. 1970. "The Central Legislative Councils in the Nineteenth Century Ottoman Reform Movement before 1876." *International Journal of Middle East Studies* 1, no. 1 (January): 51–84.

Shin, Doh Chull. 1994. "On the Third Wave of Democratization: A Synthesis and Evaluation of Recent Theory and Research." *World Politics* 47, no. 1 (October): 135–170.

Skocpol, Theda. 1979. *States and Social Revolutions: A Comparative Analysis of France, Russia, and China.* Cambridge: Cambridge University Press.

———. 1980. "Political Responses to Capitalist Crises: Neo-Marxist Theories of the State and the Case of the New Deal." *Politics and Society* 10, no. 2: 155–201.

Skocpol, Theda, and Kenneth Finegold. 1982. "State Capacity and Economic Intervention in the Early New Deal." *Political Science Quarterly* 97: 255–278.

Smith, Joel, and Lloyd Musolf, eds. 1979. *Legislatures in Development*. Durham: Duke University Press.

Springborg, Robert. 1982. *Family, Power, and Politics in Egypt: Sayed Bey Marei— His Clan, Clients and Cohorts*. Philadelphia: University of Pennsylvania Press.

———. 1995. "Legislative Development as a Key Element of Strategies for Democratization in the Arab World." *Arab Studies Journal* (Spring): 95–100.

Stepan, Alfred. 1978. *The State and Society: Peru in Comparative Perspective*. Princeton: Princeton University Press.

Stepan, Alfred, and Cindy Skach. 1993. "Constitutional Frameworks and Democratic Consolidation: Parliamentarism versus Presidentialism." *World Politics* 46 (October): 1–22.

Stevens, Mark Power. 1994. "Post-Election Seminar: A Discussion of Jordan's 1993 Parliamentary Election." Amman: Al-Urdun al-Jadid Research Center.

Suleiman, Ezra, ed. 1986. *Parliaments and Parliamentarians in Democratic Politics*. New York: Holmes and Meier.

Suleiman, Michael W. 1967. *Political Parties in Lebanon: The Challenge of a Fragmented Political Culture*. Ithaca: Cornell University Press.

Tachau, Frank, ed. 1975. *Political Elites and Political Development in the Middle East*. Cambridge: Schenkman.

Tal, Lawrence. 1993. "Is Jordan Doomed?" *Foreign Affairs* (November-December): 45–58.

Tétreault, Mary Ann. 1991. "Autonomy, Necessity, and the Small State: Ruling Kuwait in the Twentieth Century." *International Organization* 45, no. 4 (Autumn): 565–591.

———. 1997. "Designer Democracy in Kuwait." *Current History* (January): 36–39.

Trimberger, Ellen Kay. 1978. *Revolution from Above: Military Bureaucrats and Development in Japan, Turkey, Egypt, and Peru*. New Brunswick: Transaction Books.

Turan, Ilter. 1994. "The Turkish Legislature: From Symbolic to Substantive Representation." In Gary W. Copeland and Samuel C. Patterson, *Parliaments in the Modern World: Changing Institutions*, 105–128. Ann Arbor: University of Michigan Press.

Usher, Graham. 1997. "Hizballah, Syria, and the Lebanese Elections." *Journal of Palestine Studies* 26, no. 2: 59–67.

Viorst, Milton. 1996. "The Storm and the Citadel." *Foreign Affairs* (January-February): 93–107.

Waterbury, John. 1970. *The Commander of the Faithful: The Moroccan Political Elite*. New York: Columbia University Press.

———. 1983. *The Egypt of Nasser and Sadat: The Political Economy of Two Regimes*. Princeton: Princeton University Press.

Weaver, R. Kent, and Bert A. Rockman, eds. 1993. *Do Institutions Matter? Government Capabilities in the United States and Abroad*. Washington, DC: Brookings.

Wedeman, Ben. 1995. "The King's Loyal Opposition? The Muslim Brotherhood's Foray into Jordanian Politics." *Middle East Insight* 11, no. 2 (January-February): 15–19.

Wenner, Manfred W. 1991. *The Yemen Arab Republic: Development and Change in an Ancient Land*. Boulder: Westview Press.

Wheare, Kenneth C. 1963. *Legislatures*. New York: Oxford University Press.

Wiberg, Matti. 1994. *Parliamentary Control in the Nordic Countries*. Helsinki: The Finnish Political Science Association.

Wilson, James Q. 1980. *American Government*. Lexington: D. C. Heath.

Wilson, Mary C. 1994. "Jordan: Bread, Freedom, or Both?" *Current History* (February): 87–90.

Young, Michael D. 1996. "Misreading the Signs: Parliament and the Second Republic." *The Lebanon Report*, no. 1 (Spring): 24–26.

Zahlan, Rosemarie Said. 1989. *The Making of the Modern Gulf States*. London: Unwin and Hyman.

Zartman, I. William. 1994. "The Challenge of Democratic Alternatives in the Maghrib." In John Ruedy, ed., *Islamism and Secularism in North Africa*, 201–218. New York: St. Martin's Press.

Zartman, I. William, ed. 1982. *Political Elites in Arab North Africa*. New York: Longman.

Ziadeh, Nicola A. 1960. "The Lebanese Elections, 1960," *The Middle East Journal* 14, no. 4 (Autumn): 367–381.

Zonis, Marvin. 1971. *The Political Elite of Iran*. Princeton: Princeton University Press.

Index

Mahgub, Rifat, 244
Mahmud II (sultan), 12
Majali, Abdelhadi, 164, 168(nn 12, 13)
Majali, Abdel Salam al-, 160, 162, 163
Majlis, 172
Majlis al-Watani (Kuwait), 186, 187
Marei, Sayed, 225, 243
Maronite Christians, in Lebanon, 85, 86, 87, 88, 90, 95, 101
Martel, Comte de (French high commissioner), 15
Marxist studies, 21
Masri, Tahir al-, 152, 154, 168(n9)
MB. *See* Muslim Brotherhood
Media, 5, 31, 34, 36, 41, 49, 118–119, 212, 213, 219, 250. *See also* Press
Military, 39, 46, 52, 92
Militias, 99, 103, 108(n11)
Minority communities, 12, 136, 149, 157
Modern Democracies (Bryce), 18
Mokheiber, Albert, 92, 105
Monarchy, 2, 40, 252, 253, 254; in Jordan, 133, 134, 137, 141, 155; in Morocco, 111, 112, 113
Morocco, 40, 42; Constitutional Council of, 116–117, 132(n13); Structural Adjustment Program in, 115; Western Sahara annexation to, 114, 115. *See also* Chamber of Councilors; Chamber of Representatives
Movement of Social Democrats (MDS; Morocco), 129
Mubarak, Husni, 36, 52, 229, 234, 240, 242, 244, 252
Mubarak the Great. *See* Sabah, Mubarak al-
Muslim Brotherhood (MB); in Egypt, 37, 42, 230, 231, 233, 234, 235, 245; in Jordan, 68, 134, 137, 144, 149, 151–152, 156, 158–159, 163, 167(n4), 168(n8), 253; in Kuwait, 189; in Yemen, 205
Muslims: in Jordan, 135; in Lebanon, 85, 86, 87, 90, 95, 98, 104, 107(n2). *See also* Islamists; Shiite Muslims; Sunni Muslims

NA. *See* National Assembly
Nabulsi, Sulayman, 140, 141, 142
Napoleon I, 222
Nasser, Gamal Abdel, 17, 36, 140, 179, 224–225, 226
Nasserism, 175, 235
Nasserite Unionist People's Party (Yemen), 217

National Action Front (Jordan), 159, 168(n12)
National Alliance Party (Jordan), 159
National Assembly (Egypt); constitutional provisions for, 224; session from 1952, 224–226; session from 1970, 226–229
National Assembly (NA; Kuwait), 2, 42, 169–170, 176, 179; blocs in, 178; centrality of, 68, 73, 74; constitutional provisions for, 169, 170, 173, 175–177, 186; and cultural issues, 194–195; dissolving/reconvening of, 170, 180–181, 182, 183–184, 185, 186, 188, 197, 198; election of 1982, 182, 200(n7); election of 1985, 182–183; election of 1992, 170, 187–191; election of 1996, 171, 195–197; electoral laws of, 182; and Iran, 182; lawmaking in, 176, 199(n4); and Lebanon, 180–181; and national integration, 177–178; opposition in, 170, 171, 179, 180, 181, 182, 183, 184, 187, 188, 190, 192, 198, 199, 200(nn 7, 17, 18); political parties in, 178, 188; and ruling family, 58, 179, 181, 188, 193, 194, 196, 197–198, 199, 253; session from 1963, 178–180; session from 1981, 181–184; and state financial matters, 194; and Syria, 181
National Bloc (Jordan), 159
National Bloc (Syria), 15–16
National Bloc Party (Lebanon), 88
National Constitutional Party (NCP; Jordan), 164
National Consultative Council (NCC; Jordan), 137, 143–144
National Council (Kuwait), 186
National Council (North Yemen), 203
National Democratic Coalition (Jordan), 159
National Democratic Party (NDP; Egypt), 52, 227, 228, 229, 230–231, 232, 234, 235, 236, 237, 238, 241, 242, 245
National Democratic Party (PND; Morocco), 131(n2)
National dialogue, 34, 38–41; in Egypt, 36–37, 40, 233–234
National identity, 15
National Islamic Coalition (NIC; Kuwait), 189, 190, 191
National Legislative Council (Kuwait), 169, 173
National Liberal Party (NLP; Lebanon), 88, 89, 108(n4)
National Liberation Front (FLN; Algeria), 39

About the Book

The vitality and significance of parliaments in the Arab world is one of the essential—but overlooked—stories of political life in the 1990s. Baaklini, Denoeux, and Springborg present the first comprehensive, comparative analysis of modern Arab legislatures.

Drawing on their extensive experience as both scholars and project consultants, the authors highlight the contribution of legislatures to the process of democratic transition throughout the Arab world. They then provide a detailed analysis of six case studies: two in North Africa (Egypt and Morocco), two in the Levant (Jordan and Lebanon), and two on the Arabian Peninsula (Kuwait and Yemen). Their work is of critical importance not only to an understanding of Middle East politics and society but also for all those interested in the institutionalization of democratic practices.

Abdo Baaklini is professor in the Nelson A. Rockefeller College of Public Affairs and Policy, State University of New York at Albany, and director of its Center for Legislative Development. **Guilain Denoeux** is associate professor of government and director of the International Studies Program at Colby College. **Robert Springborg** is professor of politics at Macquarie University (Australia).

278